ELGAR AND THE PRESS

a life in newsprint

Richard Westwood-Brookes

To Elizabeth Halls

Who made this book possible

Acknowledgements

My thanks are due to my friends Stuart Webb, Joe Tierney and Kirsty Bothma, National Trust custodians of The Firs, Elgar's Birthplace Museum who gave me access to the various newspaper archives held there, and to all the various newspaper groups who have given me permission where needed to use quotations from newspapers and journals used in this book.

INTRODUCTION

Elgar's relationship with the press was curiously ambivalent. On the one hand, he painstakingly cultivated relationships with correspondents, yet fulsomely declared he never read their reports.

This is difficult to believe. His family assiduously collected relevant press cuttings and placed them in bulging scrap books which he doubtless studied. Friends sent him press reports, his acknowledgements indicating that he read them, and comments such as these demonstrated he monitored press content carefully: *'...the press invariably misquote & assume so much that is false that it is not worthwhile to attempt to put matters straight, I fear'* - *'One of the London dailies went wrong in stating that no work by an English composer had been heard at these festivals 'for several years'.'*

He never shied from giving interviews. He also entertained the attention of reporters when abroad, sometimes creating difficulties for himself by making ill-considered remarks. When he was made Professor of Music at Birmingham University in 1905, instead of remaining within the cloistered walls of academia, he chose to make public lectures and invited the press to witness them - something which he came to regret.

He even issued his own 'press releases' – particularly to local correspondents – such as this one to the Birmingham Gazette: *'The new Choral and Orchestral Society, shows, as was expected, signs of exceptional vitality and under the exhilarating conductorship of Mr Edward Elgar will probably do much to remove the reproach that dullness and ineptitude are necessary characteristics of musical attempts in the county. The conductor has arranged to produce for the first time in England a short Cantata by Humperdinck, the celebrated composer of Hansel and Gretel; this should excite interest far outside the radius from which the Worcestershire Philharmonic Society draws its members.'*

And this one to the Worcester Herald's Harvey Marson: *"Item: 'Dr Hans Richter is paying a flying visit to Dr Edward Elgar in Malvern this week. The Neue Musik-Zeitung – which circulates most largely in South Germany has the first instalment of a long and extensive article on Dr E in the number for Dec 24. Die Musik' now the most artistic of the German musical periodicals has also an important analytical notice; this article has the advantage of plentiful musical examples from 'King Olaf', 'Cockaigne', 'Gerontius' and other compositions.'*

In another letter to Marson, Elgar made it clear that he wanted him at the 1902 German performance of 'Gerontius' and correspondence suggests Elgar paid for his travel and accommodation.

Another example of how he cultivated correspondents was this letter to Fred Kenyon of the Manchester Courier shortly after he had been interviewed by him in 1905: *'Very many thanks for your letter & the sight of your admirable article. I cannot feel anything could be altered. You have now a standing invitation & I shall always be glad to see you.'*

Some reports which appeared verbatim in a number of papers and journals seem to carry the 'Elgar Press Release' stamp – possibly because, in those days, in an era before copyright laws, a story issued to one paper would often be lifted by other journals and published word for word.

When it came to the national critics – the men who could make or break a composer's career – he was particularly careful, even to the point of being obsequious, as in this December 1903 letter to the influential critic Edwin Evans, whose main interest was Russian music, particularly that of Glazunov:

'My dear Sir

Please accept my very many thanks for your letter: I am glad to hear that some of my things have been performed in Russia & especially that they have been seen by Glazounoff [sic] whom I admire so much: if you are seeing or writing to him anytime would you kindly convey my thanks to him for his musical interest & assure him how greatly I esteem the music of his which I have heard – only two symphonies alas ! and there is so much more to hear.

'I am not surprised that my name was omitted from a truly British list of music; I am made to feel as often as possible that I have no business to even <u>live</u> far less write, but this does not go for much when one has some sympathisers who even if they do not admire all one does, at least will give an Englishman credit for being sincere & <u>meaning</u> something.

'So I was glad to receive you letter & read your best thanks for so kindly drawing attention to my music.

'Believe me

'Yours very faithfully

Edward Elgar.'

Elgar had every reason to be thankful for the treatment he received from the press. Criticism was largely positive, supportive and encouraging - despite his reaction to it. As a result, his rising career prospered and his popularity owed much to the fine words which graced the newspaper columns.

He had many supporters in the press notably the powerful critic Ernest Newman, to whom he dedicated his Piano Quintet and Robin Legge of the Daily Telegraph. His supreme champion was however, Robert Buckley of the Birmingham Gazette, who first met him at a time when he was an unknown orchestral violinist and indefatigably bolstered his career with positive articles throughout his life. It was Buckley who wrote Elgar's first biography.

Press reports, describing events as they happen to an absent public, have quite rightly been described as the 'first drafts of history'. But newspapers are ephemeral. What carries the headlines of Armageddon today, serves to wrap fish and chips tomorrow. Consequently, the words written about Elgar in those far off days, have lain largely unread and unregarded in dusty archives ever since.

Having spent a lifetime as a journalist myself, I thought it time to unearth the Elgar story as it was witnessed by my fellow professionals who were present when those events took place. Those people, mostly anonymous and now largely forgotten, were unbiased observers with no particular affinity to Elgar. They plainly reported what they saw and heard. As a result their contemporaneous reports sometimes differed from the reminiscences of Elgar's friends and associates recalled with the benefit of hindsight, and the fond moulding of memory many years later.

One major source on which many observers have relied is Lady Elgar's diary. But this could hardly be considered objective. She, more than anyone, had a partisan view, and her own comments must be taken within that context. So, where appropriate, I have cited her testimony and compared it with that of journalists who witnessed the same events.

Occasionally, I quote Elgar's own letters – showing how he reacted to events but on the whole, I have allowed the correspondents to speak for themselves. They are more than capable of doing that!

I have, however, written this as a journalist, not a scholar, and offer it as a 'good read' particularly for those who may not be familiar with the Elgar story. At times there may be surprises to long-held notions about Elgar and his music. But you won't find any of those annoying little numbers against words and paragraphs which force you to hunt through pages of annexes at the back only to be confronted with that dreadful word 'ibid'!

These then, are the words – or at least some of them – of the 'hacks' and how they reported the life and events of our greatest composer as it unfolded before them.

Richard Westwood-Brookes.

THE EARLY YEARS – 1883 – 1892

One of the earliest reports mentioning Elgar was when he was 19. The Worcester Journal of October 23rd 1876, reported on a Worcester Glee Club meeting where 'Mr J D Price sang 'The Flying Dutchman' to which a band accompaniment had been arranged by Mr E W Elgar.'

Five years later, a march called 'Pas Redouble' appeared at the Glee Club. A local report reviewed: 'The selections for the band were splendidly played and the demand for the repetition of Mr Elgar's march was a well-deserved recognition of the talent of both composer and performers.'

In December 1883 an 'Intermezzo' - known today as the 'Serenade Moresque' - was premiered by William Cole Stockley's orchestra at the Birmingham Town Hall. The programme comprised orchestral and vocal music including Beethoven's Third Piano Concerto, the Overture to 'Sermeramide' by Rossini, a Chopin Polonaise, music by Flotow, Cowan, Mozart and Gounod and boasted 'a band of over eighty performers' with Elgar himself in the first violins.

The Birmingham Gazette of December 14th reported: 'We may observe that an interesting novelty was an 'Intermezzo Moresque' by Mr E W Elgar of Worcester. Writing from last night's hearing only we may say that the work consists of an introductory slow movement and an Andante in G minor, six eight time with a middle part in the major. The composer appears to emulate the modern French style and there are passages in his 'Intermezzo' which remind us of some things by Delibes. The manner in which the performance was received by last night's audience was highly encouraging.'

The Birmingham Mail reviewed: 'The 'Intermezzo' written by a permanent member of Mr Stockley's orchestra, Mr Elgar, justifies his assumption of a place in the programme. He dubs his piece 'Moresque' but why 'Moresque'? If we eliminate some of the unimportant effects supposed to give local colour, the term goes by the board. After all, however, 'What's in a name?' and waiving this prevalent, but not always justifiable musical nomenclature, we hasten to give Mr Elgar every credit for a musicianly work. A unanimous recall served to discover quite a young composer to the audience; and as Mr Elgar is not deficient in scholarship, has plenty of fancy, and orchestrates with facility, we may hope he will not 'rest and be thankful' but go on in a path for which he possesses singular qualifications.'

The Birmingham Post commented: 'Mr E W Elgar, a Worcester violinist, and a member of Mr Stockley's Band is to be congratulated upon the success on his very graceful and tuneful 'Intermezzo Moresque'. There is nothing particularly Moorish in it, excepting in the colouring for cymbals, triangle and drums and the principle theme is rather Slavonic than Arabic in character. But the music is melodious, graceful and pleasing, and the scoring, more particularly for the strings, upon which the burden of the work devolves, is tasteful and musicianly.'

By the early 1880s, Elgar's activities were proving lucrative. A Radio Times feature published after his death headlined 'When Elgar played for £2 12s 6d', inferring that he played for pittance at this time. But this was the equivalent to £215 in today's money.

He was also commanding more local press attention. A typical report in a Worcester paper, dates from February 13th 1884:

'CONCERT AT POWICK LUNATIC ASYLUM

'Last evening a concert was given at the City and County Lunatic Asylum, Powick, by the Worcester Amateur Instrumental Society, assisted by several well-known vocalists. The large ballroom was filled for the most part by inmates and attendants, with the members of the staff and a few visitors. An excellent programme had been arranged, and the concert was in every respect highly successful, nearly all the selections being encored. However much their mental powers might be damaged in other respects it was apparent that those of the unfortunate inmates of the institution who were able to be present had not lost the faculty of enjoyment and they were not the least hearty with their applause. The Band which comprised nearly thirty instrumentalists was under the able direction of Mr Edward Elgar, who, it may be mentioned, conducted throughout without the score.'

The report listed the programme, illustrating the sort of music Elgar conducted at this time. One of the soloists was his brother Frank.

'Part I: Overture 'L'Italiana in Algierie'; Part Song 'A Soldier's Love' Messrs Barry, Weaver, Fleet and Pedley; Song 'I am a Roamer', Mr Stoyle; Presto and Minuet (strings only); 'Come into the Garden Maud', Mr C Fleet; Solo Flute 'Fantasie Ecossaise', Mr C Singleton Graves; Glee 'Strike the Liar', Messrs Barry, Weaver, Fleet and Pedley; Danse des Savoyards' (Oboe Solo Mr F Elgar).

Part II : Overture 'Haydee'; Part Song 'I Loved a Lass', Messrs Barry, Weaver, Fleet and Pedley; song 'I fear no Foe', Mr F Pedley; Hymn for Orchestra ' Largo in G' (solo violin, Mr C Hayward); Madrigal 'Ye Happy Shepherd Swains', Messrs Barry, Weaver, Fleet and Pedley; Descriptive March 'Turkish Patrol'; Song 'Estudiantina', Mr Stoyle; March 'Cornelius'; National Anthem.'

Frederick G Pedley, a warehouseman from Worcester was an amateur singer, who ironically earned himself a place in musical history as the man who gave perhaps the first ever public premiere of an Elgar piece when he gave the first performance of an Elgar song on March 17th 1884 at the Glee Club.

The event was attended by the local papers who reviewed: 'The programme possessed an exceptional interest from the fact that it included two new songs by Worcester musicians: Mr W C Box and Mr E W Elgar. Both were rendered by Mr Pedley in a manner which well displayed their merits and the applause with which they were received betokened the fact that local talent is not without honour in the 'faithful city'. In consequence of the difficulties in Mr Elgar's composition, Mr Pedley substituted another song on it being re-demanded'.

Box's effort 'My Love of Long Ago', was repeated. Elgar had produced 'A Soldier's Song'- subsequently published in 1890 under the title 'A War Song' - but despite calls for an encore, Pedley sang 'A Woman's Faith and a Woman's Trust'. Another report explained: '…the company would gladly have heard 'A Soldier's Song' again, but not wishing to unduly tax Mr Pedley's powers, they readily consented to the postponement of the pleasure…'

In May 1884, the Worcester Philharmonic Society gave the first performance of 'Sevillana' – an orchestral portrait of a Spanish fiesta. The local press reported: 'A sketch composed by Mr Edward Elgar for the orchestra expressly for this concert, called 'Sevillana' and being a curious and lively combination of a great variety of instruments was executed with spirit under Mr Elgar's conductorship and favourably received.'

It appeared again at one of Stockley's Birmingham concerts in February 1885. The Birmingham Post reviewed: 'The only other absolute novelty was a 'Sevillana' by Mr Elgar, a member of the orchestra who has before benefitted by Mr Stockley's concerts as a means of bringing his works before the public. The piece in question is based upon a dance rhythm and 'local colour' is imparted by the use of a tambourine. It is effective, tuneful and well played, but the scoring is too heavy for poetic effect.

'Mr Elgar's work is not so ambitious as its intention but it is a graceful and fanciful example of its kind, an allegro moderato in G minor, three-eight time, with a middle portion and a coda in G major. The melodies are taking and characteristic, spirit, elegance and quaintness being happily combined.'

Three years later Elgar conducted Stockley's orchestra in Birmingham for the first performance of his 'Suite in D Minor' which included elements of the early 'Intermezzo' and 'Pas Redouble'. The Midland Counties Herald reported: 'Mr Elgar's suite which is in four movements is a pleasant and highly creditable piece of writing in which the orchestra is handled with considerable skill. A few judicious cuts are needed to give it compactness and they would otherwise vastly improve the work. This delicate attention by the knife is, perhaps, most needed in the finale which is unnecessarily long and somewhat diffuse. Mr Elgar's work, even as it is, is a pleasing and clever one, and on its conclusion the composer, who conducted, was loudly applauded.'

The Birmingham Post of February 27th 1888 added: 'Mr Elgar's very promising suite in D minor consists of four movements – a mazurka, an intermezzo, a gavotte and a march – all distinguished by fancy as well as tunefulness, but in some parts over laboured and diffuse. Its faults are those of a young writer and when the work is revised by the light of his maturer judgement, it will be greatly improved.'

While the Birmingham Mail commented: '...one could readily understand that with the opportunity the composer would endeavour to show at its best his musicality and the lavishness of his scoring and the length of his several sections can be put down to this notion. Now, however that he is in evidence as an orchestral writer there is no reason why the suite before being heard again should not have judicious operations with the pruning knife...'

The Musical Times reviewed a few months later: 'Mr Algar's [sic] suite is distinguished by fancy as well as tunefulness, though in some part overlaboured and wanting in cohesion and artistic development.'

Elgar's own reaction to this was contained in a letter to his friend Dr Charles Buck on March 30th, and perhaps demonstrates a rather juvenile reaction to fair criticism: 'I had a good success at Birmingham with my suite, but the critics, save two, are nettled. I am the only local man who has been asked to conduct his own work - & what's a greater offence, I *did it* – and *well* too: for this I must needs suffer."

In February 1888 Stockley's orchestra performed Dvorak's 'Speckled Bride'. 'A Practical Accompanist' and a Mr Pinner of Moseley, had written to the [Birmingham] Daily Gazette, complaining that the orchestra had played too loudly.

Elgar replied with a letter to the paper, written from the 'Clef Club' – a Birmingham musical club whose President was Sir Arthur Sullivan: 'Sir – I have read with much interest the correspondence under the above heading, although some trouble was entailed in following the controversy owing to a change of arena. The reason for not allowing an immediate response to appear in the newspaper which printed the letter of 'A Practical Accompanist' must, of course, be well known to Birmingham amateurs but at first blush this is not patent to one living outside the extremely 'parochial' element for which your town is famous, particularly in its musical circle.

'No doubt the accompanying solos at a particular concert would have received its best consideration (with a view to possible improvement) in private; but as the matter has been made a public affair by the appearance of an anonymous letter in your contemporary's columns it may be worthwhile to hear the matter to an end.

'I write therefore to say that at the rehearsal of *The Spectre's Bride* Mr Stockley asked the members of the orchestra (of which I am the most unworthy member) to disregard the accepted meanings of the dynamic marks of expression in accompanying the solos, taking them to represent one degree of power *less* than usual – *fortissimo* for the nonce being played *forte* only: *mezzo forte* as *piano* &c. This the members of the orchestra endeavoured to do: whether they were successful or not is still a question, and one which cannot be considered satisfactorily answered in the negative until someone of more recognised critical ability than 'A Practical Accompanist' or Mr Pinner of Moseley, takes up the parable.

'The last-named gentleman's attempt to add to our general enlightenment would be beneath notice save for the revival of the ancient anecdote of the preacher in church and the braying ass. It is unfortunate for Mr Pinner that his letter appeared simultaneously with 'A Practical Accompanist's' second effusion. A new perplexity is added to the controversy: amateurs are not only asked to consider whether the orchestra does or does not accompany too loudly, but also a more interesting matter, viz: - which gentleman 'A Practical Accompanist' or Mr Pinner, represents the fabled preacher? This is a nice point; *practical* musicians see already that either gentleman fitly represents the animal outside.'

This drew suspicious praise in the Worcester Herald: 'Mr Edward Elgar's talents, both as composer and as player are evidently appreciated in Birmingham. A 'Suite' by him will be produced by a fine orchestra in the Town Hall next week: and I notice that he writes from the Clef Club in that town, a smart letter, as a contribution to correspondence in one of the local papers respecting band accompaniments. I shall hope to see Mr Elgar's name conspicuous in a Festival programme.'

This smacks of another Elgar-inspired 'press release'. Its praise of his 'talents', his 'smart' letter, reference to a 'fine' orchestra, and mention of the 'Clef Club' - all point to him being the source - together with the somewhat transparent appeal for further recognition.

In 1889 he married Alice Roberts and moved to London in the hope of establishing himself as a composer. Shortly afterwards, 'The Magazine of Music' carried this, with information once again doubtless emanating from Elgar himself.

'Mr Edward Elgar, to whom the Worcester Festival Committee have applied for a new orchestral work is a native of Worcester. Until last May when he came to settle in London, he was Principal Professor of the Violin in Worcester and Malvern, besides being leader and soloist at the concerts held in those towns. For some years he was organist at the Roman Catholic Church, Worcester, a post held for many years by his father.

'Mr Elgar has already made himself known both as a composer and conductor. In February 1888 he conducted his own Suite in four movements for full orchestra at one of Mr Stockley's Birmingham concerts and at Worcester a set of pieces for strings only. Other works of his have been performed at the Crystal Palace under the direction of Mr Manns.

'The following is a list of Mr Elgar's published compositions:

Romance for Violin with orchestral accompaniment

Gavotte, violin and piano and piano solo

Liebesgruss, violin and piano, piano solo; and orchestra

Idylle, violin and piano

Allegretto, violin and piano

Songs

As I laye-a-thinking

Wind at Dawn

Thro' the long days

Queen Mary's Song

Roman Catholic Church Music

Two 'O Salutaris'

Litanies

Ecce Sacerdos

Unpublished compositions

Suite (four movements) full orchestra

Sevillana for orchestra

Intermezzo, orchestra

Three sketches for strings

'A new song for this rising musician, entitled 'A Soldier's Song' appears in this issue of the Magazine of Music.'

The Worcester Festival commission was the orchestral overture 'Froissart', which premiered on September 9[th]1890. The prestige of the festival attracted London critics, giving Elgar his first national reviews.

The Evening Standard reported: 'The one secular concert in the present Festival took place in the evening in the Public Hall and the audience appeared only to be limited by the capacity of the building. Opportunity was afforded on this occasion for the display of the local talent which should always receive encouragement at Festival time. In the present instance it was represented by Mr Edward Elgar who was permitted a place in the scheme for a concert overture entitled 'Froissart'. Whether the piece has any definite aim or is merely intended to suggest the age of chivalry in a general sense, cannot be said, as the book of words vouchsafed no information on the matter. The motto of the overture however 'When chivalry lifted up her lance on high' may perhaps be taken as sufficient indication of its meaning. It is in the key of B flat and opens in a martial style which however quickly gives way to a sentimental and semi-tragic slow movement, leading of course to the principal section.

The leading subject of this is bright, if not very striking, and the second theme in F allotted to the clarionet [sic] is pleasing and expressive. A somewhat stormy development is followed by the usual recapitulation and coda, in which the warlike and sentimental elements seem to contend for mastery. Mr Elgar's overture is a workmanlike effort alike in thematic material, structure and orchestration and it deserved the warm applause it received under the composer's direction.'

The Morning Post mentioned: 'One composition, the overture by Mr Elgar, exhibits great promise, which may be ultimately fulfilled.' The Daily Graphic agreed: 'Mr Elgar's work, which is elaborately scored for full orchestra proved to be a composition of distinct promise. It is brightly if somewhat noisily scored and displays considerable ingenuity in the working out section.'

While the Daily Telegraph said: 'The work which properly aims at a tone of chivalry is one of considerable interest arising from promise rather than actual achievement. It is in part crude and chiefly lacks the broad outline which in music of modern character is more than ever essential. But Mr Elgar has ideas and feelings as well as aspiration and should be encouraged to persevere. Mr Punch's memorable advice to persons about to marry is that which true charity dictates in nine cases out of ten when young men propose to write overtures and symphonies. I regard Mr Elgar as an exception. Let him go on. He will one day 'arrive'.'

The Manchester Guardian thought: 'the chief fault of the work is its excessive elaboration, and a tendency to monotony would have been more marked had the performance been less effective.'

Elgar commented in a letter to his friend Frank Webb of September 28th '…I have had very good notices in nearly all the papers especially in those most to be feared & the overture was much liked by the *musicians* present.'

A few months later, the Birmingham Post reviewed a second performance: '…we think the overture would gain by compression'. Elgar agreed, commenting to Webb, 'I think it is too long but the papers speak very highly of it as a whole & I had a good reception.'

Elgar's quest to establish himself in London ultimately failed and he returned to Malvern in June 1891, re-establishing himself as a violin teacher, and performer. An impression of him at this time appeared in an anecdote in the Worcestershire Echo: 'A lady, appropriately enough named Fidler – Miss Florence Fidler, has something to say of him as a conductor. The Lady who has played under him in an amateur orchestra says: 'He is a hopeless teacher but is a fine conductor. Those who need to be taught orchestral playing need to go elsewhere. If the band is experienced and knows how to allow itself to be played on, he will play on it to some purpose. But he is at the mercy of his moods and rarely does a thing twice alike.

'At preliminary practices with an incomplete band, he plays missing wind parts with his left hand and beats time with the right. He can bear much provocation with patience and little provocation with no patience at all. If a violin player drops her mute, there is a 'rumpus': on the other-hand he is unsparing in his care for detail and will repeat a passage many times until he is satisfied.'

Another impression appeared in the Worcester Herald of November 19th 1892 with Elgar conducting an all-female orchestra: 'Under a conductor so able and sympathetic as Mr Edward Elgar, it is not surprising that the performers should show unmistakable signs of devotion to their art. Those who delight to hear Mr Elgar's masterly manipulation of the bow will rejoice, even as these ladies must do, that their musical education is once more under the control of such a competent guide.'

'I am sure that we shall have a great treat in the two concerts which are to be given next Friday morning and afternoon in aid of the City Branch of the Girl's Friendly Society. Most of us have heard Mr Edward Elgar's Ladies Orchestra and I am quite sure that those that have done so will be pleased to repeat the experience.'

New works also began to appear, including songs such as 'Spanish Serenade', 'Like to the Damask Rose' and 'A Song of Autumn'. Reviews were mixed - the Civil Service Gazette, describing the latter as 'worthy of commendation, but it is a pity that the monotony of the rhythm has not been relieved by changes in the accompaniment and some modulations in a different key.' But greater things were on the way.

THE BLACK KNIGHT

Elgar began sketching 'The Black Knight', his first large-scale cantata, shortly before leaving for London in 1889, but didn't finish it until three years later. It was based on a translation by Longfellow of a German ballad *Der schwarze Ritter* by Ludwig Uhland, and tells the story of a mysterious stranger, presumably the personification of either death or the devil, who enters the court of a Medieval King and for some unexplained reason goes about gruesomely killing at will.

It was first performed by Worcester Choral Society, on April 18th 1893, in a programme including Schuman's Symphony in D Minor, Mendelssohn's Capriccio in D Minor for Piano and Orchestra, the finale of the first act of Lohengrin and various minor pieces. Elgar's cantata closed the first half.

The Worcester Herald previewed the event thus: 'The Concert will be rendered especially attractive by the first performance of an important work by a local musician. We refer to Mr Edward Elgar's cantata 'The Black Knight'. We may be sure that the Festival Society will spare no pains to ensure a good 'send off' for Mr Elgar's interesting composition.'

And afterwards the Worcestershire Chronicle reviewed: 'As Mr Edward Elgar's cantata 'The Black Knight' was to be performed for the first time, every seat in the hall was taken by people eager to hear – and some no doubt to pass a critical opinion on this rising composer's most ambitious work. The cantata concluded the first part of the programme but it may be, as well, to speak of it at once and say that it emphasizes the characteristics of Mr Elgar's orchestral writings – sumptuous examples of orchestration, relieved by charming melodies and sparkling with bright and picturesque passages. Mr Elgar had a very cordial reception as he took the baton to conduct the performance of his work and there was no mistaking the enthusiastic cheering which followed its conclusion.

'The performance takes about 40 minutes but so realistic is its treatment in consonance with the poem that the interest of the audience increased rather than flagged till its conclusion. The cantata bristles with too many difficulties for any but a thoroughly competent orchestra to perform it. A liberal interspertion of professionals strengthened the band [which also included Elgar's father William, and his brother Frank] very much with the result that the conductor had a sympathetic interpretation of his ideas, the performance being almost without blemish. Mr Elgar has the true grasp of the principles of orchestration, and many of the passages – particularly those where the horn, flute, oboe and clarinet were used – were of striking beauty and pictueresqueness. A sincere word of praise must be given to the chorus who paid a strict attention to their leads – some of them very awkward – and gave the proper emphasis to their parts.'

The Musical Times noted: 'The work reveals qualities in the composer which are bound to bring him rapidly to the front. His themes are striking and picturesque and his command of the means whereby they can be made the most of is very considerable. The result is a work displaying power, charm and musicianship in a high degree. Its orchestration also is excellent and abounds in judiciously contrasted effects. Chorus and orchestra did their best for this, the most ambitious work of the clever composer and a performance of exceptional merit was the result.'

Reviews also derived from printed scores publishers issued to the press, such as this from the Yorkshire Post: 'Mr Elgar is already known by a cleverly scored overture produced at the last Worcester Festival but judging from the pianoforte score of his cantata 'The Black Knight' his latest production is as far beyond the earlier composition in merit as it is in scope and dimensions. It is certainly characterised by exceptional vigour and the musical interest seems never to flag. As is almost inevitable in the work of a young writer, suggestions of the influence of other composers are not absent and it would appear as if Lohengrin had made a deep impression on Mr Elgar's mind but this cannot be regarded as a fault when it is remembered that all the greatest composers have developed their distinctive styles from the best models available in their times. We look forward with great interest to hearing The Black Knight produced in a fashion worthy of so very promising a work.'

The Musical News of London reported: 'The music is distinctly modern in style; the chorus, according to present day use, being treated only as part of the means for attaining tone-colour instead of monopolising the chief attention and over-riding the orchestra. The varying expression of the words is aptly heightened by the composer's music, and we think that choral societies will be glad to add this cantata to their repertoire.'

'The Black Knight' was taken up enthusiastically, notably by Wolverhampton Festival Choral Society who performed it on February 26th 1895, with Elgar conducting.

The town's Express and Star considered the work of 'exceptional merit and originality. Mr Elgar had no easy task in setting to music Longfellow's translation of Uhland's weird *'Schwarze Ritter'* but he has attained his object with marked success.'

The first London performance, the following March, had less favourable review from The Times: 'MISS HOLLAND'S CHOIR – This body of Amateur singers which has in the past done no small amount of really artistic work within somewhat narrow limits and has raised very large sums for charitable objects, gave a concert in St Martin's Town Hall on Thursday afternoon when a choral cantata by Mr Edward Elgar called 'The Black Knight' was on the whole very creditably performed.

The work has clever points, such as the weird dance in which death takes part, but it is sadly diffuse, the words are continually reiterated for no apparent reason and very little real imagination and dramatic skill is displayed. Sound musicianship and a laudable desire to vary the musical rhythm of verses that are a little monotonous in their regularity, are the best of the composer's qualifications apart from his possible skill as an orchestral writer, which could not, of course, be judged of from the pianoforte accompaniment.'

This particular cutting, in the Elgar family album, drew ire from Alice Elgar who, having written three exclamation marks beside it, further commented: 'Not put in book until 10 Sept 1901 – foolish remarks!'

Such was the appetite for new works that it was no surprise the Birmingham Weekly Post announced in October: 'Mr Edward Elgar has accepted the invitation of the Committee of the North Staffordshire Musical Festival to write a new cantata for production at Hanley in October of next year.' This was to be 'Scenes from the Saga of King Olaf'.

However, the following year the Three Choirs Festival returned to Worcester, and the Birmingham Gazette of December 17th 1895 reported: 'At the late committee meeting it was stated that Dr C H Parry had consented to write a short work if possible. We would suggest that Mr Edward Elgar, a Worcester man, who has distinguished himself as a composer, should also be asked to write a cantata for this occasion.'

This sentiment was echoed by The Daily Argus: 'The Black Knight' which was performed by the Festival Choral Society last night, stamps the composer (Mr Elgar) as one from who we may reasonably expect still greater things, should favourable opportunity be placed within his reach. That surely might be found within the circles of the Three Choirs Festival to start with, unless the powers that be concerned with the Worcester, Hereford and Gloucester triennial event mean to supply another illustration of a prophet who can obtain honour anywhere else save in his own country.' The Festival duly commissioned the cantata, 'Lux Christi' ('The Light of Life').

At this time Elgar's choral suite 'From the Bavarian Highlands' was also going through publication. In 1895 he was suddenly a busy man.

Meanwhile 'The Black Knight' was continuing to command favourable attention. Typical was this from the Birmingham Daily Gazette of December 6th 1895. Hailing Elgar as 'a local composer of eminence', it said: 'To call the cantata clever would be to do it injustice. For cleverness in music is a quality we encounter every day. We have too much 'talent' and too little genius. 'The Black Knight' is no mere ingenious vamping up of stale and worn out platitudes. From first to last the work bears the impress of strong and original thought.

There is little or none of the quality known as elegance, but in its place is a rugged power combined with a richness of imagination and a fertility of invention which remind us of Richard Wagner or Thomas Carlyle. Without being effectively eccentric, the themes are novel and striking, their development masterly, their harmonic treatment and orchestral colouring of a great and noble type as well as modern in the extreme sense of the term.'

This was almost certainly another example of the work of Elgar's champion Robert Buckley.

'From the Bavarian Highlands' premiered at the Worcester Festival Society's concert on April 21st 1896. Under the headline: 'ANOTHER TRIUMPH FOR MR ELGAR', The Worcester Journal commented: 'The Second part of the concert opened with Beethoven's overture 'Egmont' which was followed by the gem of the evening Mr Edward Elgar's choral suite.

'The melodies are simple but always bright and pretty and the instrumentation is extremely effective as it is elaborate. The work is offered as a tribute of esteem and affection to many friends among a noble and simple people. The suite formed an attractive item in the programme and its great success considerably enhance Mr Elgar's already wide reputation as a composer…the audience were aroused to a pitch of enthusiasm in which there were many cries of encore. A double recall to the platform testified the warm approval of the composition and its rendering. Mr Elgar may be heartily congratulated on his success.'

The Worcester Herald noted: 'I always feel specially interested when we are to hear anything of Mr Edward Elgar's for the first time. One is so sure beforehand that it will be musicianly and of a high order. Sometimes indeed it happens that the music he gives us appeals less directly to the untutored ear than to the expert, but in his latest effort we have melodies and treatment that charm the popular taste and are appreciated equally by the connoisseur. At least this seemed to be the verdict unhesitatingly given by an enthusiastic audience. It is not often that we are aroused by such a pitch of excitement, and a young French lady visiting our town was immensely astonished that English people whom she has hitherto seen so coldly undemonstrative could show their delight in such a warm-hearted fashion. Indeed, the flattering reception given to the composer and the repeated recalls were probably rather a trial to Mr Elgar, who, with the modesty of real genius seems almost to shun applause.'

After this came 'Lux Christi – The Light of Life' at the Worcester Festival. Previews were appearing from the Spring of 1896. The Daily Times, of April 13th noted: 'Considerable interest will attach to the first presentation of a work by Mr Edward Elgar which we believe will achieve a gratifying success. Mr Elgar has already accomplished something that has warranted the opportunity of winning further distinction which is now afforded him; and those who are best able to predicate have no hesitation in saying that we shall have a scholarly and forceful production, and that Mr Elgar will be hailed as a musician deserving honour in his own country.'

The Festival's London rehearsals took place in the late Summer, allowing more detailed preview. The Daily News provided a full description of the work adding: 'Mr Elgar is a musician of Malvern, whose cantata 'The Black Knight' has already been heard in London and in various parts of the country. In the West and the Midlands his name is well known and his music much admired.'

The Sunday Times of August 16th reported: 'The most important novelty at the forthcoming Worcester Festival will be an oratorio of moderate length entitled 'Light of Life' composed by Mr Edward Elgar. The subject deals with the healing of the blind man as related in the Ninth Chapter of St John. The libretto has been written by the Rev. E Capel-Cure.'

The Birmingham Daily Gazette enthused: 'Mr Elgar has long been known as a composer far above the average in respect of original genius, versatility, spontaneity and general musicianship. But we venture to suggest that the committee of the coming Worcester Festival who commissioned the work under notice will hardly be prepared for the success it will undoubtedly attain. The music has an interest, a piquancy, a masterly solidity altogether unusual, the whole combined with a freshness and a power of dramatic realisation rarely met with.

'We regard Mr Elgar's latest work as distinctly his best and since he has thus far gone from strength to strength we may reasonably expect his next effort to prove still worthier. Such is our opinion, formed after long and impartial examination of the score and by our opinion we are prepared to stand or fall.'

In an unattributed, though probably local report in the Elgar archives: 'a correspondent writes: Mr Edward Elgar's new oratorio 'The Light of Life' has successfully passed the critical test of a London rehearsal, and has passed it with the highest honours. Several distinguished members of the musical world were present at the Queen's Hall and after the performance expressed their unqualified and unanimous approval and admiration. Mr Edward Lloyd surpassed himself in the exquisite solo 'As a spirit didst thou pass' and we can confidently predict a great intellectual treat for all who are fortunate to be present.

'Professor [Alberto] Randegger, another high authority, after hearing the rehearsal in London, considered it was a very great success, and said it was the best English work that he has heard in the last twenty years.

'Still further testimony is afforded by Mr Burnett, the leader of the orchestra who regards the instrumentation as most excellent and the writing for the violin (of which Mr Elgar is so masterly an exponent) as exceedingly fine. With so much unstinted praise from such competent judges it will be odd indeed if this example of the undoubtedly high abilities of a local composer does not provide a new reading of the old saw as to where a prophet gains the least honour.'

The identity of 'the correspondent' is not given, but such is the style and language of this piece, particularly the fact that it quotes praise from various other sources, and mentions Elgar's prowess with the violin, it looks suspiciously as having derived from Elgar himself.

The work was premiered on September 10th. The Atheneum reviewed: 'We shall return to the consideration of Mr Edward Elgar's new short oratorio, 'The Light of Life' when the work is performed in London, which it should be, for it displays not only excellent musicianship, but inventiveness and must not be fully judged at a first hearing.

'Mr Elgar, whose name is not yet very familiar in the musical world has evidently talent of no ordinary nature. His score is not inordinately ambitious, but it contains a large measure of fresh, that is to say, unconventional melody, the vocal part writing is ingenious without being too elaborate and the orchestration delicate and full of colour. No more pleasing or artistic has been produced at the Three Choirs for several years.'

The Yorkshire Post added: 'The most important feature of the Festival from an artistic point of view has certainly been the production of Mr Elgar's cantata which has brought a very promising young composer into far greater prominence than he has hitherto obtained. The pleasure of coming across a Festival work so fresh and spontaneous, and of assisting to discover as it were a musician who may be destined to take no unimportant place among our native composers would seem to have upset the critical faculties of many musical journalists who have been inclined to attribute to Mr Elgar more virtues than he really possesses. Still making allowance for a pardonable enthusiasm, Mr Elgar has every reason to be gratified at the impression made by his work. His cantata written for the Staffordshire Festival will be looked forward to with exceptional interest. May he not be tempted to feel he has arrived at the goal, but rather be stimulated to greater exertions and in particular to a more careful study of vocal writing by the well-deserved success of his Worcester cantata.'

The Sunday Times said this: 'Seldom does the dip into the 'local art lottery' yield a prize so conspicuously promising as Mr Edward Elgar. Here is a musician of whom Worcester has perfect reason to be proud, and the place accorded his short oratorio 'The Light of Life' in Tuesday evening's programme was eminently justified by the critical verdict of the following day. The young Malvern teacher has uncommon talent. He knows his Wagner well – sometimes perhaps a trifle too well – and he has turned his experience as an orchestral player to good account; hence the marked superiority of his scoring as compared with his vocal writing – his choruses as compared with his solos. But his sense of proportion and tone colour and his knowledge of effect are quite exceptional, and albeit his themes are not always original, they impress in almost every case by their appropriateness of character and expressive force.

'He might have done more with his representative themes, but otherwise his handling of the various situations betrays little of the novice or paucity of bold ideas. The best number in the work is the chorus 'Light out of darkness' and this is one of such excellence that I cannot help looking to Mr Elgar for a really fine work when he comes across a 'book' which appeals in every sense to his strong artistic temperament. Meanwhile his present achievement will suffice to gain him a ready and grateful hearing in quarters where his name has hitherto been wholly unknown.'

The Observer noted: 'In Mr Elgar's short oratorio, we have a work in which the higher merit of quality is conspicuous to such a degree that we are warranted in speaking of its composer as a 'coming man'.'

But The Daily News, after attributing the 'Froissart' Overture to Elgar's brother Frank, as well as getting the date of its first performance wrong, sneered: 'The Light of Life is, down to date, Mr Elgar's most ambitious effort and if not showing any great individuality it is nevertheless a remarkably clever piece of workmanship. The truth is that in these matters the provincial composer is, to a certain extent, handicapped. He has but few opportunities of hearing the higher class of orchestral and choral music, so that anything which strikes him as new forthwith takes possession of him. Mr Elgar appears to have recently assimilated a great deal of Wagner.

'Elsewhere there are traces of Gounod and even of Mendelssohn, although Mr Elgar is beyond question at his best in his choral workmanship and elsewhere where he can give scope to his musical tendency towards the dramatic in music.'

And the Manchester Courier similarly observed: 'In his oratorio Mr Elgar has made a bold attempt to be unconventional. Whatever the faults of the work it cannot be accused of dryness which pervades too many devotional works. On the contrary, he is too dramatic; sometimes, one might say, he verges on the theatrical. His subjects are melodious, but not always strikingly appropriate to the subject he is illustrating and some of the chief themes are far too sensuous in quality for a devotional work. In orchestration he has chosen for his model Wagner and Berlioz, and the colouring is laid on with no sparing hand.'

The Morning Post reviewed: 'There is something so praiseworthy in the endeavour to strike out a new line that one wishes to be able to congratulate a composer on a complete success. But here must be reservations in one's praise. In the attempt to steer clear of devotional commonplace, of the usual Festival novelty, and of the Mus.Doc. exercises, Mr Elgar has often forgotten to be appropriate. But perhaps it would be fairer to say that in striving to illustrate too closely his text in detail he has not always stopped to think that certain methods which would be suitable to a work avowedly dramatic are not quite so happily employed in an Oratorio.

'One concrete example will suffice. The scene where the Pharisees scoff at the miracle performed on the blind man by Christ is very clever but the music characterising the Pharisees is very nearly grotesque. In a drama it would have been admirable but in an Oratorio one may doubt whether it is quite in place. Perhaps this would have been less apparent in a concert hall than in a Cathedral.'

And The Times perceptively observed: 'There seems little doubt that Mr Elgar will attain to far greater heights as a composer of secular music than of sacred. At any rate, whichever he may essay, his future will be watched with the greatest interest by all British musicians, if only on account of his unquestionable skill in handling the orchestra.'

Alice Elgar, in her diary considered the event was a 'perfectly beautiful evening.

SCENES FROM THE SAGA OF KING OLAF
AND THE INVENTION OF GREATNESS

Elgar was introduced to the fee-paying public of the North Staffordshire Musical Festival in a column entitled 'Occasional Local Notes' in the Stoke Sentinel: 'Mr Edward Elgar, the gentleman who has undertaken to compose a cantata for the next Festival is a professor of music living at Malvern. It is said that Mr Elgar has selected King Olaf, the patron saint of Sweden as the subject of his new work and that he anticipates that it will show a decided advance on his existing masterpiece.'

The work was awaited with enthusiasm. Joseph Bennett, in the Musical Times commented: 'Enough that, as far as meets the eye from the pianoforte score, the composer appears to much greater advantage than in 'The Light of Life'. He writes with a freer hand, with greater confidence and boldness. He excels in the picturesque and dramatic; his vocal music rises to its proper standard of importance and the general result is satisfactory. With this indication of what may be expected the reader must visit the event and, if he will, prepare himself to witness the birth of a work of skill and power.'

The Birmingham Argus quoted 'a representative of the great music publishing firm which is bringing out 'King Olaf': 'The Cantata is one of the finest works which have been submitted to Novello's for the last quarter of a century'. The paper then commented: 'What price the jaundiced opinion of some of the 'superior persons' of light and leading from London, who, instead of dealing with Mr Elgar per se and his works on their merits or demerits, loftily dismiss him with sneers on his provincialism ?'

The Staffordshire Sentinel reviewed the rehearsal: 'Mr Elgar had a very cordial reception. He took the choir through the more difficult passages of the work, some of the parts being gone through a number of times. On the whole the choir showed a capital knowledge of the divisions they were invited to sing, and with a little more attention to the work should give an impressive rendering of it on the all-important occasion. The Cantata promised to prove a great hit and to add to the reputation of the composer. At the close of the rehearsal, Mr Elgar expressed the pleasure afforded him to conduct the choir and thanked the singers warmly for the attention given to his suggestions and the evident desire to benefit by them.'

The paper then bolstered expectation with nine extensive examinations of the work on subsequent days.

'King Olaf' premiered on October 30th. The Sentinel described the atmosphere: 'The festival was happily favoured with splendid weather yesterday morning, the sunshine smiling on the efforts of the executive in a way which those gentlemen are likely to take as another happy augury. A small knot of people assembled near the front of the Town Hall to witness the arrivals. Otherwise there was very little to indicate that a great feast of music was in progress and that the morning was to see the birth of a musical work which is certain to obtain much more than the ephemeral reputation of the usual run of festival novelties. Happily, the hall was again well filled though the arena was once more the weakest part. The President of the Festival (the Duke of Sutherland) and the Patroness (the Duchess of Sutherland) with the same party as were present on the Thursday evening arrived just before eleven o'clock.

'When this festival scheme was in its initial stages there were fears expressed that, as the chorus was made up almost exclusively of working people, it would be unwise to arrange a programme which would necessitate their attendance at a morning meeting. The fear was unjustified in the result. Yesterday morning there was probably not a chorister absent and the orchestra presented an array as brave as that recorded on Thursday night.

'Again, as the vocal principles passed to the front, the choir and audience evidenced their pleasure and delight at the sight of artists so well known. The Prince of English tenors, Mr Edward Lloyd, met with a small ovation and cheers little less intense were accorded Miss [Medora] Henson and Mr [David] Ffrangcon-Davies. The composer, Mr Edward Elgar, of course, came in for a most enthusiastic welcome as he took up his place at the conductor's rostrum. It may be said that principles, chorus and band set themselves to secure for Mr Elgar a triumphant first representation of his most serious effort in composition. All the principles were in splendid form, Mr Lloyd very early in the performance raising the audience to a great state of excitement by his magnificent version of the dramatic solo 'And King Olaf heard the cry'. Mr Ffrangcon-Davies too was immensely effective in his opening numbers, and Miss Henson absolutely brought down the house with the most wonderful piece of vocalism, ringing out with brilliance.'

Robert Buckley in The Birmingham Gazette was exaltant: 'Mr Elgar has eclipsed himself. He has produced an epoch-making work and one that will make famous among musicians the place of its production. Henceforth, 1896 will be spoken of at Hanley as the 'King Olaf' year. After 'The Black Knight' and 'The Light of the World' [sic] great things were confidently expected, but Mr Elgar has surpassed expectation. English music is lifted to the highest plane of contemporary art.'

The report then gave birth to this: 'Mr Elgar is demonstrated *the greatest English genius since Henry Purcell.'*

The Staffordshire Sentinel recycled the report under the headline: MR ELGAR THE GREATEST ENGLISH GENIUS SINCE PURCELL' and this time-honoured mantra, presumed for decades to be the evaluation of sage musical opinion, has been regurgitated as axiomatic 'fact' ever since. Yet it actually owes its origins to a partisan journalist from a Birmingham paper, who championed Elgar so much that years later the admitted almost losing his job because of it. Such is the irony of history.

Buckley's report continued: 'The new Cantata is stamped throughout with greatness. 'King Olaf' is great in detail, great as a whole, great in its mastery of modern artistic resource, great in its thematic conception and development, great in popular attractiveness, great in the occult subtleties that conquer the expert, great in originality of melody and harmony, exceedingly great in dramatic forcefulness and above all great in its aspiration and in the marvellous spontaneity and lucidity of its most complex combinations.

'We have no hesitation in classing 'King Olaf' with the greatest works of the kind extant. 'King Olaf' belongs to the fraternity of Dvorak's 'Spectre's Bride' and the 'Faust' of Hector Berlioz; and we are not sure that Mr Elgar's work is not in some respects greater than either.

'No dramatic cantata of equal greatness has ever been produced by any English composer. By 'King Olaf', Mr Elgar unquestionably takes rank among the greatest masters of the age. There is not a weak spot or a dull bar in the work. Its 86 minutes of duration commanded a rapt attention, none so rapt as the little knot of professional critics in the balcony. These one and all rejoiced to be for once present at the birth of a masterpiece. All were prepared for a striking and powerful work though the pianoforte score though being rich and full beyond the average, replete with beautiful harmonic and structural music-pictures, proved but a vague adumbration of the glowing chromatics of the orchestra.

'We regret that the credit of its production is due to North Staffordshire and not Birmingham. Dr [Swinnterton] Heap is the deus ex machina of the case. 'The Black Knight' astonished him. Just before the production of the 'Light of the World' [sic] he said to us at Worcester: - 'I had known Mr Elgar for ten years without a suspicion of his calibre as a composer. He is excessively modest.'

Joseph Bennett, in the Daily Telegraph said this: 'This morning, the one novelty of the Festival – and, I am bold to say, the novelty of the Festival year – was produced with indisputable success. I declare my intention in a hurry, because already some reader exclaims 'Mr Elgar again ! We heard of him only a few weeks ago at Worcester. Is this to be an Elgar season ?'

'No doubt and on the whole deservedly so, if there be any just pretention in the work of an earnest and able musician, who comes to the front by the sheer force of merit without organised puffery or the aid of any clique. I say this with especial emphasis, because I do not on every point of musical faith and practice see eye to eye with the Malvern musician. He adopts methods which I cannot recognise as of ideal value. But behind all his work lies the power of living talent, the charm of an individuality in art and the pathos in one who, in utter simplicity, pours forth that which he feels constrained to say, and leaves the issue to fate. Than this, I know no more interesting combination. It goes far to disarm the hostility of criticism, or, at any rate, to blunt its darts by sheer force of human sympathy.'

Bennett devoted two and a half columns in his report, providing examination of the work, scene by scene. He then gave his opinion of the composer and his methods, and in particular Elgar's use of the 'representative theme' or 'leitmotiv' – a device where a theme, or combination of notes is used to represent either a person or a mood within the action. It is a device which is characteristic of Wagner, and which Elgar adopted in his choral works.

'A mere glance through 'King Olaf' proves that Mr Elgar is much more at liberty in it than in the sacred work he composed for the recent festival at Worcester. The limitations of religious music, as is now obvious, fettered him. In the secular work he is entirely at large giving an impression that we can see the man following his own instinct and method and working out results as it pleases him. That is a great point gained. To begin with, not more often in art than in social life does the real man appear in each case. There are conventionalities embodied in public opinion, which issues edicts as from another Sinai, threatening penalties against transgressors. It must not be supposed however, that Mr Elgar has struck out new paths. He has merely allowed us to see the methods which his sympathies and judgements endorse and has followed these with the utmost frankness and simplicity. This may be said in particular with regard to this representative theme, that most conspicuous feature in the structure of modern music as applied to personages and events. Let me now repeat what I have said many times before, namely that the representative theme, sparingly used for a particular and well-defined purpose, is capable of doing good service, but that when profusely employed as the cardinal feature of a musical design, it limits the composer, makes him the slave of his own mechanism and places his work in subjection far more irksome and unworthy than those of the old *contrapuntists*, who, after all, had learning on their side. But while holding this opinion, I do not fail to recognise that the representative theme and its related usages have become established and the best must be made of it til another change takes place. In one sense Mr Elgar has made the best of it by inventing themes which are distinctive and characteristic, by so using them that the analogue of the scriptural wayfaring cannot easily err therein.

His *leit-motives* are many. Every personage has one. There are subjects which stand for creeds and qualities for this and that, till, as in Wagner, the music is given up to the enforcement of an applied significance and it is all done so cleverly, with such an easy command of resources and with such a happy skill in dovetailing the *motive* that no gaps and consequent jerks disturb the flow of the music. And let it stand that Mr Elgar has a right to use the method adopted – the right which comes from ability and which only ability can confer.

'So far I have dealt only with a matter of procedure lying within the lines, of so to speak, musical architecture. Now it is necessary to go beyond and above. It was said of Mr Elgar's Worcester cantata, not without reason, that the composer sacrificed vocal melody to the exigencies of orchestral effect. The remark does not apply to 'King Olaf', or, if at all, only in a very limited sense. It now appears that Mr Elgar knows how to write effectively both for vocal solo and chorus and that, as a matter of fact, he shows a peculiar sensitiveness to the effects which can be produced by such means. This is perhaps the most important revelation made by the new work because found in connection with a rare gift of writing for the orchestra. We have plenty of musicians who can score cleverly; indeed, no musical ability is more common thanks to examples set in abundance by modern masters. But it is one thing to fill in a score and another to conceive ideas that lend themselves to the highest orchestral effects. Mr Elgar as now convincingly shown, can do both and combine with that power the not less important one of bringing orchestra and voices into masterly association.'

Other reports concurred with Bennett's assessment. Elgar did, however, receive one further accolade – and one which he could not have expected – he had a mention in 'Punch'.

'What next ?' it declared in a column of jokes featured in its November 7th edition – 'Mr Elgar's new Cantata having been successful at the North Staffordshire Musical Festival, *King Olaf* will probably be followed by *Queen O'Smile*'

After it was all over, the Staffordshire Sentinel reproduced a letter from Elgar to the Festival Committee in which he heaped praise on them for organising such a platform for his new work and wishing them well for the future. He then added this: 'Please say to the chorus that I came among strangers, but, if I ever come to the Potteries again, they have given me the right to feel I shall be among friends.'

Twenty-five years later, they invited him again, to conduct a Silver Jubilee performance of the work, offering what they could afford in the post First World War potteries – 15gns - about £350 in today's money plus travelling expenses and free overnight accommodation in their chairman's house. They were tersely told by Elgar's concert agents, that unless they offered 50gns -or £1200 in today's money - the great Sir Edward Elgar could not even consider the matter.

THE IMPERIAL MARCH AND THE BANNER OF ST GEORGE

After the success of 'King Olaf' the press wanted to know more about this hardly-known Malvern musician so introductory biographical features started to appear.

The Musical Standard of November 21st 1896 offered this, headed 'Musicians of the Day'.

'To some extent, he inherits his musical faculty, several members of his family being more or less interested in the youngest of the arts. If not quite a prodigy, young Elgar took to the pianoforte at an early age. Although while still a child, he could extemporise in such a way as to astonish those privileged to hear him, there was no encouragement held out to him to devote himself to music with a view to adopting it as a profession. As a matter of fact he was intended for the law; and, indeed, spent twelve months in a solicitor's office with a view to being articled. The work, however, was uncongenial. Having taken up music in earnest he mastered the organ and rapidly became organist of the St George's Church at Worcester.

'Much of his time was taken up in composition. He composed, indeed a good deal of church music. He also wrote several orchestral pieces all of which he had the good fortune of having played by Mr A Manns at the Crystal Palace and by Mr Stockley at Birmingham – a certain hallmark of the intrinsic value of those early efforts of his. About this time, he took up the violin and studied this beautiful instrument under A Pollitzer, with such enthusiasm that in a comparatively short time, he became the recognised leader in Worcestershire.

'In 1889 he married the only daughter of the late Sir Henry G Roberts KCB of Hazeldine House, Worcestershire and took up his residence in London. Not overburdened by professional duties which have proved disastrous to the development of so many musicians, Mr Elgar was left to turn his attention to composition of a more serious import than he had hitherto undertaken. It is to this period that we owe the romantic concert overture 'Froissart'. This work was first played in Worcester in 1890 and was received with great favour as promising much for the future.

'The following year, Mr Elgar removed to Malvern. Here he has since resided devoting himself almost exclusively to composition. He has published much, the chief works being a cantata for chorus and orchestra, produced at Worcester in 1893, and since heard at Walsall, Hereford, Wolverhampton, Tenbury, London (with pianoforte accompaniment) and at the Birmingham Festival Choral Society's jubilee concert last December. Other large compositions are a large sonata for organ, serenade for string orchestra (published by Breitkopf and Hartel of Leipzig) romance for violin, with orchestral accompaniment, several solos, published by Schott & Co, of Mayence and some violin studies published by Chanot. Messrs Novello have published several smaller choral works.

'Among these may be mentioned two extremely popular part songs for ladies' voices with obbligato for two violins, in addition to the usual piano accompaniment. A choral suite 'From the Bavarian Highlands' (published by J Williams) was produced with great enthusiasm this year at Worcester. Mr Elgar has likewise produced many songs for all voices which have found a publisher in C Tuckwood.

'The composer's life in Malvern is an ideal one for a musician. In addition to the time devoted to composition, his life is taken up teaching composition to a limited number of pupils and in general country pursuits. He keeps in touch however with the modern musical world by frequent visits to Munich, Paris, Bayreuth etc., and all that is worth hearing in London he manages to hear. We may add that Mr Elgar is no man's pupil either for harmony, counterpoint or orchestration. All that he has achieved in music has been entirely through his own efforts, and without any recommendation, save that of Dr C Swinnerton Heap, the well-known musician of Birmingham. We trust that the Royal Choral Society will see its way to a performance of 'King Olaf' on one of the dates still open, as such an interesting and uncommon work should certainly be heard in London.'

The impression that this was either written by or heavily influenced by Elgar is inescapable. Apart from the biographical details the subtle references promoting his status bear his hallmark: his ability to extemporise on the piano which 'astonishes' those 'privileged' to hear him; how he 'rapidly' became organist at St George's – when the post was held by his father; how 'much of his time was taken up with composition', and that 'several' of his pieces were performed by Manns at the Crystal Palace.

The piece elevates him to the 'recognised leader in Worcestershire' on the violin, which, according to this, he apparently only took up when he studied under Pollitzer – despite playing the instrument and teaching it for years. The disastrous London adventure is reinterpreted as an exercise which led him to be 'not overburdened by professional duties' allowing him 'to turn his attention to composition of a more serious import than he had hitherto undertaken.'

The dismal retreat to Worcestershire is highlighted almost as a career elevating decision allowing Elgar to devote ' himself almost exclusively to composition' – no mention of eking out a living teaching violin – but it is also keen to point out that he kept in touch with mainstream musical life via his quoted visits to Europe and 'hearing all that is worth hearing in London' Of his published compositions there is special indication that some of them were published by overseas firms – so therefore subtly suggesting that his music had already achieved international appeal.

The article also ensured that his self-taught educated is highlighted and ends with the plea 'We trust that the Royal Choral Society will see its way to a performance of 'King Olaf' on one of the dates still open, as such an interesting and uncommon work should certainly be heard in London.'

Another article appeared in 'The World'. It was a little more incisive.

'Mr Elgar rose to fame at one bound when 'King Olaf' was played at Hanley last Autumn. Twelve months ago, a few knew him as a teacher of the violin in Malvern; today all the world knows him as a composer to be reckoned with. I cannot help thinking he has chosen the better part. Perhaps if he had settled in London he would by now be a Professor giving eighty lessons and dining out seven times a week and scribbling Royalty ballads in his scanty leisure. As it is, he has composed 'King Olaf'.'

During 1897 – Queen Victoria's Diamond Jubilee year – he produced two new works : the Imperial March and the choral piece 'The Banner of St George', with libretto by Henry Shapcott Bunce writing as 'Shapcott Wensley'.

The Imperial March was first performed at a Crystal Palace concert on April 19th 1897 and was cautiously well received.

The Musical Standard reviewed: 'Mr Edward Elgar has proved himself a clever composer and his 'Imperial March' is at once a clever march. New marches are frequently 'too terrible for words'. Their commonplaceness, their mock force and their bareness are a source of wonder even to a hardened soul. What Wagner did for the form of the march is now well recognised. Mr Elgar in his well-formed march would appear to be almost the first British musician who has studied the march as Wagner made it. The result is unquestionably satisfactory and highly interesting. It is a composition for which one has sincere admiration. It has been customary to look upon a march in a very free and easy way, as if you must not expect much in such a comparison. As in the 'Kaisersmarch' we found in the 'Imperial March' impressive development and a polyphonic earnestness and thoroughness that makes one feel inclined to praise the composer's work highly.

The scoring, happily, is most able and effective; but Mr Elgar has shown himself elsewhere a master of modern orchestration. But it is not intended to be understood that the themes are new: they are not! One simply admires the *form* of the composition and the scoring; not the themes. The opening theme is not at all original or fine and the Trio (curiously Bruneauesque [as in Alfred Bruneau, the French composer]in melody) is also not thematically novel. This is a pity; but we have strong passages derived from these themes – which is something. It is truly safe to say that one can hardly expect to have a more powerful or representative Jubilee march from the pen of any British composer. One should indeed be thankful for what Mr Edgar [sic] Elgar has achieved in his spirited composition.'

The Musical Times added: 'To write an original march is almost as difficult as to write an original chant, but Mr Elgar has made a bold, and in a considerable degree, successful attempt to impart freshness to a stereotyped form. The music possesses considerable dignity, and the melodious nature of the themes, is enhanced by the harmonic freshness of their setting.'

The 'Banner of St George' premiered by St Cuthbert's Hall Choral Society in London on May 18th, received competition from the well-established composer Sir John Frederick Bridge, the organist at Westminster Abbey, with his 'Flag of England' for soprano, chorus and orchestra, to words supplied by Rudyard Kipling.

The Bristol Evening Times commented on the Bridge work: 'Not only are the poems striking in character and of high literary merit, but the musical settings are marked by individuality, strength and effectiveness and well illustrate the sentiment of the words.' Elgar's was also well received, the Times declaring: 'The work is quite good enough to be heard independently of this year's commemorations, to which, indeed, only passing reference is made.'

The Yorkshire Post commented: 'We have two cantatas by well-known musicians. 'The Flag of England' by Dr Bridge of Westminster Abbey and 'The Banner of St George' by Mr Edward Elgar. The authors of the words are respectively Mr Rudyard Kipling and Mr Shapcott Wensley and all we shall say of the cantatas at present is that we wish librettists and composers had been better sorted. Mr Elgar's power would have been worthy of Mr Kipling's splendidly vigorous verse and Dr Bridge's cleverness would have been equally well expended in endeavouring to give interest to Mr Shapcott Wensley's blameless lines'.

The Manchester Guardian commented: '[Elgar's] music is carefully written and the different dramatic moments in the ballad are well emphasised. It is rather a pity, nevertheless, that in several instances the composer has let the orchestra move in unison with the chorus; an independent accompaniment would have been preferable in all cases and would have added greatly to the aesthetic value of the work.'

Elgar commented in a letter to his editor August Jaeger on August 4th 1897: 'You praise my new work too much – but you understand it – when it is performed will anyone say *any*thing different from what they wd. say over a commercial brutality like the 'Flag of England' for instance: naturally no one will & the thing dies & so do I.'

And two days later: 'Please do not think I am a disappointed person, either commercially or artistically – what I feel is the utter want of *sympathy* – they i.e. principally critics, lump me with people I abhor – mechanics. Now my music, such as it is, is alive, you say it has heart – I always say to my wife (over any piece or passage of my work that pleases me) 'if you cut that it would bleed!' *You* seem to see that but who else does?'

This was an unfair reaction from Elgar and illustrates the almost juvenile sensitivity he had to public assessment his works.

The press had given perfectly reasonable reviews of 'The Banner of St George', as they had done to Bridge's work. The mere fact that both had appeared at the same time meant that reviews were naturally contemporaneous – there was no deliberate attempt or conspiracy amongst the press to 'lump' Elgar with people he abhorred. It was merely the nature of how things had worked out. At the time of these reviews Bridge was held in high esteem, having been organist at Westminster Abbey for many years, and distinguishing himself in his organisation of the music for Queen Victoria's Diamond Jubilee that same year. It was natural that a new work from his pen should receive press attention. Elgar, though a rising star was still somewhat unknown quantity, particularly in London.

Bridge, a near contemporary of Elgar, also came from Worcestershire. He taught many fine musicians from the time, including two whom Elgar regarded as particular friends – the composer and organist Herbert Brewer, and the conductor Landon Ronald. It was also Bridge, in his role as Conductor of the Royal Choral Society who introduced performances of Elgar's works to London audiences.

In June the 'Imperial March' was played at the Queen's Jubilee Garden Party at Buckingham Palace, and the State Concert held at the Palace on July 15th – both events organised by and featuring programmes chosen by the vilified Bridge.

Elgar's march was the only work by an English composer so chosen. The Musical Standard commented: 'I notice with pleasure that Mr Edward Elgar's Imperial March was included – with pleasure because British composers have been too much neglected at these State Concerts and also because this particular march is quite the best of the occasional music which the Diamond Jubilee brought forth.'

So much for Elgar's work being 'lumped' together with music by those he abhorred.

CARACTACUS

On January 19th 1898 The Leeds Mercury reported: 'The Leeds Festival executive, after considering the question of new works, had deemed it advisable to communicate with Mr Edward Elgar, whose name was favourably received by the Provisional Committee eighteen months ago. Mr Elgar who already occupied a high position as a composer, had agreed to write a new cantata for the Festival. It will be entitled 'Caractacus'. The Executive Committee unanimously recommended the adoption of this work, which will occupy one part of a concert.'

The Yorkshire Post on the same day enthused: 'The most interesting announcement is that there is a prospect of a new work by Mr Edward Elgar. With this and the new works promised by Sir Arthur Sullivan and already composed by Professor Stanford and Mr Humperdinck, there seems a prospect of festival novelties of more than common interest.'

The Musical Times added: 'The new cantata for Leeds will furnish Mr Elgar with a splendid opportunity to still further demonstrate his remarkable dramatic powers, and we may rest assured that he will fully realise all the expectations that have been formed of him as one of our foremost native composers.'

On March 5th, the Yorkshire Post published two columns entitled 'Mr Edward Elgar at Home' providing this impression: 'In person Mr Elgar is tall and spare, in feature favouring the aquiline and with an air of distinction. As he appears I note that he is arrayed in rough tweed with leggings and looks so much like a country gentleman given to field sports that a couple of pointers and a gun seem inevitable concomitants. His study has a piano, books, books, and more books. He is not a one-sided man, but an omnivorous reader; was the first member of a sort of book club, a literary federation, which enables Malvern people to know each other's libraries; [novelist] Mrs Lynn Linton is an enthusiastic member. There is a big portrait of Wagner, and a board over the fireplace displays, in poker work, an ascending flash of chromatic semi-quavers; the 'Fire-motive' from the *'Ring of the Nebelungen'*. A cosy room with quaint *bric-a-brac* from foreign lands; bits of carving from the Bavarian Highlands, the composer's annual resort: with other suggestive features of artistic life and artistic proclivity. An intensely amusing cartoon from a German newspaper is conspicuously but carelessly posted on the wall – clearly a temporary feature. A photograph of a 13th century sculpture of the Crucifixion from Worcester Cathedral, the figures instinct with life and expression, seems to be a permanent joy. Mr Elgar's tastes are evidently distinguished by their universality.

'When wearied of the composing tent with its beautiful outlook to Bredon Hill, to Pershore, and Evesham, the historic Edge Hill, and its memories of the Civil War, he admits a strong inclination for golf which he claims to pursue with praiseworthy perseverance and though by no means phenomenally successful, he is wont to declare that he is at any rate animated by the best intentions. The American craze for kite-flying; with its aerial photography and its quasi-scientific aims, had for some time a follower in the composer of 'King Olaf' who desired to invent a compensating kite that should automatically adapt itself to whatever currents it might meet with in its upward course. Kites, it would seem, are not to be relied on during sudden and unexpected emergencies. Sailing away in a suitable wind and apparently giving promise of steady and irreproachable conduct, they are apt of a sudden to jib, to fly in the wrong direction, to bolt, to kick, to plunge, to cavort and to be guilty of other deplorable excesses. It was Mr Elgar's hope to restrain these unregenerate tendencies to break in and bridle the innate diablery of the fiery untamed kite that might be scientifically useful. But nothing came of it, or rather nothing satisfactory. All he achieved was to bring down his neighbour's spouting and on another occasion to afford employment to a powerful navvy, who in dire extremity helped the composer and a scientific friend to pull down a heavy flight of kites from the central blue. *Eripuit coelo fulmen* [A bolt rescued from heaven] may truly be said of Mr Elgar but if he has snatched fire from heaven the feat was not accomplished with 'square tailed' or 'long tailed' or 'bob tailed' kites.

'As to Mr Elgar's musical opinions and convictions, he delights in everything that is good whatever its school or period; would gladly go a hundred miles to hear a Wagner opera, and would enjoy a Haydn quartet, if a good example. Among the hierarchy of the masters, he placed Beethoven first, then Bach, then Mozart, then Wagner. Replying to the objection that Wagner was one-sided, and had only done opera, he is emphatic on the point that Wagner has done it supremely, once and for all. Replying to a reminder that Bach is usually put first by cultured musicians, he admits the Leipsig [sic] cantor's general supremacy and says he plays three or four of the Immortal Forty-eight every day. Concerning the Philharmonic Choral and Orchestral Society of Worcester of which he has recently accepted the conductorship, he says that though he is desirous of bringing forward new works he has no wish to slight the old masters. He wants the best of everything. When new works are worth hearing, let them be heard. We cannot eternally give 'The Messiah', 'Elijah', Beethoven's Fifth Symphony and Schubert's 'Unfinished' without any change. Wherefore the Society is producing Humperdinck's *'Die Wallfahrt nach Kevlaar'* (a ballad of Heine) for the first time in England; the German words to be used, which fact strikes me as unusual in this country. The people of Worcester, it seems, are cultured and would as soon sing in German as any other language, and so saying, Mr Elgar takes a dip at the bird's-eye seen dimly half-way down a Titanic canister. 'King Olaf' he says, 'went like a flash at Bradford. Mr Cowen conducted splendidly – nothing could have been better – and both band and chorus, as well as conductor have my warmest gratitude.'

'From Bradford to Leeds and from Leeds to the new cantata 'Caractacus', is an easy transition and he is kind enough to give a few musical indications of the style and manner of certain movements. The whole is sketched thematically, but the working out still demands time and energy. 'Easy composition, laborious correction' is said to have been the motto of Robert Burns and Mr Elgar works on similar lines. Not far from his house the great Herefordshire Beacon with its wonderful trenches of the Silures and its vast system of prehistoric fortifications rears its scarred flanks to the clouds; and this may have inspired him with the 'ancient British' idea. There will be a 'British March', perhaps a 'Roman March', certainly a 'Druid Chorus' and a 'Sword Song' by Caractacus. Those who know how skilfully Mr Elgar writes for the orchestra would fain have an Overture but the inclusion of this feature is somewhat uncertain. Nevertheless, the cantata will present much noble music and though it could hardly surpass 'King Olaf' it will probably possess more popular features. True it might not be heard on the barrel-organs but there is every reason to believe that 'Caractacus' will do honour even to the Leeds Festival and that, like 'King Olaf' it will be found that the cantata has 'come to stay'. Not everyone can appreciate the Elgarian muse at a first hearing; this is the inevitable drawback of individuality of style, a point which is fully discussed in Mr Balfour's 'Foundations of Belief' a great work whose title scarcely promises musical criticism. But Mr Elgar's work is both scholarly and inspired and improves on deeper examination and repeated hearing. And as the composer has gone from strength to strength there is every reason to anticipate a great success for 'Caractacus'.'

Rehearsals began on July 9th – more than a month before he completed the full score. The Leeds Mercury reported: 'Another full rehearsal of the Festival Chorus was held in the Town Hall on Saturday afternoon when Mr Edward Elgar appeared in person to direct a trial of his new cantata 'Caractacus'. Mr Elgar who came before the Festival Chorus in Leeds for the first time, acknowledged a warm welcome by declaring that he did not appear as a foreigner but as a fellow countryman. To be called upon to write a work for the Leeds Festival he esteemed the blue ribbon of his profession and the highest honour a composer could secure. He had looked forward to that meeting and he hoped the experience would be mutually profitable. The rehearsal then began in the presence of the sectional chorus-masters and a goodly number of the public. The trial was a thorough one, entailing many repetitions, and once at least eliciting a cry of 'Bravo !' from the conductor-composer who briefly expressed his satisfaction ere quitting the platform at the close.

'The interest of the occasion of course centred on the opportunity it afforded those present of making some sort of acquaintance with the new work. Criticism is out of the question at this early stage but it may be permissible as well as worthwhile to indicate a few general impressions derived from the rehearsal.

'Thus, it appears that 'Caractacus' contains little or no actual part-writing for the voices which are treated on something resembling orchestral lines. Mr Elgar is free from whatever cramping influences may be held to accompany an academic training, and perhaps, as a result, he has dared to be original in several directions. 'Caractacus' certainly embodies some of the best music Mr Elgar has written and it is already evident that the novelty furnishes a worthy successor to 'King Olaf'.

By the end of August, rehearsals were attended by the Festival's Chief Conductor, Sir Arthur Sullivan, who in 1890 had, according to fond belief, so infamously denied Elgar the opportunity of rehearsing his music by arriving unannounced to commandeer the orchestra. Now, eight years later, he witnessed Elgar taking centre stage amidst continued praise from London critics – even though the work had yet to be heard.

E A Baughan in the Musical Standard: 'I have no hesitation in saying that 'Caractacus' is not only the most important of the novelties but, viewed quite apart from the Leeds Festival works, is a composition which definitely determines Mr Elgar's position as the first of modern British composers. Such praise may seem exaggerated in view of the excellent work done by Stanford, Parry and others during their career, but there is just that real musical creation in 'Caractacus' that is lacking so often in the work of the more pretentiously academic of our native composers. Again, if ever a national opera were established in England, Mr Elgar is the one man to whom I should look to give us something worthy of our nation.'

Elgar reacted to this in a letter to his friend Troyte Griffith: 'I will send you a M. Standard which is the first to give me the place I've fought for.' Griffith replied: 'I am glad that you have at last satisfied the critics – and yourself, but remember I am one, what have you been feeding them on in London ?'

Baughan's article also produced damning verdict on the enormous festival programmes and rehearsal organisation: 'By beginning at ten o'clock and finishing at two o'clock, you certainly get four solid hours. But four solid hours are too long a stretch both for the instrumentalists and the conductor, and yet four hours a day are quite insufficient for the work to be done. It would be better to have a working day of six hours or more than a whole day of rehearsals. It may be that some of the orchestral players could not give so much time in one day. If that be so then undoubtedly it should have been arranged so that the rehearsals might have begun last week.

'As it is one is reluctantly brought to the conclusion that artistically, these festivals, of which as Englishmen we are excessively and naturally proud, are too much of a farce. Everything that can reasonably be expected has been done to make the choral performances as perfect as possible. And yet when such efforts are made towards perfection it is depressing to find that to a great extent the goal must necessarily be missed through the fashionable parsimony toward adequate orchestral rehearsal.

'Saturday and Monday are considered sufficient for the rehearsal of the chorus and orchestra together when the programme contains no less than eleven choral works : 'Elijah' Elgar's 'Caractacus', Stanford's 'Te Deum', Otto Goldschmit's new Ode, Alan Gray's 'A Song of Redemption' Bach's 'Mass in B Minor', Brahms's 'Rhapsody', Cowen's 'Ode to the Passions', Faure's 'The Birth of Venus' the Choral Symphony [of Beethoven], and the 'Hymn of Praise'. When it is said that these eleven works contain six which are absolutely new both to the orchestra and chorus, and one, the Choral Symphony, which experience has always shown requires an enormous amount of rehearsal it must be admitted that when I said these festivals under present circumstances are artistically a farce, I was not going too far.'

Baughan heaped similar derision on the orchestral programme: 'To show how absurd are the ideas of the organisers of these festivals as to the amount of rehearsals required for the orchestra, it is only necessary to say that on Monday four hours were evidently considered sufficient for the rehearsing of no fewer than five overtures including Dvorak's 'In der Natur' Liszt's 'Les Preludes' and the duet between Wotan and Brunnhilde at the end of 'Die Walkure' besides the Beethoven Symphony and Mozart's 'Prague'.'

And he added: 'Then came the rehearsal of Miss Clara Butt's song : 'Divinites du Styx' which was quite a waste of time as Gluck's score is simple enough in all conscience and, as the result proved, nothing had to be corrected. Miss Butt could easily have explained her ideas to Sir Arthur [Sullivan] without going through the whole song and so wasting precious time which could easily have been given to Mr Elgar's 'Caractacus' a work which bristles with difficulties both for the soloists and the orchestra.'

He continued: 'A somewhat strange incident in the 'Song of Redemption' [by Alan Gray] was the finding by the composer much to his surprise of a couple of final chords that clashed. The last I saw of the tall Yorkshire musician was his sitting down with the full score on his knee ruefully putting matters right. Then came the Spring Song from 'Die Walkure' and to suit Mr [Edward] Lloyd the orchestra was ordered to transpose the music a semitone upwards. Apparently Mr Lloyd set the tempo which to my mind was in places ludicrously slow.

'I could not help wondering what Humperdinck thought of our English rehearsals. He wandered about all morning somewhat disconsolate for he was in some trepidation about band parts of his Moorish Symphony.

'The composer's disconsolate expression was justified. The symphony is in three movements and the band parts of the last two were not complete on Thursday, the parts for the brass and some of the strings not having come to hand. The composer is promised a special rehearsal and this will make it all the more difficult for Mr Elgar to obtain something approaching perfection in the performance of his 'Caractacus'.'

Elgar did not escape either: 'The composer is not a very experienced conductor and probably did not do himself justice knowing that hardly two hours remained for the rehearsal of his work. At any rate the stoppages were incessant and even then it was quite evident the composer did not attempt to do more to correct obvious misreadings for too many a passage. One could see from the score he would have liked to have given more point and spirit. As it happened the rehearsal came to an end before his work had been gone through and the remaining number had to be left over to Thursday morning.

'It is a pity, I think, that 'Caractacus' is not to be conducted by a professional conductor at Leeds, for Mr Elgar is not a good conductor at all, and during the rehearsals it has been evident that he cannot make the men under his command understand to the full precisely the effect he desires to obtain; but the festival fashion puts a premium on the suicide of composers and Mr Elgar will be the latest victim of that fashion.'

The Sunday Times also criticised the rehearsals, both in Leeds and London, saying that the way they were handled 'was laudable enough but it did not do; nor was there a man in the orchestra, I fancy, who would not have preferred to take an interval for lunch at one o'clock, returning at two and going on till four – thus putting in altogether five hours work per diem – rather than rehearse for four hours at a stretch and wind up in a state of mental and physical exhaustion with the unpleasant reflection that some portion of the morning's programme had been left over for another day.

'Even Sir Arthur Sullivan, quick and sweetly reasonable as he is, found last Monday morning's task a heavier one than he could accomplish. Fancy – only four hours for putting the polish on – not to say achieving a 'reading' of – two symphonies, one symphonic poem, five overtures and four other instrumental and vocal pieces! It was obviously beyond human power; the two symphonies had to be left untouched.

'But it is difficult to say what would have happened if all the novelty-composers had been fidgety and exacting in the same degree as Mr Edward Elgar. Somehow, Mr Cowen, with his 'Ode to the Passions', Dr Stanford with his 'Te Deum', Dr Alan Gray with his 'Song of Redemption', Herr Humperdinck, with his 'Moorish Rhapsody' and M. Gabriel Faure with his ode 'La Naissance de Venus' contrived to make satisfactory progress and finish off their various works within an approximately just space of time.

'Not so Mr Elgar. The Malvern musician is one of those conductors who understand what they want a great deal better than the art of getting it. His idea, apparently, is to worry his forces into a comprehension of his intentions. He stops at every third bar and calls for repeats until the band fairly loses its temper (without perhaps showing it) and there ensues a general feeling of impatience and dissatisfaction. 'Caractacus' maybe a work of great ability but it had no right to occupy the time of the Leeds orchestra to the extent that it did last Tuesday and Thursday.'

The Leeds Mercury observed: 'It is a long work and exceedingly difficult and thoroughly deserved an entire morning. As it happened, Mr Elgar, after being introduced to the orchestra by Sir Arthur [Sullivan] in a charming little speech only had two hours and ten minutes to run through his ambitious composition, with the result that the rehearsal was not finished. This is very unsatisfactory not only for the unfortunate composer but also for the band. Mr Elgar in the earlier part frequently stopped the instrumentalists, his chief complaint being of under accentuation. Certain passages he went through three or four times, and in one instance this repetition caused a considerable amount of amusement. It was where Eigen describes her meeting with the Druid maiden. Madame Medora Henson was singing the music and at the line, 'When we came to the oak' Mr Elgar several times stopped the band. Some of the audience remarked that the daughter of Caractacus and her lover took a long time reaching that oak!

'Applause is supposed to be prohibited at these rehearsals, Sir Arthur [Sullivan] remarking that they are private gatherings and that the audience is only invited to listen and not to express appreciation. Indeed in these matters, the distinguished musician tries to be very severe and asked two ladies to cease chattering! Mr Elgar's work was, however, such a surprise, that at the close of nearly every section there was applause. This was specially loud in the second section after Caractacus's stirring solo 'Leap to the Light' which was tastefully rendered by Mr Andrew Black and after the exquisite love duet in the third for Madame Henson and Mr Edward Lloyd.'

The Yorkshire Herald added: 'At the conclusion of one very fine scene between Miss Henson and Mr Edward Lloyd the audience broke all restraints and applauded vociferously bringing up the Hon. Secretary with a protest.'

While The Yorkshire Post noted: 'The love duet, sung by Madame Henson and Mr Lloyd provoked a storm of applause which the entire force of police were unable to quell. But what audience could resist the high G with which the duet ends, even were the music less beautiful than it is?'

Then came the performance. The Leeds Mercury carried a full-page feature providing a vivid picture of what that day must have been like.

'It was a muggy day yesterday and the Victoria Square has seldom looked muggier or the Town Hall more black and majestic or the shops opposite more tumble down than they did on the opening day of the Leeds Musical Festival.

'In the grey, the dirty grey of the morning curious wayfarers waded their way to the Square which all day possessed a magnetism that was only equally the general dismalness of its surroundings and of the atmosphere. The finishing touches were being given to the temporary erections, the last piece of red baize was smoothed out and tin-tacked tight and hammer in hand the joiners and the carpenters stretched themselves with a sigh and contemplated the glory of a completed task.

'All was ready for the Festival. A tremendous effort had been made to lend an air of poetry to the ghastly materialism of the Victoria Square. There is, as all the world knows, a fountain in the centre. Yesterday it was a fountain no more. No stream of water gurgled despondingly from its pipe to drop dejectedly into the dirty water in the dirtier basin beneath. The tap had been turned off and the glories of this cascade were for the nonce suspended. Instead, a pile of fern leaves – or was it bracken ? – had been strewn generously over the surface of the basin and potted evergreens waved – or would have done so had there been anything to wave them - proudly on the parapet and every possible ledge. Green though it all was and inexpensive, it was an obvious improvement on the efforts of the 'fountain' even at its happiest moments.

'The crowd stared with awed admiration at this oasis in a desert of dreary brick and mortar and then turned their attention to other matters. And of these there was an abundance.

'The policeman's gloves never looked whiter, their bearing never more lofty nor responsible, their helmets never so metropolitan. All day long in gentle persuasive accents they implored entreated and directed. Now it was 'Please Ladies, not so close in' – to the poor folk who had no tickets and less money – or 'Not this way!' to the cabby who would take the shortest route in flagrant violation of all the printed regulations that were ever concocted. All the carriages, and the cabs, or whatnot began to roll up for the opening concert in the morning, the crowd and the interest correspondingly grew in volume. Women in discoloured attire, with shawls over their heads divided their attention 'twixt the opening and closing of carriage doors and the disinterested cries, groans, gurgles, and shrieks of countless unhappy-visaged babies to whom the Festival was as nothing compared with the gratification of the inner-man – one ought to say, inner infant.

'Young girls, hatless and arm in arm stood patiently and laughed and talked and waited. What did they expect to see? Goodness knows. That is what a policeman said, adding that anything would draw a crowd. It was a remarkable demonstration of British endurance one way or another, that crowd, outside the Town Hall, all day long.

'Eventually they must have got home to bed and one wonders whether their bosoms at that late hour throbbing with satisfaction that having realised all that they had undoubtedly anticipated. It is impossible to say.

'Assuredly they looked happy and delighted enough. Possibly the festival was to them, perhaps more as it was to some of those on whom Fortune had smiled with all her teeth showing but who nevertheless wore a very blasé look at everything that was going on within the walls of the sombre-looking Town Hall.

'There were plenty of cabs and sufficient carriages during the half hour preceding the morning concert to satisfy the most critical judge of horse flesh harnesses and hides. But it was nothing to the evening. The magnetism of the City square was then beyond all calculation. Whole streets were blocked with vehicles, on hire, on loan, and on exhibition. The indifference of the horses was only equalled by the hauteur with which their drivers bore themselves and the eagerness with which their living freight disembarked and lightly strode over the various steps of their respective entrances.

'It was here that the crowds – for there was a crowd outside all three main entrances – gaped most and stared and jostled and pushed in their energetic attempts to see the Festival from without. And in sooth it was a brave sight to see the gaily dressed ladies tripping from the steps of the broughams and up over the red-carpeted steps with the gentlemen behind shouting directions to the Jehus and giving a final pat for the satisfactory adjustment of their white ties.

'There was the same exclamation as is popularly attributed to a wonderful exhibition of the magic-lantern – a long drawn-out attenuated crammed-with-admiration 'Oh-h-h'. It was almost with regret that the policemen – it was all policemen – implored the wonder-stricken crowd to keep off; it seemed so inhuman to deprive them of the joy that is borne of genuine admiration for the real yet unattainable – an admiration which in most cases, was unalloyed with a single pang of envy.

'Hither and thither hurried people – greybeards, youths, elderly ladies, and maidens – with 'scores' rolled under their arms. This Festival must be a 'fine strike' for the music-sellers. But this is merely by the way. All the while the concerts were in progress the waiting assembly outside scarce diminished either in numbers or patience and not until the last cab or carriage had gone did the crowd dissolve – a gossiping, chilled, wondering congregation, the greater part of which will doubtless repeat their self-imposed practices today and for the remainder of the Festival.

'Everywhere one went within a score of yards of the Town Hall, one was warned in staring monotonous tones of black 'Beware of Pickpockets', who, if they were there at all were sufficiently cute to let no one know it. In all respects it was a well behaved, orderly, respectable crowd – for these are days when one does not have to be a company-promoter or anything else which might be deemed to qualify as respectable. The police on the whole had no trouble. When they worried they worried in a merely official sense and nobody minded. It was all good nature the whole day through. Such is the direct and indirect outcome of the influence of music that whether it be heard or not, so long as it is there, somewhere, its harmony will force its way into the heart and the hand of the pickpocket with be stayed. A fellow-feeling makes us wondrous kind, save, as somebody has said when there's a fellow feeling in one's coat behind. But as far as could be gathered, there was nothing so sad as that in all yesterday's proceedings.'

The article then provided a vivid impression of what the atmosphere was like inside the hall, as Elgar came to the rostrum to conduct his new work.

'With every seat again occupied, as it appeared, the Victoria Hall presented an even more brilliant spectacle in the evening, when fashion enjoyed full sway. There was, too, a certain pleasant air of expectation and excitement observable for the first of the specially commissioned works was awaiting judgement. This was Mr Edward Elgar's 'Caractacus' which promised to be the most important of the novelties brought forward during the week.

'It was a triumph and everyone admitted it. There is always someone, however, who has a rider to add. The rider last night was to the effect that it was a most amazing noise. Exclamations were to be heard all over the crowded hall at the conclusion of every scene. 'Tremendous isn't it?' said one lady to a bosom friend. 'Yes that it is and so dramatic' was the gushing response. But in spite of everything, in spite even of the noise of the brass and the crash of cymbals, perhaps in consequence, hands were clapped as seldom as they are in evening-dress circles, and the chorus rose en-masse and cheered Mr Elgar for all he was worth.

'The composer was most modest. His bow was hurried, almost nervous and he seemed only too glad to be able to get away from it all. Even in the hour of his triumph he remembered the share of the chorus and of the orchestra in the success achieved; and thus it was that Mr Elgar combined one bow to the enthusiastic audience and another to the cheering occupants of the orchestra, with a clap of the hands on his own part – a pretty little tribute to all that the chorus and instrumentalist had done for him in the rendering of an ambitious and altogether striking work.

'Coming to the audience it was a sight worthy of the best traditions of Leeds or of anywhere else. A compact mass of brilliancy will best, and not exaggerately, describe it. The Victoria Hall never looked more resplendent. Nor will the spectacle ever be surpassed there. How could it be?'

And then, after this scene setter, came the verdict on Elgar's work:

'Having written at length in a preliminary article followed by some later remarks at rehearsal it is not easy to find anything fresh to say upon the actual performance of 'Caractacus'. Now however, what were assumptions and inferences are replaced by verities and from the depth of actual intimacy one can speak with some conviction of authority.

'Thus fortified we hasten to record our impression that 'Caractacus' is a work of which our native art has good reason to be proud. It is, we think, the best that Mr Elgar has yet accomplished, and, with 'King Olaf' in mind, this is significant.

'The pictorial qualities of the cantata are very great – indeed we are inclined to rate them as chief among the many features that clamour for attention. Mr Elgar can of course be directly dramatic when he likes as almost every other page of his score testifies but he is even more obviously concerned with the pictorial than the emotional phrases of his subject and the whole work moves with the atmosphere of the graphic and picturesque.

'Mr Elgar is not the product of a school. Some may hint that this is his misfortune but we prefer to consider it rather as an advantage and to see in the individuality of his style something that an academic training would have undesirably modified.

'As with Dvorak's music it is not the solo passages in 'Caractacus', effective as they may be, that primarily excite attention so much as the fine texture and changing depths and masses of colour in what, for convenience sake, may be called the orchestral background, though in some instances background is about the last term to apply with any approach to propriety.

'The very strength of 'King Olaf' proved in a measure its weakness. There was such a wealth of idea and such a free use of the full symphonic orchestra in that remarkable work that the mind rather wearied in the attempt to grasp it all.

'With 'Caractacus' the same strenuous style of treatment prevails but the utterance is more direct and the thought conveyed is of a simpler though not less significant kind. At times it might be urged the voice parts become well-nigh drowned by the orchestral commentary; but while Mr Elgar's method naturally makes for the exaltation of the orchestra as an illustrative medium we are inclined to attribute such apparent over-weighting to the present festival band which is disproportionately large. Be that as it may, all will agree in recognising the score of 'Caractacus' as being remarkably interesting and rich in colour.

'Here brief consideration must be given to the representative theme [aka 'leitmotif'] for it forms the all-pervading feature of 'Caractacus' and by the value of its application Mr Elgar's work must either stand or fall. Though there are some to whom the representative theme is as odious as the Turk, its significance is not impaired by that fact.

'Just think of what it can do for the dramatic composer or teller of a musical story! Among other things it enables him to depict what is passing in the mind or life of a character without that character appearing or uttering a word; it forms an explanatory connecting link between one phase of the story and another and by its use and development all the threads of dramatic action or emotional feeling may be suggested within a page or even a few bars of the score. Had the pre-Wagnerian composers discerned its infinite possibilities who can doubt they would gladly have adopted the device!

'The only reasonable objection to it lies in the method of its application. If its use causes the music to move, as if upon creaking hinges, the representative theme is but a delusion or a snare.

'Mr Elgar demonstrates his right to employ it much as though he were some Siegmund, and the representative theme, figured as the buried sword in the ash tree – to be used only by him who can draw it forth. Mr Elgar is of course not the first to draw forth this great weapon or the only one to cleave its way to artistic victory by its aid, but we know of none in this country who have wielded it quite so consistently or well.

'Within half a dozen bars of the opening chorus we got nearly as many representative themes and yet the melodic phrase moves so naturally that the joinings are scarcely apparent. The average auditor who hears so little might sit through a performance of 'Caractacus' without suspecting that a single phrase was repeated or that its repetition signified anything but poverty of invention.

'To such, of course, the method upon which Mr Elgar has constructed his cantata conveys no meaning. On the other-hand those who grasp the underlying design together with the fact that the representative theme is a veritable guide to and commentator upon the dramatic situation will be wonderfully helped even if many themes escape their notice; whilst the musician will marvel at the extreme ingenuity with which the composer has set himself in this respect to tell his tale. Apart from its construction, 'Caractacus' is – as should be the case – thoroughly interesting.

'Mr Elgar's melodic gift is very great and often highly happy and original in its manifestation. In proof of this we would point to the 'Druid Maiden's Theme'. Less important however is this fascinating subject than the 'Song of the Sword', which is alike manly and musical, though the popular verdict is in favour of the love duet in the third scene and for once the popular verdict is not wrong for it would be hard to conceive more beautiful or more passionate music of the kind than is to be found in this remarkable episode. Here Mr Elgar touches high water mark though performance brought out the final scene in a way we had not ventured to anticipate. To think that such an amazing wealth of thought and idea as is revealed here should be largely spent in vain is indeed saddening.

'And yet we are afraid it is only too likely that 'Caractacus' will be treated with neglect if only for the very obvious fact that it exacts much from even the best-equipped Festival forces.

'It is indeed an irony of fate that works with not a thousandth part of the artistry and brain power embodied in 'Caractacus' are likely to have the preference because they involve less preparation and slighter executive means.

'The currency of Mr Elgar's work is, however, a matter for the future to decide. For the time being it is enough to pronounce 'Caractacus' to be a remarkable creation which is enough to make the present Festival memorable in musical history. At such a triumph for our native art all with unfeignedly rejoice.

'The performance may fairly be described as gratifying and in some instances even excellent. The score is a most elaborate one and crowded with detail and that the band got through it so well and after so slight rehearsal is a proof of what our native players can do when subjected to a severe test. Though it was not apparent that Mr Elgar had reduced the number of his strings, as he thought of doing, the effects gained were much more satisfactory than at rehearsal on Saturday evening.

'For this Mr Elgar has probably to thank himself for a greater measure of self-possession was evident in his conducting and the players could not but reap benefit from the confidence thus inspired. Mr Elgar's system of treatment necessitates much dove-tailing of themes and the accompaniment thus provided is often of but slight assistance to the singer. Probably on this account much false intonation was heard chiefly it must be said on the part of the principals. Mr Andrew Black as 'Caractacus' was, however, free from this, and his rendering of the role proved to be one of his best-judged efforts, at once manly and artistic and endowed with some touch of tenderness as well as desirable vigour and utterance. Mr Edward Lloyd hardly came up to his rehearsal level but that was remarkably high even for him and for the rest it must be conceded that he sustained the part of Orbin, the bard, warrior and lover with much warmth of expression and beauty of vocal tone. As Eigen, the King's daughter, Mdme. Medora Henson did her utmost but she hardly appeared to grasp the idiom and sang in a manner to suggest she had not been thoroughly familiar with the part though her rendering of the love duet with Mr Lloyd was remarkably effective and captured the fancy of the audience in an unmistakable way.

'As the Archdruid, Mr John Browning had a congenial task to perform and acquitted himself well, more particularly in the scene about the sacred oak in which, as we have said, a subdued gong-roll is employed with happily suggestive effect. Mr Charles Knowles, in a dual role also justified the confidence reposed in him by his dramatic style and vigorous utterance.

'As for the chorus they enjoyed the work and did full justice to its demands. The call of the sentries afar was hardly subdued enough but the chorus of the spirits of the hills was wonderfully well managed, whilst the grandiose peroration with the basses fairly revelling in their work created an imposing effect and was followed by a scene of warm enthusiasm, Mr Elgar being recalled to the platform and congratulated in the heartiest manner by audience and executants alike.'

So much for Elgar's music, but the libretto, by his Malvern neighbour, the retired Indian Civil Servant Harry Acworth, had different review.

As the Observer noted: 'It is to be feared that the libretto of Mr Edward Elgar's new cantata 'Caractacus' will militate against its popularity. The scheme, in as much as it provides a series of scenes which lend themselves to musical treatment is good; but it is carried out in an amateurish manner.

'An invocation by Druids in a forest stirs the imagination but when at the climax of the rites the chorus declare that 'The curse is spoke' the solemnity of the scene banishes with the celerity of a magic-lantern slide. Again the happy-to-be-ever-after ending is doubtless consoling to those who take an interest in the fate of lovers but it is not heroic and suggests a Roman suburban villa with Caractacus as grandpapa. The final chorus, too, of the Romans, who, after ferociously vociferating for the death of the Britons, suddenly declaim a long prophecy for the future greatness of the conquered land, is absurd.

'These failings may account for the want of character and in certain instances, commonplace nature of some of the principal themes; but when this has been said, there remains nothing but what excites admiration.

'The triumphal procession music at Rome seems to yearn for spectacular illustration and the whole scene is conceived and carried out with great dramatic power. It should close the work, the clairvoyant remarks of the Romans forming an anti-climax, although their setting is a fine piece of choral writing. Every page indeed, shows the hand of a highly imaginative and accomplished composer and whatever be the fate of Caractacus, it will always excite the esteem of musicians.'

The Athenaeum Magazine, after discussing Elgar's liberal use of 'representative themes' said this: 'We must own to a feeling of disappointment with the 'Caractacus' theme: it does not appear to us sufficiently imposing, a few places excepted. Then the orchestral accompaniment, although this is not a very appropriate term – appears at times over elaborate; a further careful application of the pruning knife would, if we are not mistaken, improve some of the earlier scenes. But this difficult matter could only be undertaken by the composer. After hearing his work it is possible that he may be of our opinion.'

The Times concluded: 'Mr Elgar's music has the inestimable merit that it seldom if ever conveys even a momentary suggestion of any other composer's work. All that he has to say is his own. It suffers if at all, from an excess of detail not from any absence of interest or individuality. The librettist has occasionally led him into a somewhat undue prolixity in the development of the dramatic or musical material and several of the six scenes would be none the worse for a little compression.'

The Daily Mail declared: 'Mr Elgar, who almost at a bound, has arrived in the front rank of contemporary composers. The power and originality of his works are unmistakable. He is the Rudyard Kipling of the musicians.'

E A Baughan, in The Westminster Gazette in an often quoted review which has long suggested that 'Caractacus' was generally badly received by the critics, commented :'He has strength of execution and his ideas though tending towards the sentimental and even now and then to the commonplace are dramatic enough. It is only when we expect really original and strong invention that Mr Elgar fails. His power of making music covers up his poverty of direct and thematic invention. All through the work we are brought to a standstill by a theme which has not risen to the dramatic and poetic situation and the music as a whole gives on the impression that a second-rate mind has by some freak of nature been endowed with a capacity for expressing itself which we do not expect to find in anyone who is not a genius. For in 'Caractacus', that capacity is very marked.

'There can be no doubt of the immense cleverness of the work and it must be emphatically stated that this cleverness is no mere pedantic expression of a certain mastery over the art, for Mr Elgar's individuality is that, above all else, he is a musician and always writes *music*. To sum up, there is much fancy and poetry in the music and quite extraordinary technical expression but that the musical conception, the themes, the general atmosphere of the work swing so much to the sentimental and facilely melodious that the music does not convey the ideas the composer intended.'

Rosa Burley, Headmistress of the Malvern School where Elgar had taught violin, gave her own account, written many years later. It is often quoted as eye-witness testimony but its veracity is surely questionable in the light of this press reaction and indeed Alice Elgar's diary.

In her published memoir 'The Record of a Friendship', Burley recalls: 'Edward, who never enjoyed any festival of his earlier years was particularly unhappy at this one. Nervous and never too sure of himself, he needed an immense amount of encouragement before he was at anything like his best and while in Worcester, where by now he had become something of a lion, this stimulus was always forthcoming, it was a different matter at Leeds which had known and entertained most of the greater composers of the 19th century. Here he was merely one of a group and by no means that most important member of it, with the result that although the committee treated him with courtesy and such committees consisted of very cultured people, he felt insulted and hurt.
'The fact is, of course, that this was one more example of the absurd injustice which necessitates a composer's attempting to be a performer. The Leeds committee found Edward ill-tempered and difficult but it may be that they did not realise the state of his mind. After the nervous strain of creating one of his major works he was in no mood to supervise the details of its performance, still less to listen to the chatter of either admirers or detractors.
'When it was all over he rushed back to Malvern with the air of one who has fought - and is inclined to think he has lost - a heavy engagement.'

Alice Elgar's diary cites Edward and herself visiting the Town Hall the day after the performance, where in the gallery they heard a work by Palestrina and Stanford's 'Te Deum' – then going to a lunch with the Lord Mayor at which Alice introduced Lady Mary Lygon to Gabriel Faure. The following day they attended the performance of Bach's Mass in B Minor and then dined with the Festival Secretary along with Sir Hubert Parry before going back to the Festival where they heard Parry's 'Blest Pair of Sirens' and Handel's 'Alexander's Feast'. The next day they attended the festival again, heard Cowen's new Ode, met him, and spent time with Sullivan before leaving for London where they stayed for ten days, attending concerts at the Queen's Hall – where the Bavarian Dances were performed and the Crystal Palace – and where the Triumphal March from 'Caractacus' was performed in London for the first time - 'Great Success. E. had a *real* ovation', according to the diary - and then wound up their stay in the capital by visiting the Savoy Theatre – presumably at Sullivan's personal invitation – to hear 'The Sorcerer' and 'Trial by Jury'.

On his return, Elgar sketched in his mind the 'Enigma' Variations.

THE ENIGMA VARIATIONS

On February 24th 1899 the Daily News reported: 'Mr F G Edwards has, for the March number of the Musical Times, obtained from Mr Elgar certain details concerning his forthcoming works. For a London concert in the spring Mr Elgar has, for example, written fourteen orchestral 'Symphonic Variations' intended, it is said, as sketch portraits of his friends or rather he has 'looked at the theme through the personality, if not the spectacles of thirteen other men and women'. The idea opens up infinite possibilities. An orchestral portrait by Professor Bridge or Professor Stanford – and vice versa - would, for example be especially interesting.'

Various other papers announced the arrival of the Variations and by April adverts were appearing in the nationals for the June concerts at the St James's Hall where Hans Richter was to give the first performance as part of a series of concerts including works by Tchaikovsky, Rimsky Korsakov, Glinka, Glasounov, Siegfried Wagner, and Svendsen. Elgar, as the press rather pointedly complained, was the only British composer included.

Novello's released the published piano version of the score, which further tantalised the press concerning the way in which Elgar had constructed the work. One report commented: 'These Variations are supposed to be more or less descriptive of certain of Mr Elgar's friends. The composer goes so far as to provide initials to his variations, but the clue thus supplied does not point in the direction of any celebrities. 'C.A.E.' 'R.P.A.' 'B.G.N.' and 'Ysobel' gratify the curiosity but little and 'Nimrod' even less.

'After all however, this is a small matter compared with the fact that these Variations – fourteen in number – are highly artistic and conceived in the true modern spirit that disdains the merely ornamental treatment of a chosen theme. Whilst never losing sight of the original subject Mr Elgar contrives to place it in quite an astonishing variety of aspects.'

The Yorkshire Post, reviewing the piano score shortly before the first performance commented: 'These fourteen variations possess an interest that is quite apart from their intrinsic musical value. Each represents the composer's characterisation of one of his friends so that the whole is a portrait gallery translated into music. The idea cannot be described as a new one after Schumann's 'Carnival' in which the personalities of his wife, Chopin, Paganini and of Schumann himself in different moods are reflected by the various movements.

'Mr Elgar's application of the idea differs however, in one important respect. His 'portraits' are of his private friends and are not of public characters as such. We shall, therefore listen to his variations in much the same spirit in which we visit the National Gallery for the sake of the pictures rather than that in which we study the National Portrait Gallery for the sake of the subjects. It need not be added that this is the artistic, as distinguished from the merely historical, point of view. Mr Elgar, we take it, has chosen his subjects chiefly as affording varying types of character – an excellent method it must be acknowledged, of securing variety of musical treatment.'

The Birmingham Gazette exulted: 'The work is a masterpiece of its kind and confirms our oft-stated opinion, that Mr Elgar is exceptionally strong in orchestral writing and admitting his unusual versatility, that in the region of the symphony will be found the climate most likely to develop his genius to the highest perfection.'

The well-known story concerning the work's conception appeared verbatim a week before the first performance suggesting it emanated from a press release bearing Elgar's hallmark: 'Dr Richter is so delighted with Mr Edward Elgar's Variations, Op 36, which are to be first played at St James's Hall on the 19th inst. that he is giving the work extra time at rehearsals in order to ensure a perfect performance. Mr Elgar, it is said, displays a curious vein of humour in this composition. It happens that he was extemporising on the pianoforte one evening and 'chanced upon' a pleasing theme. Turning to a friend in the room he remarked that a certain person would play the melody in a particular way, that somebody else would play it differently, that a violoncellist might make it an agreeable solo and that a Cathedral organist could embellish it with pedal notes. Mr Elgar has now shown in type what his friends might have done with this theme, or 'Enigma' as he calls it.'

A different version appeared in the Musical Standard shortly after the first performance: 'The composition owes its origins in the composer extemporising one day. For the amusement of a few friends present he gave a series of variations showing how a theme could be treated to express the character of some of his friends.'

The Variations closed the first half of a mixed programme preceded by Dvorak's 'Carneval' overture, Svendsen's Legend for Orchestra 'Zorahayda' and the closing scene from 'Gotterdammerung' by Wagner. The second half also featured the first UK performance of Rimsky-Korsakov's Suite 'Snegoroutchka' and Mozart's 'Prague' Symphony.

This was the press reaction.

The Times: 'An abundance of novelties was provided for last night with the natural result that the audience was very large. The most important of the new works was a set of orchestral variations in which Mr Elgar has worked out the humorous idea of giving musical portraiture to a number of his friends who are designated in the score by initials or sobriquets only.

'The theme upon which the variations, or portraits, are professedly based (for we are informed that a yet more important theme exists, though not audibly) is a succession of notes not unlike the subject of the G minor fugue in book I of Bach's '48'; it has an inner meaning, for it is inscribed 'Enigma' and in a beautiful movement headed only with asterisks a certain phrase is enclosed in inverted commas so that it is evidently impossible for the uninitiated to discuss the meaning of the work fully. On the surface, however, it is exceedingly clever, often charming, and always original and excellently worked out. The composer was warmly applauded at its close.'

The Daily Telegraph: 'Well wrought and ingenious are all of these variations exhibiting in a very high degree Mr Elgar's fertility of resource and the ample freedom of his method. As those who had previous experience of their author expected, the variations are quite modern in style and texture. We like best at a first hearing the ninth of the set [Nimrod] of suave and meditative character, which suggests a cheery personage, beaming through gold rimmed spectacles; while the next in order [Dorabella] provides with its lightness elegance and daintiness, plenty of contrast. The fourteenth variation [EDU] at once bold, jubilant and martial, brings to a close this able work which will certainly add to the composer's reputation.'

The Morning Advertiser: 'English musicianship was payed a direct compliment in the playing for the first time, a set of variations by Mr Ed. Elgar. Steadily, modestly, but with irresistible certainty, Mr Elgar is pushing aside the buckram coated Academici who would monopolise the open paths of honour and is taking his rightful place as a chief among composers of native birth.

'According to Mr Elgar's printed statement 'The principal theme is not played but goes through and over the whole set', an occult remark which inclines us to the belief that Mr Elgar is having a humorous dig at the modern writers of programme music. We did make some effort to realise the subtle presence of this astral subject, but the variations on the theme that was in evidence were so replete with charm, with grace and technical beauty that we found sufficient for the moment was the beauty thereof.'

The Atheneum: 'The theme displays dignity and at the same time simplicity while of the variations we may say there is not one that could be termed feeble; they are remarkable for charm, variety, character, rather than for the skill both of structure and orchestration, by which, however, these qualities are enhanced'.

But: 'We regret that the composer has dedicated his work 'To my friends pictured within'. There was no harm in his working, like Beethoven, to pictures in his mind; but it would have been better not to call attention to the fact. The variations stand in no need of programme; as abstract music they fully satisfy. If the friends recognise their portraits, it will, no doubt, please them; but this is altogether a personal matter. The variations will, we feel sure, be often heard and as often admired.'

The Morning Post went further: 'The programme book informs us that 'over the whole set another and larger 'theme' goes, but is not played…So the principal theme never appears even as in some late dramas e.g. Maeterlinck's 'L'Intruse' and 'Les Sept Princesses' – the chief character is never on the stage' These, it appears, are the composer's own words.

'The peculiarities of Mr Elgar's work does not stop here, for each variation is supposed to depict the idiosyncrasies of one of his friends. Now, the point of a joke is lost if no one can understand it but he who makes it and as the identities of Mr Elgar's friends are not disclosed it is impossible to say whether their musical portraits do them justice or not.'

The Sunday Times agreed: 'It would have been as well to omit certain mysterious suggestions', while the Illustrated Sporting and Dramatic magazine wondered whether Elgar was 'slyly poking fun at his contemporaries who imagine that music has a Jules Verne-like aptitude for ascribing the marvellous'.

The Daily News concluded: 'Mr Elgar's Malvern friends must be a diversified though interesting party, the most remarkable perhaps being a graceful personage bearing the initials 'W.N.'; a meditative, not to say melancholy, character boasting the wholly inappropriate name of 'Nimrod'; a delightful and possibly a very young lady called 'Dorabella' (the best number of the piece); 'B.G.N.' who is graceful though rather slow; and an anonymous personage who may possibly stand for any friend whom the composer had forgotten to include in his gallery, and for whose sake is quoted a phrase from 'Calm Sea and Prosperous Voyage'.'

The Star added: 'There seems to be no disagreeable person among them, unless it is disagreeable to be a little noisy and very, very energetic; not even a pedant or a prig (one really would like to know what a clever man like Mr Elgar would make of the musical formula for a prig). Not all are equally successful. I myself liked those best which are gay and fanciful and dainty preferring them to those which are big and strong. In fact Mr Elgar seems to have been more happy with the Variations which represent women than with those representing men. He might be called in the best sense a 'feminist' in music.'

While the Pall Mall Gazette – still calling Elgar 'Edwin' – went even further: 'They are exceedingly clever but we could have wished that he had not chosen to accompany their publication with a certain amount of extraneous self-criticism, which we frankly own to find unmeaning and unintelligible. 'Through and over the whole set', says he, 'another and larger theme goes and is not played'.

'That, we submit, in music is a rank impossibility. Mr Elgar compares his idea to that in Meaterlinck's 'L'Intruse in which the chief character never appears. But in a play such a situation can obviously be suggested where in music is can never exist. No, we take up a firm stance with Mrs Gamp; the theme that never appears is Mr Elgar's Mrs Harris: it is impossible for us to believe that there is any such person.'

The reference to Mrs Gamp and Mrs Harris is to characters in Dickens. The former is a nurse in 'Martin Chuzzelwit' who has a supportive but entirely imaginary friend called 'Mrs 'Arris'.

Of Elgar's friends, the Pall Mall Gazette critic concluded: 'Some are brilliant creatures, one or two frankly frivolous, one as light as any ballet dancer, two or three rather sentimental, one or two bores, and one a man of exceeding great unhappiness.'

The World commented: 'Mr Elgar rather upset my temper by allowing some nonsense about his clever work to be printed in the programme. He warned us that the dark saying of his enigma, or theme, must be left unguessed by us and that the apparent connection between the variations and the theme is often of the slightest texture. He added – in order to confuse us all as much as possible – that the principal 'theme never appears, even as in some late dramas – the chief character is never on the stage'.

'Mercy on us! What foolish words be these! A theme and variations and the composer tells us that the theme 'must be left unguessed', and that 'through and over the whole set another and larger theme 'goes' but is not played'! This sort of would-be profound and quite unutterable twaddle sets all sensible people against the composer who gives vent to it and against his music. It bemuses the mind. One sits listening for that theme which is over all, like a storm cloud – 'goes' like George Meredith's *Diana* and is not played.

'Where does it go? Perhaps to limbo. Mr Elgar ought to be above such egregious nonsense and ought to let his brilliant music talk for itself. I cannot speak as to the value of the theme that is not played. Since it is not played it cannot be criticised.'

And the Musical News chirped: 'Why distract public attention from the work itself by saying 'I meant something by all this: but you cannot follow my meaning as you do not know my friends.' To quote Schumann by way of apology is beside the mark, for, with few exceptions everyone knew the 'friends' he depicted musically.'

While the Daily Mail complained: 'A musical riddle with twenty-five answers – none of which are guaranteed correct – almost rivals the Sphinx.'

The Guardian commented: 'It may indeed be regretted that the composer should have attempted to describe in his fourteen variations the personal characteristics of several intimate friends who are represented in the score by initials or sobriquets and being unknown to the majority of the audience do not add much to the interest of the music.

'It is aggravating too, to be told that the principal theme is a 'dark saying' or that through and over the whole set of variations another and larger theme 'goes but is not played'; or again to find a certain passage in the thirteenth variation written as a quotation between inverted commas.'

The Westminster Gazette also raised a point which might explain why Elgar *didn't* include any well-known people: 'The possibilities of this sort of thing are obviously considerable and in the hands of certain practitioners one could even conceive libel actions – or would it be slander? – resulting.'

Hans Sachs, writing in the Musical Courier commented: 'The general impression of this score on the whole was that of earnest purpose, ample technique, a judgement founded on study and experience and a facility both in finding and in developing musical ideas. The work is decidedly more intellectual than emotional. There is more self-criticism than self-abandon in it, and the climaxes sound more like a well-planned attempt to reach an effect than the result of strong emotion curbed in and directed by the will.

'Was it not Lord Chesterfield who said that weight without glitter was not gold, but lead? Now I do not think that Mr Elgar's variations are not without brilliancy, but I *do* think that weight plays too preponderant part in this score. The theme, entitled 'Enigma' is by no means ear-haunting or soul-searching, but a few jerky phrases, such as Brahms might have written as a counterpoint to a more important theme.

'Brahms in fact dominates throughout the first five variations and elsewhere in addition. An echo of the early Beethoven, the Beethoven of the first movement of the eleventh piano sonata crops up in Variation 6 [Ysobel]. The 'effects' of Variation 7 [Troyte] are those of the last number of Grieg's first 'Peer Gynt' suite. In Variation 10 [Dorabella] the influence of Tchaikovsky begins to assert itself; the Casse-Noisette suite and the G minor variations being now and then suggested.

'I am well aware that many of these seeming plagiarisms are noticeable only at first and that a better knowledge of the work would in all probability reveal more of the composer and less of the sources of his inspirations. This work, then, to sum up, is in my opinion one in which the critic can find little to blame and an almost unlimited number of excellencies. But, at the same time, I fear that above and beyond all this freedom from blemish there is not to be found that charm of personality and that inexplicable attractiveness which alone endear and artwork in the affections of the public.'

Elgar's public popularity was by now well established, as the Sheffield Independent bore witness after a local performance of 'King Olaf' shortly after the Variations premier: 'Mr Elgar was seen by our reporter on the conclusion of his work in the evening. It was with the greatest difficulty that the composer could be approached. The ante-room was besieged by ladies anxious to get Mr Elgar's signature, and, 'If he would be so kind, a bar from 'King Olaf''. Mr Elgar is a patient and long-suffering man, and he seems unable to say 'no' to a lady, so while he used one hand in wiping his brow, he drove a fountain pen with the other.'

Richter again performed the Variations, in an October 1899 concert also featuring Dohnanyi's Piano Concerto and Tchaikovsky's Pathetique Symphony. The World summed up the general mood: 'Mr Elgar's Variations improve on acquaintance enormously.'

But it added: 'The first time one was, perhaps, too much occupied with the novelty of his attempt at musical portraiture and was perpetually diverted by the curious felicity of some of the orchestral details. The second time one took the brilliant details for granted and listened undisturbed to the work as a whole.

'At the first hearing, again, what struck one most was the success with which many various characters had been drawn in sounds. But this very success carried with it a great danger. For there was but little of that feeling of inherent unity amid diversity without which no work can really be good.'

But for the Morning Leader, the problem with the 'friends' still existed: 'I still think that they contain the best music the talented composer has yet written, but the composition as a whole does not impress me so much as it did at first. There are, to begin with, too many variations, and they do not cohere. The composer set out to describe the idiosyncrasies of several of his friends who are designated by initials but he does not think this fact need have been publicly mentioned. But I fancy it has a great deal to do with the scrappy ineffectiveness of the composition as a whole.

'Mr Elgar has thrown together a number of sketches some of them the merest 'impressions' and the concluding variation has the air of a tacked-on climax. It is all very clever and ingeniously scored, but so continuously epigrammatic as to be a little tedious. And I like Mr Elgar when he is not epigrammatic, but serious as in the opening enigma, the ninth variation [Nimrod] (the best of the lot) and the finale, and when he is frankly light, as in the Dorabella variation. I would suggest that these four sections should be played as a kind of suite for most of the remaining variations are too scrappy in effect, and kill one another, as it were.'

Elgar's reaction appeared some years later: 'When the Enigma Variations were produced the names of the friends 'pictured within' were a puzzle to music critics altho' it was expressly stated that the music might be considered without reference to them. One supercilious young man said: 'I can't criticise your music because I don't know your friends.' The answer was really vitriolic and stern 'Of course not – they are ladies & gentlemen.' Somehow that critic is still cold to the charms of Elgar's music.'

The 'friends' identities remained secret as far as the general public were concerned for 25 years, only being revealed when Elgar wrote accompanying notes to a set of piano rolls in 1924.

The Daily Telegraph reviewed: 'We know or thought we did, each variation apart from its purely musical interest, to be very much a musical portrait of somebody known to the composer. It is not too much to say that after reading what Sir Edward tells us on these rolls, every writer on Elgar, every annotator of the 'Enigma' variations, will need to revise what he has written.

'Every pianist with a soul above musical trash will delight in the rolls for the music he can win from his instrument with their assistance. But every student of the music of our time simply must know what Sir Edward has to say about these variations.

'The issue, indeed is of a first-class importance on the literary side of the art, these variations being, when all is said for the oratorios, the work by which Elgar is best known by the world in general. It was also the first serious work by an English composer to win anything like world fame for a couple of centuries and more.

'On the 'Enigma' as hitherto understood, Sir Edward throws no light. He says nothing about the other and larger theme we never hear but which goes with, not only the theme of the variations, but with each variation. Exactly how a theme which 'goes with' the theme actually used can go with the 'Dorabella' is explained, of course, by the fact that, though usually included in the numbering, the 'Dorabella' in which the theme makes no appearance, is an intermezzo rather than a variation.

'Attempts have been made, it is understood, to cajole Sir Edward into disclosing the secret, but without success. We are not yet to know whether or not the correct answer is to be found in the Gregorian Tone whose first four notes – C,D,F,E -are the basis of the last movement of Mozart's 'Jupiter' Symphony and as a combination are among the germinal themes of music.

'Elgar at any rate is fond of the little phrase, for it crops up in many of his larger works and at a particularly significant point in the very personal 'The Music Makers'. If it is embedded in the variations the writer has not noticed it. Those interested are invited to examine the first four notes of the basic theme of the variations and not to overlook the shape they assume in the 'Nimrod' variation.

'All this, however, is speculation and probably well off the mark. Perhaps, too, we are not entitled to probe into a matter Sir Edward evidently strongly prefers to keep to himself. What he now says is simply that the theme he uses is his own and nothing is to be gained in an artistic or musical sense by 'solving the enigma' of the personalities indicated by the pseudonyms or initials prefixed to the variations in the score.

'These personalities have been a source of inspiration and their idealisations a pleasure intensified as the years go by. They are almost certainly West Country people – men and women of Malvern, Hereford and Worcester and thereabouts so that in a peculiar sense the variations spring from the soil that is our own. Moreover, the work was written at Malvern – within fourteen days of February 1899 – an achievement that even in the days of Handel and the small score would be remarkable.

'It is interesting to note that he sent the score to Richter, though he had never met him, and that a discerning conductor, after suggesting a stronger ending, put them down for performance with small delay.

'He tells of their genesis. He was playing with the theme on the pianoforte and had turned it into the form in which it appears in the fourth variation. The late Lady Elgar, listening, asked who it was like, and could not say, but – 'it was exactly the way W.M.B. goes out of the room.' As the story is usually told, she did not use the initials but referred to W.M.B. more familiarly. But she went on to say that Sir Edward was doing something she thought had 'never been done before'.

'But we have reason for gratitude that Elgar took the hint his wife threw out and gave us the 'Enigma' of our delight. Not that every expounder of the variations has reason to bless the composer for the veil of mystery he has thrown over them. Now that he has thrown the veil aside it emerges that these friends of his we thought 'pictured' in the music are not in every case so portrayed. Some characteristic of theirs, some incident associated with them, fired the composer's musical imagination.

'Probably the only full-length portrait is that which bears the initials C.A.E. (the late Lady Elgar). Hers is the first variation and her music returned in the self-portrait which is the finale of the work. As an instance the case of G.R.S. is worth noting. The variation is a rumbustious affair; the original was a cathedral organist. One annotator asks us 'to note how his active organ peddling is suggested almost throughout in passages given to 'cellos, double basses and bassoons'. Another refers to vigorous organ peddling here.

'Both were written for the benefit of gramophonists and had a certain amount of reason on their side. Sir Edward, however, tells us that it is G.R.S's great bulldog that is pictured, his wild rush down a river bank, his scrambling out of the water and the bark he gave when he landed.

'In some cases it is the musical proclivities of a friend that engages the attention – a 'cellist, a pianist, a viola player. One is mere banter, the most boisterous of them all. Its title 'Troyte', along with the information that he is an architect, will prevent his identity being hidden from Malvernians. The recreations of the very noisy personality portrayed in the music happen to be chamber music and chess.

'There were variations, it seems, for Sullivan and Parry, but Elgar elected not to include them. One would like to hear them.'

One further aspect of this was contained in the piece: '…in 'Musical Opinion' ten years ago there was quoted under 'Peeps into the Past' a review from the 'Harmonicon' of June 1825, of a work entitled –

'The Enigma Variations and Fantasia, on a favourite Irish Air, for the Pianoforte, in the style of Five Eminent Artists, composed and dedicated to the Originals, by Cipriani Potter.'

The reference to this work by Potter, who was, despite his Italian sounding name, an English composer, seems remarkable, considering that it not only used the word 'Enigma' in its title, but also was based on the idea of depicting people in its various musical movements – in this case leading musicians of the time including Rossini and possibly Beethoven.

It is quite plausible that Elgar would have known this work. It was very popular at the time and could have been the sort of work sold at the family music shop. Despite the varying versions of the story of how Elgar's 'Enigma' initially came into his mind, there is no dispute that it emanated from improvisation at the piano, and Potter's composition was a piano piece.

It is quite possible that Elgar could have either consciously or sub-consciously adopted the title for his own work – so perhaps the 'Enigma' is not so 'Enigmatic' after all!

THE GORDON SYMPHONY

In February 1899 The Atheneum announced: 'Mr Edward Elgar's new symphony for the Worcester Festival will be entitled 'Gordon' based on the career of General Gordon. His martial elements, his restless energy and his religious beliefs have inspired the composer. This, like Beethoven and his admiration of Napoleon which led to the 'Eroica'.'

The Sunday Times commented: 'Mr Edgar [sic] Elgar's new symphony is to bear the title of 'Gordon' and will form a dignified musical tribute to the memory of the revered soldier-hero whose martyrdom was happily avenged at Omdurman some months ago,' while The Daily News, alluding to Gordon's connections with both China and the Middle East, commented: 'It will, it is hoped, be free from the characteristics of either Chinese or Arabic music.'

By May, however, The Worcester Journal reported: 'It has been announced that Mr Elgar will not write a new symphony for the Worcester Festival as originally arranged, possibly because he is too much occupied by other work.'

Further comment ceased, but in September, just as the Festival began, the Daily News, under the headline 'The Payment of Composers', commented: 'It is becoming more and more the question how much longer the urgent claims of art are to be sacrificed to those of charity. The question has indeed, at this festival, arisen in another form. In the earlier prospectuses, a symphony or some important composition of that character was announced from the pen of Mr Edward Elgar.

'It was afterwards withdrawn, and the reason, as I am credibly informed, is that the committee declined to pay an adequate fee for it, thinking British musicians should contribute their brainwork gratuitously. This, I believe, is the beginning of a campaign on the part of British composers which may have far-reaching consequences upon our annual festivals. Composers notoriously are not the wealthiest members of the community and they, at least, fail to see why they alone of the professional musicians engaged at the festival should be expected to work for nothing, in order that the funds available for charity may be thus unfairly augmented.'

The Glasgow Herald amplified: 'Mr Elgar is just now extremely popular with his brother musicians owing to the withdrawal of his promised Symphony from the Worcester Festival on the grounds that the committee were not willing to pay properly for his work, £100 being the sum mentioned [about £8,000 in today's money]. Mr Elgar, it is true, is a man of considerable private means but it is claimed that men of fortune are often the readiest to work for nothing and thus spoil the markets. Besides a poorer composer might have been afraid to take so strong a stand, lest he might be boycotted by festival committees. The foreign contributor to English festivals is invariably well paid, for the intelligent foreigner has a very healthy objection to working for nothing.'

In reply, T L Claughton wrote to The Worcester Echo : 'My attention having been drawn to a paragraph which, I am informed, has been copied into many newspapers, stating that the withdrawal of Mr Elgar's promised Symphony from the Worcester Festival was due to the fact that the ' Committee were not willing to pay properly for his work, £100 being the sum mentioned'. Will you allow me as a member of the Committee and having acted as Chairman at its meetings, to give the most unqualified contradiction to this statement? No proposal of the kind was brought before the Committee and no such sum was ever mentioned there as a condition of the fulfilment of Mr Elgar's promise.'

The source of this detailed 'credible' information is a matter of speculation. But Elgar received no more major commissions from the Worcester Festival.

SEA PICTURES

The song-cycle 'Sea Pictures', premiered in an evening concert considered 'absurdly long' by the Times, at the 1899 Norwich Festival. Also included were: the overture 'Mignon' by Ambroise Thomas, 'Trio des Flutes' by Meyerbeer, symphonic suite 'The Seasons' by Edward German, 'Ode to the Passions' by Cowen, 'Vorspiel and Liebestod' from 'Tristan and Isolde' by Wagner, 'The Dream of Endymion' by Cowen and 'Overture di Ballo' by Sullivan,

Daily Telegraph critic Joseph Bennett reviewed: 'The Malvern composer leaves roaring to the ocean. He deals tenderly, sometimes with an effect of infinite sadness upon such themes as 'A lullaby on the waters', 'In haven, Capri', 'A Sabbath morning at sea' 'The place where corals lie with the bones of Lycidas' 'The bottom of the monstrous world' and the swimmer who floats in 'sleepy swirling surges hidden.'

'I could have wished that the gifted composer had chosen at least one lyric, salt in flavour, one verse, if no more eloquent of the ocean when its waves dance in the sunshine, and the ship, as Jack Hatton once sang, 'goes with a pleasant sail – give it to her boys, now give it to her'. But it is scarcely wise to complain that the songs are not other than those we heard tonight, seeing with what beauty, Mr Elgar has invested with the thoughts of his poets, one of whom, C A Elgar has contributed an exquisite flower from the garden of verse.'

The Standard, along with others, saw an oriental influence in 'Where Corals Lie', concluding: 'The work will undoubtedly add to Mr Elgar's reputation and should be heard in our concerts throughout the land.' While the Morning Post commented: 'Beyond their reference to the sea, these songs have nothing in common and the words are by different authors. Though not of equal value they all exhibited that excellence of workmanship their author has taught us to expect from him.'

Generally, the critics agreed the most effective song was 'In Haven', the Daily News dubbing it 'a delicious little number in which local colour is sought to be imparted by the employment in the accompaniment of a guitar.'

The Pall Mall Gazette thought: '[The songs] are not all equally fine; but the finest, perhaps 'In Haven', is extremely fine. Only those who understand (in Henley's splendid phrase) how all the universe can be 'narrowed to the compass of a ring' will see how, in this slight-seeming creation, there is housed so great an artistic emotion. The poet saw in the smallest of flowers just the one shut door that kept him from all the mystery 'of this unintelligible world' so in one short song this exquisite composer houses the even more unintelligible mystery of artistic beauty.'

'Sabbath Morning at Sea' fared less well: 'by far the longest and by no means the most inspired of the series' according to the Times - a view echoed by the Morning Post.

Joseph Bennett, having mused over the performance for another day said: 'I may as well add that Mr Elgar's music made a deep impression upon the best judges here. The note of praise was sounded aloud this morning in the conversation of musicians, who discern, perhaps, more readily than the general public, such beauties of the work as are not quite on the surface. I think, however, that the songs will have a better chance when given individually, rather than as a group. The persistent seriousness, sadness even, which pervades them, may appear monotonous to the majority, whereas, taken, not as a cycle – and they are not a cycle in any sense – but separately, their beauty will know no hindrance.'

THE DREAM OF GERONTIUS

In July 1900 The Birmingham Post announced: 'The only important novelty to be produced [at the Birmingham Festival] will be Mr Edward Elgar's sacred cantata 'The Dream of Gerontius' based on Cardinal Newman's inspired poem and though Mr Elgar has given abundant proofs of his possession of the imaginative faculty demanded for such a task, it is none the less gratifying to learn from the chairman of the Orchestral Committee that a high musical authority who has examined the work pronounces it to be one of 'great beauty and originality'. This was more than a month before Elgar had actually finished orchestrating it.

Anticipation grew. The Birmingham Gazette on August 28th eulogised: 'The Festival Chorus is making great progress with the new work 'The Dream of Gerontius' which is winning golden opinions from all who hear it. Of course, the orchestra is wanting and as everybody knows, the orchestra is a strong point with Mr Edward Elgar. But even without the orchestra, the greatness of the music is discernible. The foot of Hercules is there.

'It would be contrary to etiquette and to the statute in such a case made and provided to attempt a detailed description of the work. But there can be no doubt as to the quality. Even in the bald unaccompanied choruses the solemn impressiveness of the music is abundantly manifest and we venture to predict that 'Gerontius' will prove to be Mr Elgar's best work since 'King Olaf', which so far in our judgement holds the palm.

'There is a lofty earnestness about 'Gerontius' which grows upon the hearer, week by week. Here and there we perceive the individual touches for which Mr Elgar is especially famous – beautiful bits of modern chromatic writing. He seems to have done the work in the most sincere spirit, caring nothing for mere effect apart from a just rendering of the words.'

But the paper added: 'One doubt only remains: will the music be properly appreciated at a single hearing?'

The Birmingham Post added: 'The chorus had to work in faith that all would in time become clear and were ready and obedient to every indication and correction of the conductor. Mr A J Cotton, at the pianoforte gave every assistance to the singers in what was not an easy task by any means.'

The Sheffield Independent questioned Elgar's decision to allow Hans Richter, the Festival's Chief Conductor to direct the work: 'Respecting handing over of the baton to Dr Richter, we are reminded that at a certain Leeds Festival Sir Michael Costa once conducted a new cantata by Henry Smart; the performance was an indifferent one; Costa got the blame for it and made a vow that he would he would never again undertake the direction of the first performance of music by another. This decision has had more or less influence upon Festival conductors of a later day, who have usually made way for the composer himself when the introduction of a new work was in question.

'While of the opinion that a conductor of today is a far abler man and more anxious to serve the interests of the young composer than was the great and mighty Sir Michael, who had an idea that there was but one musician in the land and that one was Costa, it is to be regretted that Mr Elgar has not accepted the position which was his by precedent. With a real live chorus master to prepare the choristers, if the musician can compose music worth hearing at a festival, he can direct his forces. Given that ability, he should neither be robbed, nor suffered to rob himself, of the honour.'

Further concerns came privately. Nicholas Kilburn, a seasoned choral conductor, wrote urgently to Elgar: '…for such a work's rendering dare we hope for that which is worthy? Alas! I fear, I fear! Were I dictator, state funds should provide the means full & adequate, and a stately cathedral, & I wd. summon only musicians, only artists to listen, & not once only; and thus should justice be done.'

All appeared well however. Birmingham Mail a week before the premier noted: 'It is at the request of the composer that Dr Richter will conduct and the admirable manner in which the music was rendered this morning demonstrates the wisdom of that choice. It would be difficult to improve upon the interpretation given to many of the most important and inspiring passages of Mr Elgar's work and both the composer and the conductor appeared well satisfied with the manner in which the orchestra fulfilled its task while the small audience privileged to occupy seats in the gallery was enthusiastic in its approval.

The Pall Mall Gazette of September 24th marvelled that Elgar had 'found so noble an inspiration in what is after all, a somewhat inferior literary work; for Newman was really no poet and the peculiar materialist moulding of his thought which comes out so strongly for example in his sermon on 'The Neglect on Divine Calls and Warnings' found its full expression in this set of verses, which, to do him justice, were rescued by a friend from the wastepaper basket. It will be found however that precisely this materialist attitude towards the greatest mystery of life, which is death, has touched Mr Elgar's muse with no uncertain sincerity of emotion. We shall be very much surprised if this work does not come to be regarded as a noble contribution to the masterpieces of art.'

Two weeks before the premier, The Birmingham Post enthused: 'An advanced stage of the preparations was reached last night, when Mr Edward Elgar paid a visit to the Masonic Hall to rehearse the choral portions of his sacred Cantata 'The Dream of Gerontius', so ably and so thoroughly prepared by Mr W C Stockley, the chorus master. Mr Elgar, as he stepped to the conductor's platform was received with enthusiastic applause and cheering. He thanked the choristers for the cordial reception accorded to him and said that it was in Birmingham when associated with Mr Stockley's orchestra that he learned all the music he knew and he always cherished a friendly feeling for Birmingham. At the close of the rehearsal he thanked the choristers and said that he was extremely pleased with everything they had done.'

In the Elgar family archives this report carries Alice Elgar's vehement exclamation marks against the reference to the 70-year-old Stockley who was chorus master only because Charles Swinnerton Heap died in the early stages of preparation. His alleged lack of understanding of the music is often quoted as a contributory factor in the eventual disastrous performance. Her ire is similarly present where 'Chorus of Anglicans' is printed rather than 'Angelicals'.

London orchestral rehearsals began barely a week before the premiere. The Birmingham Gazette reported: 'They had grandly accomplished a noble feat and one that a critical and technical audience knew how to appreciate. They had played 'Gerontius' at sight, counting all their rests and coming in at the right moment with surprising precision.' It was the first time they had seen the music.

A joint rehearsal of orchestra, chorus and soloists had still not taken place however. Rehearsal time was also required for the rest of the three-day programme which included: Mendelssohn's 'Elijah', Bach's 'St Matthew Passion', Handel's 'Messiah', Brahms' 'German Requiem', sections from Handel's 'Israel in Egypt', Dvorak's 'The Spectre's Bride', Coleridge Taylor's 'Song of Hiawatha' and various orchestral pieces.

The Musical Standard four days before the 'Gerontius' premiere, mused: 'It is late in the day to speak of the rehearsal arrangements at Birmingham. It was stated, not officially it is true, that both 'Messiah' and 'Elijah' were to be rehearsed otherwise than chorally but we note that neither of these masterpieces figures in the printed order of rehearsals although the selections from 'Israel in Egypt' do. That is rather a pity as no festival has yet taken place at which the fashion of giving these familiar works without full rehearsal has not had bad results – at least if one expects perfection.

'But when two novelties 'The Dream of Gerontius' and 'The Song of Hiawatha' are in the programme, which also contains such exacting choral works as Brahms' 'Requiem', Bach's 'St Matthew Passion' and Dvorak's 'Spectre's Bride' all to be rehearsed with soloists, chorus and orchestra within the space of a full day, an evening and a morning it is difficult to understand how time could be found for the rehearsal of familiar pieces.

'The question is of very old standing but while a balance has to be made for charities and while that aim is really the motive force of our festivals, the question remains academic. It may be discussed but no good comes of its discussion. Still, in listening to the orchestra trying over the orchestral music of 'The Dream of Gerontius' and afterwards to the soloists running through their parts and with the knowledge that the only full rehearsal of soloists, chorus and orchestra will take place at Birmingham this Saturday afternoon when the work is bracketed with Sir Hubert Parry's 'De Profundis' one could not keep feeling strongly once again that the rehearsal arrangements at our festivals entirely prevent them taking the stand they should.

'Dr Richter is a fine conductor in his mastery over a score and over his men and what he managed to get out of his forces on Monday last was quite wonderful. But it seems to us that all he could do was to pay attention to the difficult points and on these he concentrated himself. There was room for much more light and shade, better graduated crescendos and more delicate pianissimos. The spirit of the thing was there, no doubt; but more could have been got out of the work. How all this is to be obtained from the single rehearsal at Birmingham, we do not understand, but rest in the placid hope, that it will be 'all right on the night'.'

The Sunday Times commented on yet another deficiency in its preparation: 'The full score is said to be the most complicated that an Englishman has ever written. It was only available practically at the last moment for the purposes of the analytical notes and the preliminary band rehearsal held at Queen's Hall on Monday. As a matter of fact, Dr Richter had never set eyes upon the score until last Sunday evening.'

The first joint rehearsal took place on September 28th – five days before the premier – when an incident, often considered a major contributor to the disastrous premier, occurred in the first Demon's Chorus.

The Birmingham Mail commented that Elgar wanted: '...more fire, more effect, and entreated the choristers not to sing as if they were in a drawing room. The chorus took the lesson to heart and infused wonderful power into this remarkable scene.'

But other papers noted differently. The Birmingham Post commented: 'The rendering of this part did not satisfy the composer and he addressed the executants on the subject from the front of the orchestra. We venture to think that this was a mistake and showed want of tact, more especially as the baton was in Dr Richter's hands. A repetition brought out all the points desired.'

Festival Chairman G H Johnson, responded immediately with this letter to the paper: 'Sir – Your musical critic in this morning's issue assumes that Mr Elgar made a mistake in addressing the choir while the baton was in the hands of Dr Richter, and charges him with want of tact. Dr Richter desires me to say that it was at his request that Mr Elgar addressed the choir so as to give them his view of how the work was to be rendered. I have no doubt you will be willing to correct the wrong impression conveyed by your notice.'

But the paper remained unrepentant: 'We have received the following letter in reference to a comment made in this column yesterday on Mr Elgar's indiscretion in lecturing the chorus on the conclusion on Saturday's rehearsal of his work. Mr Johnson tells us that Mr Elgar addressed the choir at the request of Dr Richter, but there was no evidence or intimation of the fact at the time and in any case of course, Dr Richter is not responsible for Mr Elgar's criticisms, which have been the subject, we understand, of much discussion among the members of the choir.'

Alice Elgar wrote in the family's copy of the paper 'atrocious and insulting paper, no apology at all.'

Another unattributed paper commented: 'It was amazing how the composer's directions were set at nought. He (poor man) had the temerity to upbraid the chorus at rehearsal last Saturday. With Dr Richter's permission he addressed them and among other things he said: 'You sing my music as if it were a drawing-room ballad'. It was lenient criticism. For to the interpretation of drawing-room ballads you must bring more than negative qualities: a want of imagination, a want of expression, a lack of dynamic light and shade.'

Musical Opinion commented: 'And then the composer made matters worse at the final rehearsal by putting up the backs of the choir. He told them that their singing was 'all wrong' and the Chorus of Demons was sung as if it were a drawing room ballad.' But the article continued: 'The fact is that the choir were over-worked and they had not a conductor in Dr Richter who could inspire them with new life at the last moment.'

A slightly different version was carried in the Worcester Chronicle: 'There appears to have been some difficulty at the Birmingham rehearsals in getting the chorus to realise the composer's ideal of certain passages of the work, and Dr Richter, who conducted, invited Mr Elgar to explain his views personally to the chorus. Whether it was the tone adopted by the composer or some unfortunate phrase used which was unpalatable is not clear; but the chorus seems to have thought there was cause for resentment.

'Remarks appeared in the press about their having been 'lectured', 'brought to book so sharply' and as to whether they deserved a rebuke so severe. To be told that their singing 'wanted point' and that it was in fact 'drawing-room singing' must have been decidedly unpleasant; at the same time if a composer to put those in front of him 'on their mettle' it must be expected that he will speak his mind. As Mr Elgar spoke at the request of Dr Richter, who wielded the baton, of course no question of etiquette could arise.'

The Morning Leader discussed the incident at some length, following a letter its music critic received from a member of the chorus: 'He very kindly says that as one who has read my notes and criticisms in these columns he feels he is almost writing to a personal friend. That puts things on a nice kindly footing. I am glad it is so because in this particular instance of Elgar I cannot agree with my correspondent.

'He says that the composer has not studied the voices and in places has written notes almost impossible to sing. That the choral work is difficult I admit but I can see nothing that is at all impossible, provided that a sufficient number of rehearsals are held. But I must say my eyes were opened when my correspondent informs me that only seven rehearsals of the work were held. Seven! Why, seventy would hardly have been too many. I do not think that seven rehearsals were a fair share to be devoted to so difficult a composition.

'And now as to the quarrel between Mr Edward Elgar and his chorus. The composer does not seem to have had an ingratiating manner and when asked by Dr Richter to express an opinion on the reading of the chorus at rehearsal he 'grossly insulted' the singers by telling them it was 'all wrong' and by saying that the chorus of demons was sung like a drawing-room ballad. 'And that' adds my correspondent, 'after we had fairly shouted ourselves hoarse'

'But 'fairly shouting themselves hoarse' is probably not what the composer wanted although the earlier part of the chorus is liberally marked fortissimo. In fact, this shouting was the fault of the chorus in every work given at the festival. It seemed impossible to restrain them.

'At the same time, Mr Elgar's outburst though justified enough by the performance was ill-advised. It took the spirit out of the singers without giving any suggestion as to what he wanted. But my correspondent must remember that it is extremely mortifying to a composer to hear his music sung as if it had no meaning, for no modern composer looks on his music as so much material on which a choir may exercise its lung power.'

After Elgar's death in 1934, letters appeared in The Birmingham Post from members of the chorus that day. 'Second Soprano' wrote: 'On the morning of the performance, Dr Richter came and stood on the steps leading to our dressing-rooms and with unforgettable voice and gesture besought us to do our very best 'for the work of this English genius'. Elgar's words at the rehearsal: 'It is no better than a drawing-room ballad', were not received in the large-minded spirit that their truth demanded from a body of loyal singers.'

W R Smith recalled: 'The late Dr Richter was conducting the final rehearsal for band and chorus when suddenly the composer appeared on the platform; and, turning to the male voices, who were struggling with the 'demon' music, shouted excitedly: 'Gentlemen you are singing it all wrong!' We were far too 'polite' in our rendering of such curious and difficult music and had not grasped at all what it was intended to portray.'

Frank Richards of Stourbridge commented: 'My memory of the incident is rather different. At the last rehearsal in the Masonic Hall, Sir Edward was quite pleased with the effect produced. At the final rehearsal in the Town Hall, his actual words were: 'Gentlemen you are all wrong; you are singing like a party of school children' Not only I, but many others of the chorus recognized the fact that Sir Edward had failed to allow for the disparity in the size of the two halls. The chorus filled the Masonic Hall, but only the stage in the Town Hall. However that may be, the male members of the chorus were disgruntled and didn't hesitate to show it. Dr Richter did not seem very pleased either.'

'Gerontius' made its debut on the morning of October 3rd 1900. The Morning Advertiser reviewed: 'Those who have a belief, a sanguine faith in the development of English musical art will take a solid pleasure in Mr Edward Elgar's new work 'The Dream of Gerontius' and the more so because coming to the end of a time expired century they can point to it as the corner stone of musical thought and progress of the Victorian era.

'Since the production of the 'Golden Legend', Sullivan has practically passed out of the domain of intensely serious music, and no one has been found to fill his place as a composer endowed with a genuine spontaneous gift for melody as well as possessing a complete mastery of the art of orchestration. The academical school has had its say and failed. We cried to the gods even as the heathen cried to Baal to send us a prophet and they remained silent. Our professors and our Doctors of Music have laboured zealously and lovingly to make good the deficiency, they have given us Requiems and Te Deums and, according to their lights, they are entitled to our warmest praise. But they lacked the vital spark of genius; they were not and are not full-souled men.

'A new star, however, appeared over the horizon in 1896 and now Birmingham has won distinction for its festival by its performance of 'The Dream of Gerontius'. I will not go so far as to say that Mr Elgar's latest work is going to achieve a widespread popularity. To award it the appreciation and approbation which it is due, the music needs attentive study. Once, however, it has penetrated the mind, once the reader or listener has become impregnated with its vital characteristics then does it control the senses and capture the intellect. '

'I do not think the work will ever become widely popular *because it is far too difficult for the average choral society to even attempt*. It is too elevated in thought and musical diction to make any direct appeal to the public at large and its religious bent is opposed to the convictions of an essentially Protestant community. Nevertheless, I heartily and unreservedly congratulate Mr Elgar on his noble achievement and the place it gives him among the world's composers.'

The Daily Graphic thought that it was: 'a work of ambitious scope and imposing dimensions and in it Mr Elgar showed himself more completely master of his art than in any of his previous works. He shows a true appreciation of the limitations of art and his discretion has carried him securely through difficulties which at first sight might seem insurmountable.'

The Daily News, commented that '"Gerontius' shows Mr Elgar in a stronger light as a musician and a thinker than anything he has before done will be generally admitted. Sometimes, indeed, the work reveals real genius. On the other hand it is commendably free from claptrap, from any straining after cheap effect.'

The Globe thought 'there can be no question that the work is one of great power, full of beauty and a decided advance upon anything which Mr Elgar has yet written.'

The Pall Mall Gazette went further: 'I am about to speak words which may seem exuberant and enthusiastic; but I have thought over them carefully before setting them down for the public eye, and I will venture to say that since the death of Wagner, no finer composition (I am quite remembering Tchaikovsky and his great symphonies) has been given to the world. I am proud that Mr Elgar is an Englishman, for his has justified Purcell's early career; in a word he has produced a genuine masterpiece.

'I have spoken of Wagner and indeed that latest and most wonderful work 'Parcifal' has undoubtedly influenced Mr Elgar in the composition of 'The Dream of Gerontius'. The *motif* associated with the suffering of Amfortas is produced almost note for note in this new work, and, strangely enough under circumstances (so far as letter-press goes) which imply very much of the same sort of suffering. Beyond this almost captious comparison the spirit of the two works is curiously in accord, and it is a fine consideration to think that an Englishman has taken up art at precisely the point where the immortal author of 'The Ring' and of 'Parsifal' laid down his arms: for I claim all this for Mr Elgar.'

The London Musical Courier considered: 'I have no hesitation in saying that the composer of 'Gerontius' is a genius of whom England ought to be proud', while the Manchester Guardian commented: 'Edward Elgar's dramatic power admits of comparison with the great masters.'

Correspondents also commented on the audience reaction. The Morning Leader: 'It is not usual to applaud in the Town Hall in the morning but the audience insisted upon calling for the composer after a performance that extended over an hour and three quarters.'

The Daily Graphic: 'Mr Elgar was called on to the platform at the conclusion of his beautiful and impressive work and loudly applauded.' A sentiment echoed by the Daily Telegraph: 'At the close of the performance the audience, distinguishing between composer and executants, summoned Mr Elgar to the platform where customary honours were bestowed upon him.'

The Star claimed Elgar was 'cheered loudly' by the audience, while the Sunday Times mentioned: 'At the close there were loud calls for the composer, who did not appear for some minutes but eventually was the recipient of an enthusiastic ovation.'

As to the performance, the critics were unanimous as to its deficiencies. Some mentioned it only briefly while praising unreservedly the music, and to some extent the performance of the orchestra and soloists, notably Marie Brema who sang the part of the Angel. But others made no secret of their feelings about the choir.

The Sunday Times asked: 'What was the matter with the Birmingham choristers? Nobody could quite tell. I heard a dozen different stories during the week but none that satisfactorily explained why an intelligent, well-balanced body of first-rate voices should do its good work only by fits and starts, singing at one concert in really capital style and at the next going to pieces as completely as a German band caught in a thunderstorm.

'The crisis came early in the proceedings. The 'Elijah' performance at the opening concert told no tale of doubtful efficiency or of strength and quality below the average. Full justice was done to the familiar oratorio by everyone concerned and there were general anticipations of sustained excellence all along the line. That same evening however, in Sir Hubert Parry's 'De Profundis', we were rudely awakened to the fact that something was wrong. Either the choir did not know the work or it was unequal to the exigencies of twelve-part choral writing. It got astray at the outset and was more than once so near disaster that I for one expected the genial composer to throw down his baton in sheer despair. Happily, his courage and tenacity did not fail him. By a miracle he contrived to pull his wavering forces together and ultimately the end of the difficult Psalm was arrived at without a break.

'This unpleasant experience augured ill for the 'safe delivery' of Mr Edward Elgar's still more exacting contribution on the following morning. Here indeed rumour had already prepared us for serious shortcomings. The final rehearsal of 'The Dream of Gerontius' had, it was said, been so far the reverse of satisfactory, that the composer lost patience with the chorus and told them in good plain English that they either knew nor understood his music. And this the actual performance proved to be the case.

'A more perfunctory rendering of a new work it has never been my lot to listen to at a big Festival. The tenors began flat in the very first semi-chorus and set an example of doubtful intonation that prevailed throughout most of the many in the cantata where awkward intervals and trying dissonances lay a trap for these unwary choristers. Nay more; their attack was rarely unanimous and their rendering of passages requiring the most delicacy often offended the ear by a grating harshness of tone and slovenliness of phrasing.

'In a word, a spirit of hesitancy permeated the entire performance and wrought material harm at its birth to a composition which demands in a peculiar degree the absence of those distracting influences which accompany a faulty interpretation. So much, apparently for the value of the extra day's rehearsal which Dr Richter was in such pains to secure in order to make all safe!

'But it is the irony of fate that the best laid schemes for good in this world should sometimes be thwarted. The probabilities are that an additional month of preparation would not have strengthened the weak spots in this particular Birmingham choir. A local critic remarked to me that its ranks contained too many 'green' singers – young men and women with good voices but too little experience, too little stamina, too little training in the subtleties of really high-class choral singing. If this be the true explanation of the state of affairs – and the death of the chorus-master, Dr Swinnteron Heap, only a few months ago would in measure seem to confirm this – then the Festival Committee must look to it that both choice of material and methods of discipline and study are placed upon a more severe basis before 1903.

'That Birmingham needs to go further afield for its choristers I am not inclined to think. The point is that it must have a choir capable of doing the Festival work in consistent fashion. It was the lack of consistency that made the *laches* of last week so particularly irritating.

'On the evening of the same day that 'The Dream of Gerontius' received such scurvy treatment, we were listening to a magnificent rendering of the choruses in 'The Song of Hiawatha'; yet the very next morning in the St Matthew 'Passion' we heard passages blurred, sung out of tune, and given what a want of steadiness and precision worthy of a fourth-rate provincial choral society.'

But he added: 'When everything is said and written I fancy the Birmingham Festival of 1900 will be remembered as the meeting that witnessed the production of 'The Dream of Gerontius'. If this cantata does not belong to the type of works that live and flourish in the full light of day, then I am greatly mistaken concerning the present trend of musical opinion and feeling in this country. Apart altogether from the religious point of view, Cardinal Newman's poem is a 'Chef d'Oevre', and to pay Mr Elgar the highest compliment in my power I consider his music eminently worthy at all points of association with it. He has reproduced with marvellous fidelity its deep spirit of mysticism, besides striking with a certain touch that extended gamut of human emotions that runs through it.

'It will be necessary to wait for a better performance of the choruses before one can properly appreciate the grandeur of Mr Elgar's conception or gather the full meaning of the tremendous polyphonic numbers in which he has set forth the praises of the heavenly host. For the moment I have naught to add in the way of admiration for Mr Elgar's technical equipment to what I have already said. On the other hand the extraordinary wealth of colour and rare sensuous charm of his orchestration were brought into clear relief at Birmingham and so was the new-found lyrical quality of his writing for solo voices.'

Other critics were equally damning of the performance. The Daily Telegraph commented that the chorus 'went all to pieces' and added: 'It is humiliating for any friend of English music to have to express such an opinion but there is no escape from it and no concealing truth without deeper abashment. True, the music was difficult but there had been time to prepare it and the reason for so grave a choral failure has to be sought elsewhere. It is not my business to discover why the chorus could not sing six lightly accompanied bars without losing the pitch or why all the concerted music was rendered in a hesitating and pointless fashion. That task belongs to those who have followed processes and not simply witnessed results.'

The London Musical Courier added: 'The unfortunate performance of 'Gerontius' was followed after the interval by as beautiful a rendering of the wonderful 'Unfinished' symphony as I have ever heard. It was as though Richter had said to his audience 'See it was not my fault this bad performance as proof whereof I will show you perfection'. This again was followed by 'Israel in Egypt' to the massive choruses of which, no subtlety of emotion being required, the choir did ample justice.'

Musical Opinion commented: 'It may be that choral singing in general is in a backward state compared with that of other branches of the art and that it will be a long while before our choirs can undertake music of the calibre of Mr Elgar's'.

The German critic Otto Lessman who, after following the reactions of his English counterparts had little to commend the performance added: 'Proud England rejoice! You have an important composer in Mr Elgar!'

Elgar's reaction was contained in an often-quoted letter written to August Jaeger: 'I have not seen the papers yet except one or two bits which exuberant friends insisted on my reading & I don't know or care what they say or do. As far as I am concerned music in England is dead – I shall always write what I have in me of course. I have worked hard for forty years &, at the last, Providence denies me a decent hearing of my work: so I submit – I always said God was against art & I still believe it. Anything obscene or trivial is blessed in this world & has a reward – I ask for no reward – only to live & to hear my work. I still hear it in my heart & in my head so I must be content. Still it is curious to be treated by the old-fashioned people as a criminal because my thoughts & ways are beyond them.'

After Jaeger replied telling him he was both 'weak' and 'wicked' to react in this way, Elgar claimed it wasn't the performance which had drawn his reaction, but that he was upset about his wife's throat condition.

As far as the papers were concerned, he reiterated: 'as to the papers I've not seen one year & shan't see 'em for a long time -stay – I lie – I saw, under compulsion the Manchester Guardian [the one saying 'Edward Elgar's dramatic power admits of comparison with the great masters'] that's all.'

A second performance, at the Crystal Palace, was planned for a few weeks after the premiere. The Worcester Chronicle reported: 'The difficulties of the work are acknowledged on all hands - indeed, owing to the great amount of preparation required, it is announced that Sir Augustus Manns has indefinitely postponed the performance which was announced to take place at the Crystal Palace at the end of the month.'

Even Elgar himself shied away from a full performance with his own Worcestershire Philharmonic Society giving only a 'selection' from the work the following May. Berrow's Worcester Journal commented: 'Dr Elgar, as conductor, obtained from the large chorus and powerful orchestra an interpretation of his masterpiece which gave the completest satisfaction to the audience – and, it may be believed, to himself.

The Worcester Herald commented: 'Dr Elgar kept all up to their work and not only did he keep a firm hold on the chorus and orchestra but on the audience also. By an imperious wave of the hand he silenced untimely applause and when the buzzing chatter and shuffling which always fill up the interval failed to cease when he took his stand at the conductor's desk he called for silence and waited with arms folded gazing at the audience until they relapsed into comparative stillness.

'The chorus singing was exceptionally good whether in the subdued passages or giving forth the bold massive harmonies which are a striking feature of the work. At the close of the cantata, the audience were most enthusiastic but though the applause was kept up for four or five minutes the composer declined to bow his acknowledgements.'

Another local report commented: 'One could quite understand Dr Elgar's objection to any applause between the parts and even at the end. It seems something of a desecration of the religious spirit which pervades the work, and yet, of course everyone was anxious to let the composer know how deeply he had stirred them by the wonderful beauty and mysticism with which he has treated the grand poem.'

William Green, as 'Gerontius' had struggled with a cold. Elgar showing his public relations skills sent all the local press cuttings to the Editor of the Musical Times with a covering letter:

'William Green did really splendidly – you need not mention his cold which existed only in the minds of the reporters. You know in certain circles – connected alas! with the futile Birmingham Chorus – a great point has been made of the supposed exceptional difficulty - our amateur chorus sang *well* – in tune throughout & with real devotional feeling – the work made a *profound sensation* really & was a noteworthy event. The audience was the largest ever assembled in the Hall I believe.

'P.S Our performance of the Selection shews that the work is within the means of an intelligent chorus with a (fairly) intelligent conductor.'

This was the report which resulted:

'The practicability of Dr Edward Elgar's setting of 'The Dream of Gerontius' was fully demonstrated at a performance of a selection of the work given by the Worcestershire Philharmonic Society at the Public Hall, Worcester, on the 9th ult., under the composer's direction. The Worcester amateurs sang well in tune throughout and with real devotional feeling and the work proved to be well within the capabilities of an intelligent choir. The audience, one of the largest ever assembled in the Hall was profoundly impressed by the performance in which Miss Helene Valma, Mr William Green and Mr F Lightowler were efficient soloists.'

The first full performance after the premier was set for the 1902 Lower Rhine Festival in Dusseldorf.

In order to ensure that he had the best press coverage, Elgar arranged for Harvey Marson of the Worcester Herald, to be there writing to him on April 20th 1902: 'I received the message copied on the other side this morning. I hope you can go to Dusseldorf. The 8vo copy in German will reach you soon – the new edition is not yet ready.'

The note reads in translation: 'Your wish that a place be reserved for the critic of the Worcester Herald, Mr Harvey Marson will, of course, be notified.'

Marson subsequently cabled the paper after the performance: 'Dr Elgar was enthusiastically called after the first part and at the end he was received with a storm of applause in which the chorus and orchestra joined as well as the huge audience. The orchestra greeted the happy composer with the inspiring cacophony called a 'Thutch' (flourish) and a splendid laurel wreath of enormous size was presented to him. The greatest impression received was from the singing of the chorus which proved the absurdity of the charge frequently made against the composer after the Birmingham performance of 1900 that his work was impossible to render.'

The Daily Telegraph commented: 'No work could have been received with more whole-hearted enthusiasm than 'Gerontius' was last night. The composer, who was present, was not only recalled several times at the ending but after the first part, an honour I am told, hardly ever bestowed on a composer by a public here. And very gratifying too was the impression made by the work on the musicians present. No one was louder in praise of it, than Richard Strauss himself, the leading composer of the day; and many there who asserted that of living composers Strauss and Elgar stand in a class by themselves.'

The Morning Leader concluded: 'Yesterday was a memorable day in the history of English music. The triumph of 'The Dream of Gerontius' with an audience containing many of the most distinguished musicians of the Continent, including Richard Strauss himself, will cause English music to be treated with more respect throughout Europe for the future, and will serve to open to it many avenues hitherto closed.'

The paper, like many, mentioned that as a result 'Gerontius' was set down for performance in Cologne, Aix-la-Chapelle, Liege, Utrecht, Breslau and Heidelberg, and, like many others bemoaned the lack of apparent interest from English venues, and the whole musical culture which existed in England at the time: 'By this way perhaps, it may reach us (though it does not do to be too sanguine): but it is a circuitous route from Birmingham to London, via Belgium and Silesia.'

'I remember that in October 1900 in Birmingham everybody said: *'How difficult these choruses are! How will they ever be sung?'* Last night I kept on wondering whether my memory was not playing me a trick – and if people really did say so, why on earth they did. It all seemed so lucid, so direct, and to convey its message of lofty thoughts so unmistakably and so beautifully.

'Where were the obscurity and extravagance, the unnecessary complexity of which British Beckmerserdom had made so much? A few hundred Germans with brains and an intellectual conductor had attacked them and they had crumbled away as the walls of Jericho before the trumpets of Joshua. The truth which is not flattering to our pride is that the chorus singers here have long been familiar with the newest ideas in music and music like Elgar's which comes as a shock to those whose musical horizons is bounded by the 'Elijah', 'The Messiah' and Novello's Anthems appeals to their heart and their brain.'

'Such music as this – otherworldly and mystical – must not be attacked as if it were a foursquare Handelian chorus. It needs men and women who not only understand the symbols on the notepaper but the ideas which have inspired them.'

It added: 'As an influential German musician said to me last night: *'This is epoch making. It is the sort of thing no musician can afford to ignore.'*

The German press were equally enthusiastic. The Cologne Gazette hailed Elgar as 'one of the leaders of musical art in modern times.' The Dusseldorfer Zeitung commented that Elgar 'has been acknowledged a master of immense learning and great depth of feeling, while the Rheinisch Westphalische Zeitung said 'he is a master of polyphonic structure and one who knows how to steep his contrapuntal art in such genuine feeling that the listener hardly notices the skill with which these tone pictures are wrought.'

Die Musik added: 'In all that he does, Elgar has the immense advantage of originality. There is personal style in the composition, which is stamped by the greatest artistic seriousness, and the instrumentation is so brilliant that one may with confidence call it the best to be found in any modern choral work. Our concert institutions cannot neglect the Englishman's work if they would be followers of the progressive principle.'

The Neue Freie Presse quoted Strauss: *'With that work England for the first time became one of the modern musical states. Up to now England has always received German music without giving us anything in return. Now for the first time an Englishman has come to the Continent who deserves to be heard.'*

After the performance, there was a banquet in Elgar's honour and there followed a famous incident in which Richard Strauss, who had conducted Liszt's 'Faust' Symphony in the second part of the programme, rose unannounced and delivered an impromptu speech praising Elgar and his achievement.

August Jaeger, covering the event for the Musical Times, reported Strauss' words to open his report: *'I raise my glass to the welfare and success of the first English Progressivist, Meister Edward Elgar, and of the young progressive school of English composers.'*

Jaeger continued: 'The speech, spoken in clear ringing tones that carried conviction to all that heard it was sprung upon the assembly as a complete surprise. The generous words of the most distinguished living German musician were received with real enthusiasm by the assembled musicians and dilettanti; but the few English visitors present were filled with delight at the unexpected great honour paid to their gifted countryman.

The Times also covered the speech: 'A short speech was made quite unexpectedly by Herr Richard Strauss, in which he deplored that England had hitherto not taken her proper place among musical nations because of the want of *Fortschrittsmanner* – that is, of men who represent forward movement in art at every given epoch – ever since the period of England's musical greatness in the Middle Ages. The creation, however, of a work like 'The Dream of Gerontius', he added, showed that the gap had been filled and the day of reciprocity in music between England and the rest of Europe was dawning; and he concluded by asking those present to drink the health of the British musical renaissance, and especially of Dr Elgar, to whom he applied the most flattering epithets that one composer could bestow on a brother in art whom he is proud to welcome as a fellow-worker. *Laudari a laudato viro* ['the praise praised'] – the proverb is something musty, but it has a very real application to the matter in hand.

'I must anticipate the charge that in thus emphasizing Herr Strauss's words I am magnifying mere after-dinner amenities into a profession of faith. But we do not realise in England – it is the kind of thing we never do realise till it has ceased to be – that Richard Strauss is, whether for good or for evil, the dominant factor in the musical life of Germany today. What he says on an occasion like this to an audience containing many musicians will be canvassed eagerly in every musical society in the Empire, and it cannot fail to have a share in bringing about a result for which all British music lovers have been hoping.'

Elgar's own reaction to this was contained in a letter to the head of Novello's Alfred Littleton, which displays his innate ability at self-promotion: 'For me, I understand , the thing was a triumph ! But I feel rather dazed at the success & will think of it when six months more hard work have rather dulled the memory of these wonderful days.

'Richard Strauss, who never speechifies if he can help it, made a really noble oration over Gerontius – I wish you could have heard it – and it was worth some years of anguish – now I trust over – to hear him call me Meister!'

However, Strauss's speech, while lauding Elgar and his work, made no reference to Parry, Stanford or any other English composer who had come before, and who were still producing works, prompting the composer C W Orr many years later to recall that it 'caused some fluttering in the academic dovecots'.

Elgar's take on this was contained in a letter to his friend Nicholas Kilburn: 'We had a glorious time in Dusseldorf – Strauss's speech has been misunderstood (deliberately?) by the village organist type in England.

'Strauss is absolutely great – wonderful and terrifying but somewhat cynical – his music I mean. *He* is a real clever good man.'

THE CATHOLIC CONTROVERSY

The first full British performance after Birmingham was at the Worcester Festival the following September. In order for the performance to go ahead in an Anglican Cathedral, the Cathedral authorities required textual changes to the libretto removing certain Catholic references.

The changes were carried in the Daily Chronicle : 'Some of the lines in the book of words were disfigured by asterisks which on further examination were found to indicate 'omissions of a doctrinal nature'. Twice in the first of the vocal numbers asterisks were noticeable. For 'Jesu Maria' with which Gerontius begins his anxious utterance, respecting the future, 'Jesu, Jesu' was substituted, while instead of the line 'Jesu have mercy ! Mary pray for me' the vocalist was compelled to sing 'Jesu have mercy ! Be with me in my extremity ! There were other instances of such petty tinkering with a devotional poem to some extent known and admired by all present. Thus, the words 'And Masses on the Earth' occurring in the Angel's final song, were excised; but perhaps the silliest interference with the work was the description of the chorus of the 'Souls in Purgatory' as that of 'Souls' merely. The authority responsible for these weak alterations was not announced but it can be guessed.'

The Yorkshire Post, commented on the unusually high demand for tickets, resulting in the Cathedral being full: 'Indeed for once the public seems to have transferred their allegiance from their customary favourites 'Elijah' and 'The Messiah' for which I understand the booking of places has been lighter than usual and to have given it for the time being to their own townsman. Whatever may be the reason whether it be local feeling or curiosity concerning a much-discussed work or perhaps even a spice of scandal in hearing a Papistical poem in an Anglican Cathedral, the result was the biggest crowd of the Festival.

'To revert for the moment to the point, it must be confessed that it was not a wholly immaterial one, as long as these Festival performances are officially regarded as 'services' and preceded and followed by prayers, Cardinal Newman's poem with its invocation of the saints, direct prayers to the Blessed Virgin, and chorus of souls in Purgatory is undoubtedly not in accordance with the teachings of the Church of England. It is however a pleasant indication of how much the two branches of the Church Catholic have in common that a very few verbal omissions and alterations, including one short cut, sufficed to make the text wholly acceptable from the Anglican point of view.'

The Standard echoed: 'Interest and curiosity were further excited by the objections raised by the clerical authorities at Worcester to certain supplicatory passages addressed to the Virgin Mary and the Saints being sung in the Cathedral. The excised portions had little detrimental effect on the music and practically made no difference to the character of the work which is deeply imbued with the spirit of the Roman Church.'

But the Pall Mall Gazette thought: 'Newman's poem was written as any poet might write it, from one particular and religious point of view. He attempted to embody (and in one special feature with conspicuous success) the Roman Catholic belief in mortality and immortality. Frankly, his work was an essay; but there it was completed and definite. He embodied poetically the religious essence of his own private and individual persuasions. Now here was obviously to the outsider a merely academic affair. Newman's beliefs had nothing to do with the proprieties of the matter, once granted that Elgar's setting of the Cardinal's work was to be produced.

'Yet with a solemn folly worthy of the heroes of Pope's 'Dunciad' – it will be remembered by the reader that Pope had two heroes in succession for his immortal satire - every reference to Roman Catholic beliefs was carefully excluded from the poem. 'Jesu, Maria, I am near to death' – thus the poem begins; the second name of this invocation, incredible as it may seem, was omitted in performance. To so curiously petty a level did this prejudice descend that where Newman had written a chorus for 'Souls in Purgatory' the last two words were actually omitted in the printed copy supplied to the public.

'A Roman Catholic priest of known wit, who was present this morning at the performance, suggested that instead of omitting the words 'in Purgatory' the difficulty might have been better solved by simply putting 'Fried Souls'. The story is authentic.'

And writing in the Catholic publication, The Tablet, the Rev T A Burge OSB complained: 'The annoyance felt in the audience was unmistakable. If the words were offensive to Protestant ears and therefore unsuitable for a Protestant Cathedral it would surely be more honourable to refuse the performance altogether than to treat it so cruelly. The incongruous part of the affair – there is always some amusing incongruity in these matters – comes out when we hear that on the previous Sunday, Canon Knox Little made the Cathedral resound with the praises of 'Our Lady' and the 'Mother of God'. And in the evening the 'Stabat Mater' of Dvorak was given in its entirety; the sanctities of the Cathedral not being supposed to be violated by the invocation of Our Blessed Lady when uttered in Latin!'

Under the headline 'A Festival Absurdity', the Musical Standard commented: 'The mutilation to which Dr Edward Elgar's 'The Dream of Gerontius' was subjected at Worcester has aroused a deal of protest in the press. From a common-sense point of view the Dean and Chapter of Worcester Cathedral have not a leg to stand upon. They alter Cardinal Newman's poem and even omit some verses from it in order that the most conservative of Anglicans may not have their sensitive conscience shocked, and yet they allow Dvorak's 'Stabat Mater' to be performed in its entirety because it was sung in a language not understood of the people.

'They even allow Tchaikovsky's 'Pathetic' symphony to be performed in the Cathedral although that work breaths a spirit totally at variance with accepted Christian ideas. And moreover, with Philistine complacency the Dean and Chapter imagine that by altering a line here and there in 'The Dream of Gerontius' they had purged the work of any special reference to Roman Catholic tenets. That was hardly a complement to the sincerity of Dr Elgar's music for that work does not image the religious faith of its composer in spots and patches but draws a clear psychological picture of it as a whole.

'You may alter the words and excise a number or two but you do not thereby change the essential character of the music which is a musical illustration of the spirit of Cardinal Newman's poem as it appealed to the sympathies of the composer.'

COCKAIGNE

After 'Gerontius', Elgar turned to his preferred medium of orchestral music and produced one of his most brilliantly accomplished works, the overture 'Cockaigne' – a musical depiction of London at the turn of the century, which premiered at a Philharmonic Society concert in June 1901.

The Daily Telegraph noted: 'The composer evidently considers that poetry and painting have no rightful monopoly of London within the region of art and in the present case he fully asserts the claim of music to a share in the same great theme. In striking out this new line for himself, Mr Elgar may have done more than he knows; or, at best, he may only be half conscious of an idea that the amazing and ever enlarging phenomena of urban life offer the most vital subjects to contemporary art, and that upon them the artist must work, if he would reflect the spirit of his time.

'The composer has here attempted a musical picture of London at the present time – a picture embodying his conception of the overwhelming vitality and energy of our great metropolis. He has not of course sought to do this on, so to speak, a single canvas. No stretch of that material could comprehend the entire vast field, and we have instead a succession of scenes such as might present themselves in the course of a ramble through the interminable streets.

'We are to suppose that a pair of lovers, fresh from the country perhaps start out to inspect the great City in light-hearted mood. They are naturally somewhat bewildered by the turmoil that rages around and presently step aside into one of the parks, the repose and beauty of which revive their own special and particular romance. So, Mr Elgar gives a place to the 'old old story' in his description of the new, and not only so, but suggests the humours and impertinences of younger generation of Londoners to whom lovers have always been fair game.

'Entering again into the streets, our visitors soon hear the distant music of a military band, which coming nearer and nearer, passes in all due pomp and circumstance. Their attention is next arrested by a church, into which they go, not, like the immortal Mr Wemmick [i.e John Wemmick in Dickens' 'Great Expectations'] for the purpose of getting married but for another spell of quiet. The organist is practising and his instrument with its improvised counterpoint contends with the rumble and roar of passing traffic.

'Without carrying description further, it may be said that generally the composer, recalling his own experiences of life in London, and in a mood to idealise his Cockney friends, has, like Hope, told a flattering tale. But the work, while of humorous bent is a perfectly serious effort, and neither a 'pot boiler' nor a mere jeu d'esprit.'

'It is conceived and worked out in such a genial mood as to cast some doubt upon the belief that Mr Elgar is thoroughly a man of the time. There is no suggestion here of a city of dreadful night; no thought of tragedy or vision of terror such as the modern composer is wont to indulge in because supplying him with cheap material for assaults upon the nerves of his neighbours. On the contrary, the overture is bright and cheerful, humorous withal, distinguished by fine appreciation and overflowing with enthusiasm for its subject. One listens to it smiling and comes away exhilarated. This is dreadfully unfashionable not to say vulgar. Popular pessimism should not be insulted and Mr Elgar must consider his obligations.

'Seriously – 'Cockaigne' is a remarkable work – remarkable alike in the nature of its subject, the fullness of its treatment and the obvious sincerity underlying all. It may be said that in all this the element of reality is slight and the drawing vague. Realism is not the business of a composer, who, even more than the poet is 'of imagination all compact' and he cannot be held responsible for the indefiniteness which is, in some aspect, the weakness, in others the unique and splendid strength of his art.

'Again, it may be urged that the composition of street scenes is not activity on the highest plane of music. Granted but we cannot have everything at once. Mr Elgar is yet at an early stage of his career as a creative musician and he must be allowed freedom. We may be sure that he does not choose his subject at random, and that having fixed upon it he studies it profoundly, and works it out with infinite care sparing nothing required by a finished work of art.

'Someday the composer will give us symphonies but on the way to that achievement he is in no more hurry than was Brahms. The pace is for himself to determine. 'Cockaigne' may be regarded both as a representation of scenes and as a creation in purely musical form. As to its first aspect, the observer is perhaps most struck by the manner in which the spirit of the music helps the intended suggestion. Cheerfulness and humour pervade the work and are assisted here and there by most felicitous device. Happy for example is the thought of intruding the London children upon the lovers in the park and of showing the street-boys gambolling in the rear of the military band.

'Best of all, perhaps, is the device which represents the small folk by the theme which serves for their elders with each note reduced to half its original value; so that where the men and women walk 'magnanimous' the youngsters go with a run. Then there are the lovers, valuable as being always present to our consciousness and so linking scene with scene in a manner at once effective and non-obtrusive. We can convey no way in words the applicability of the music to the varying sections of its 'programme'. For that the overture must be heard: but let us say that we do not clearly see how, in this respect, the music could be improved upon.

'No doubt there are many other ways of drawing the same series of pictures, but Mr Elgar, in his own way, is thoroughly satisfying. We speak, of course, for ourselves only. From a purely formal and technical point of view the new overture is equally if not more interesting. The composer might have elected to treat his theme on the basis of a 'Symphonic poem' which would have enabled him to dispense with form. It is to the credit of his musicianship that he did nothing of the kind.

'Mr Elgar's artistic sense thus gives his work an enormous advantage, redeeming it from rhapsody, and imparting to it, order and the organic life which belongs to regular development. As an orchestral piece, 'Cockaigne' is one of the finest achievements of our day. Granted that it is exceptionally difficult – that there are passages in it for various instruments which ordinary performers would find trying – yet there is nothing impossible to skill, as Thursday's performance proved, and it is only for a skilled orchestra that Mr Elgar has written.

'Of course, we do not now learn for the first time that the composer is a master of orchestration. He was born, perhaps, with an instinctive sense of it. From him no secret of scoring is hid and he uses combination and colouring with a sure hand and certain effect. This makes his work delightful hearing, even when the piling up of sound seems carried to excess.

'And now it is time to say how well, 'Cockaigne' was played under Mr Elgar's direction, notwithstanding its large demands upon the performers. The execution of the overture, like its composition, was distinctly an achievement of high rank, but is not the work dedicated 'to my many friends, the members of British orchestras' and on that account did not the Philharmonic band do its very best?

'The overture was received with tumultuous approbation, the composer being recalled again and again and yet again, and still once more.'

The Referee noted: 'Technically the score is a masterpiece of contrapuntal science and the orchestration is so rich and full as to suggest comparison with the overture to 'Die Meistersinger'. Better than all its science, however, is its powerful expression of healthy and exuberant life. It is music that does one good to hear – invigorating, humanising, uplifting.'

The Morning Leader, however, said this: 'I was sensible of a want of strikingness in the thematic material. Also, although the overture is in the sonata form the effect of the composition is spasmodic and episodical. There is no large design and not sufficient voice in the music – by lack of voice I mean that its melodic outline is feint and the clever polyphony is not employed as a means to an end but is an end in itself. The effect is that the composer does not say anything definite. Too often the music sounded as if it were the orchestral accompaniment of a music drama with the voices omitted. But all the same 'Cockaigne' is a work of extraordinary cleverness and spirit.'

The World commented: 'There is romance and there is passion mixed in his description of London streets, or the London urchins, the London parks where lovers woo and listen to a military band and the London church where lovers pause and meditate. It is not a city of Dreadful Night that Dr Elgar asks us to contemplate; it is not a London dim under the pall of a November fog or shivering under a March east wind. It is London almost in a Mafecking mood. It is almost the mood of Rome in Berlioz's Carnival Overture – only that is more idealised; and the individual is not unlike the Eulenspiegel whom Strauss has pictured – with a dash of the Nurembergers imagined by Wagner.'

But for the Orchestral Times, Elgar's London vision was not romantic enough: 'Where then does the work fail? Why can we not say without reserve that it is a great work for in many ways it is actually so? The reason is I think that either Dr Elgar has not been sufficiently impressed with the poetic side of the great city or he does not love it sufficiently for it to have caught his imagination in its giant grasp and to have swept him off the plane of mere virtuosity into the higher realms of poetic truth.'

Elgar had given the original autograph manuscript of 'Cockaigne' to a friend. In December 1909 it was sold at Sotheby's for £24 – about £1,900 in today's money. In the same sale, a group of 24 autograph letters of Beethoven were sold for £660 [£52,000], prompting the Daily Telegraph to observe: 'When the Elgar manuscript of 101 folio pages is as old as a Beethoven opus, it will be valued at a much higher sum than £24.'

POMP AND CIRCUMSTANCE AND
THE CORONATION ODE

The first two Pomp and Circumstance Marches emerged at a Liverpool Orchestral Society concert on October 19th 1901. Elgar's friend, Alfred Rodewald, who ran the Society, had hoped in vain for a symphony but Elgar produced the marches. By now he was styling himself 'Dr Elgar', following his receipt of an honorary Doctorate of Music from Cambridge.

Musical News considered: 'It is stated that Dr Elgar's idea has been to blend the practical and artistic into one – to make the marches in every way adapted for marching purposes, while not sacrificing any of the qualities required for performance in the concert room. The first of these intentions is certainly realised, especially in 'Pomp' [No 1] which is spirited-exciting-throbbing-pulsing almost maddening in its insistent rhythm. The Trio is quite Elgarese in its melody and a relief from the rather brassy glare of the Quickstep proper in which the full orchestra is kept hard at it, and the organ also requisitioned.

'Circumstance'[No 2] seems musically the better of the two. The vivacity is no less extraordinary but is suggested with lighter touch not that the brass and drums are forgotten in any way. It is surely difficult for a composer to find something that has been left unsaid or some new way of putting something which has been said in march form. That Dr Elgar can do this with success is attested by his 'Imperial March' and the world will be all the better for his new Quicksteps for they are bright, lively, clever music, summed up by one auditor in the word 'jolly''.

The Daily Post reacted: 'Both are quick steps and are scored for the full orchestra. The first, which is the longer of the two, has not the well-marked beat of the second, although in the trio portion there is a fine swinging melody for violins, clarinets and horns. There is a plentiful use of percussion and at times the general orchestration seems thin but this was evidently not the opinion of the audience who applauded the march enthusiastically. The second march is in A minor and contains delightful writing, a charming melody in thirds for reeds and flutes being most delightful. The second march went even better than the first and Dr Elgar was accorded quite an ovation.'

The Manchester Guardian reported: 'The first of the two is an extremely telling piece. It begins with an unmistakable 'Tommy Atkins' theme, somewhat perky and swaggering in gait but frank and genuine withal – a highly original and effective piece of musical characterisation. The second is more popular in style and in some ways more effective but less original than the first.'

The marches were performed again shortly afterwards at the London Proms, under Sir Henry Wood - Number One becoming the stuff of legend. As Wood recalled: 'The people simply rose and yelled. I had to play it again – with the same result; in-fact they refused to let me go on with the programme. After considerable delay, while the audience roared its applause, I went off and fetched Harry Dearth who was to sing Hiawatha's Vision; but they would not listen. Merely to restore order I played the march a third time. And that, I might say, was the one and only time in the history of the Promenade Concerts that an orchestral item was accorded a double encore.'

Press reports carry an anomaly, suggesting the first march was actually played second. This might have been an error but it appeared in several different papers so Wood possibly performed the marches in reverse order.

The Manchester Guardian, written on the night of the performance stated: 'The two marches are respectively in the keys of A minor and D major; and the last, which is perhaps the more striking, pleased so well tonight, that it had to be repeated.

The Daily Telegraph: 'If the clash of contending rhythms and themes endures through the first of the marches and the opening portion of the second, there comes with the final trio a melody of broad and surpassing beauty which the composer displays in the simplest and most sweeping fashion. Here again it is not the march of British soldiery that the music illustrates. To some ears the fine theme will suggest a song of thanksgiving for victory, to others the inspired hymn of some great pilgrim band. But whatever the interpretation the passage remains one of real and moving magnificence.

'Hearing it, the audience caught fire and when the march's coda had brought forth the tune again in ever more majestic shape, no one spared his applause. To refuse an encore was impossible and Mr Wood repeated the piece to the satisfaction of all.'

The Observer: 'It is not too much to say that the second of these pieces – the march in D – and perhaps even both of them – will carry Dr Elgar's name and fame to every part of the world where there are people capable of appreciating virility, strength of characteristic expression, nobility of style and robust, healthy sentiment, as expressed in music. The marches were played for the first time in London on Tuesday last and literally 'brought the house down'. In vain were Mr Wood's bows – five times acknowledged – in vain his last resource of inducing the band to rise and bow – March No 2 had to be repeated. An even greater furore was produced last night when the march in question was played for the third time (its second performance had been given in the afternoon).

'The enthusiasm was greater than we can ever remember to have been evoked by any work by a British composer. And in this case there is no difference of opinion between the cognoscenti and the hoi polloi. The marches have the popular ring - are just the music for the man in the street and at the same time satisfy the musician by their magnificent orchestration, harmonic texture and sureness of effect. It would be a crime to contribute to any artist's downfall by praise of the kind likely to lead to what our American cousins call 'swelled head', otherwise we should have no hesitation in saying that Dr Elgar is the greatest composer England has produced since Purcell.'

An unattributed report added: 'If Dr Elgar is like other people (which fortunately he is not) he should be a happy man this week, for it has fallen to his lot to do what no one has done before him. He has composed two marches which were produced at Queen's Hall on Tuesday night, when the second of them had to be repeated in deference to deafening clamour. They were heard again on Saturday afternoon at the Symphony concert, and the second of them was repeated at the evening's Promenade Concert, when an audience that was large, in spite of the fog, insisted on hearing it twice. Has any English composer ever done the same except in the theatre?'

Just why the tune which we know today as 'Land of Hope and Glory' struck so much accord could possibly be explained by the continuation of this anonymous report as it described the two marches and what the critic thought they represented : 'The dark fateful tones of the first bring before us men marching grimly to meet the foe, as it were, through the fabled terrors of some enchanted forest or some rockbound pass. Then there are bugle calls and we seem to hear the shock of arms.

'In the second all is bustle and excitement as of an army marching gaily homeward knowing its work well done. Then in the trio and the coda we seem to see a triumphal progress through a city 'all on fire with sun and cloth of gold' amid the blare of festal trumpets and the shouts of a nation making holiday. We have often been told that the 'Kaisermarsch' and 'Huldigungsmarsch' such be considered as Symphonic Poems rather than as marches, and so I should prefer to consider these, for all their strict march form.'

This was the time of the Boer War. People also remembered foreign conflicts, particularly Afghanistan, where the British army had been wiped out only a generation before, and the name of the Khyber Pass was etched onto public memory. So perhaps the reference to 'some rockbound pass' and 'men grimly marching to meet the foe' which the critic saw in the A minor march resonated with the audience. The other, with its major key and uplifting anthem-like trio section, similarly resonated positively, evoking feelings of an end to conflict, and the prospect of fathers, husbands and sons returning home, alive and in triumph.

In the following year Elgar used the tune from the D major march again, in his 20 minute, seven-element, choral Ode commemorating the Coronation of Edward VII – in a triumphal finale for which librettist A C Benson produced words beginning 'Land of Hope and Glory.'

The Daily Telegraph reported: 'The work as was to be expected is essentially British in origin and character. An Englishman, Mr Arthur Christopher Benson, has written the words and of the same nationality as everyone knows, is the distinguished composer. The Soloists will be British also, with Madame [Nellie] Melba, it is hoped, to represent the Colonies. All this is as it should be on an occasion so particularly national.'

'In the finale 'Land of Hope and Glory' all available means are used to the end of an imposing finish. An interesting feature here is the use of the theme of the Trio of the March in D, from the composer's 'Pomp and Circumstance'. In compliance with a request, Dr Elgar has used it as representing the climax of national feeling.'

The King has long been thought to have made that 'request', but, Clara Butt, who popularised the song in the form we know today, perhaps unsurprisingly suggested it was her.

The Ode was planned to open a 'Command Performance' at the Royal Opera House, Covent Garden, otherwise featuring opera excerpts. The Truth magazine complained: 'Some extraordinary nonsense is being written about the 'Command'. In one of the halfpenny morning papers I read the other day that the whole performance would be in English – a perfectly preposterous idea, considering that the large majority of the operatic vocalists are not conversant with that tongue. Elsewhere too it has been stated that there will be a series of Galas – another idiotic invention, for it would of course be impossible to secure either the artists or a ten-guinea audience for more nights than one.

'Then again I have seen an absurd report that Dr. Elgar's 'Ode' will occupy nearly the entire evening. If it did it would truly be a Gilbertian sort of Gala. It may in fact be taken for granted that apart from the entr'actes, when, as an enthusiastic lady once declared 'uniforms jostle with coronets' every minute spent without Jean de Reszke, Calve or Melba, will, by this army of courtiers, be deemed a minute wasted.

'I believe that it is true there are seven numbers to this 'Ode' but they will have to be remarkably brief, or some of them, masterpieces though they may be, must inevitably be omitted, for the entire performance of the 'Ode' is twenty minutes, or, including the National Anthem half an hour. In the finale in which the Coldstream Guards' band will enter – Dr Elgar – or as by that time he probably will be Sir Edward Elgar – has, it is said, introduced the theme of one of his 'Pomp and Circumstance' marches.'

The question of an Elgar knighthood was soon debated in the Pall Mall Gazette: 'The list of Coronation Honours includes the names of but few musicians – Sir Hubert Parry who rises a step in obtaining his baronetcy, and (as one must now call him) Sir Charles Villiers Stanford who obtains his knighthood. The choice is, of course, naturally an official one; but it is nonetheless one which will arouse interest, discussion and possibly controversy.

'Sir Hubert Parry, who is in a certain sense a musical representative of all that is sound and fittingly constructive in English music, of course takes a quite natural place. In point of knowledge and of general accomplishment he is rightly famous, just as well known, and is a pillar of academic strength.

'Sir Hubert Parry has laboured hard at his chosen and appreciated art; but his lines can scarcely be said to run along the ways of popularity. It is all very well for demonstrative writers occasionally to set his scoring above that of Mendelssohn; but the fact remains that Mendelssohn has survived all the shocks which are likely to dim the immortality of the new Baronet.

'Let us grant at once that Parry is a learned man; but as we have before said it is his critical writings that we like best; and we therefore prefer to think that a music critic has been honoured in his person. Not for a moment would we detract from Parry's musical accomplishment from the view point of musical accomplishment; but the honour is a very special one and therefore naturally provokes one to inquiry.

'We should have liked to see Sir Alexander Mackenzie make a further step in civil promotion. Mackenzie like most men of creative power, has done now good, now more indifferent work, but the good work is undoubtedly of most excellent stuff composed. We have before written from the general standpoint, of Mackenzie's work; but at its best that work assuredly shows the musician as possessed of a fine talent for absolute musical construction, no less than of an exquisite sense of beauty and of melody.

'That Mackenzie has had his failures is to record of him a human commonplace that is inevitable with all human endeavour based upon a large scale. But his sound musicianship and his widely extended interests, literary as well as musical made us rather desire to see his name included in the Coronation list.

'Sir C Villiers Stanford probably gets what many people would have expected him to get. We are sure that we have never hesitated to praise him for many excellent qualities, but some may have doubted if Stanford has ever done a really *big* work. 'Shamus O'Brien' was a charming opera of course, but it was not an 'Aida' (shall we say?) nor yet even an 'Ivanhoe' forgotten and in disuse though that work be. 'Much Ado' was fascinating in parts and throughout was musicianly. And there have been many delightful instrumental and other works, though some have hesitated over the 'Requiem'. So that we may range ourselves here on the side of them that heartily approve.

'We should approve with more complete wholeheartedness if we did not rather miss one name upon whose inclusion some had very confidently counted – that of Edward Elgar.

'A knighthood for Elgar was something upon which some had, as we say, counted. The very fact that he was officially connected with the Coronation with the composition of his Ode seemed guaranteed. But apart from this fact he is certainly a musician of most remarkable, most exceptional and most extraordinary merits. We have often written of him in these columns, but the occasion may serve to repeat our opinion.

'We can do so with the greater feeling of sincerity because we frankly do not like his Coronation Ode. It seems to us to be lacking in Elgar's customary terse and spiritual inspiration. Now and then of course, he hits out a fine phrase, but the general trend of the composition is, we fear, towards the kind of music that is rather loud and rather machine-made. The repetition, too, of the big march from his own 'Pomp and Circumstance' seems to detract from it on the score of originality.

'This is not work which is worth of the man who wrote the 'Light of the World'[sic] with its magnificently meditative prelude, or 'Caractacus' or yet 'The Dream of Gerontius'. Nevertheless it would be absurd to judge a man by any official work (who would judge Horace, for example, on the merits of his 'Carmen Seculare' ?) that we need only state our not very enthusiastic feeling towards Elgar's 'Coronation Ode' and still grieve somewhat that his name which is so much honoured abroad, especially in Germany, should not have received on such an occasion as this public recognition in company with the names of Sir Hubert Parry and Sir C Villiers Stanford.'

In the event the Ode's premier was cancelled. The King developed appendicitis and the Coronation was postponed. Elgar reacted in a letter to August Jaeger: 'Don't for heaven's sake *sympathise* with me – I don't care a tinker's damn! It gives me three blessed sunny days in my own country (for which I thank God or the Devil) instead of stewing in town. *My* own interest in the thing ceased, as usual, when I had finished the M.S. – since when I have been thinking mighty things! [i.e. 'The Apostles'] I was biking out in Herefordsh: yesterday & the news reached me at a little roadside pub: I said: 'Give me another pint of cider' I'm deadly sorry for the King, - but that's all.'

The Ode finally appeared at the October Sheffield Festival. The Morning Leader said: 'Elgar has attempted something that to a great extent lies outside himself. Perhaps patriotism, as Schopenhauer thought, is only individual selfishness magnified. However that may be, no composition written in honour of the Coronation has been worth its performance. That is a hard thing to say but had not the programme stated the fact I should not have thought the composer of 'The Dream of Gerontius' had written 'The Coronation Ode'. He has played to the gallery.'

The Times commented: 'The work does not look good on paper, but in performance every note tells and in its entirety the composition sustains the composer's reputation,' while The Athenaeum, calling the work 'Dr Elgar's setting of Mr A C Benson's 'Coronation Ode' concluded: 'The freshness, skill and charm of the music are undeniable – the composer indeed would find it difficult to write anything that was not in many ways interesting – but somehow or other, the 'Ode' music lacks soul.

'In Gerontius, Dr Elgar was evidently deeply moved by a poem which treats of subjects which have excited strong emotions of hope and fear in the greater portion of mankind: expressions of loyalty and well-wishing to King and Queen, however strong and sincere, cannot stir one's nature to the same degree. In 'Gerontius' there is more heart. In the 'Ode' more head.'

An unattributed cutting in the Elgar archives called it 'a peculiarly empty and unsatisfying production without a dignified bar or an original one from beginning to end and in every way, unworthy a concert of artistic aim'

Even the Birmingham Post said: 'The writing is 'cheap' for a composer like Elgar.'

LAND OF HOPE AND GLORY

'Land of Hope and Glory' has long caused division. Some view it as a quasi-National Anthem - others, the epitome of a hateful imperial past. In both, Elgar is identified with applause or condemnation. Yet, he merely produced a tune. Benson wrote the words.

This was his original version as used in the Coronation Ode:

Land of Hope and Glory,
Mother of the Free,
How may we extol thee,
Who are born of thee?
Truth and Right and Freedom,
Each a holy gem,
Stars of solemn brightness,
weave thy diadem.

Tho' thy way be darkened, Still in splendour drest,
As the star that trembles
O'er the liquid West.
Throned amid the billows,
Throned inviolate,
Thou hast reigned victorious,
Thou has smiled at fate.
Land of Hope and Glory,
Fortress of the Free,
How may we extol thee,
Praise thee, honour thee?
Hark, a mighty nation
Maketh glad reply;
Lo, our lips are thankful,
Lo, our hearts are high!
Hearts in hope uplifted,
Loyal lips that sing;
Strong in faith and freedom,
We have crowned our King!

The tune had already achieved such popularity that it was played on street corners throughout the land and sensing lucrative rewards, publishers asked Benson to re-write the lyrics to create a popular ballad. Benson duly obliged:

Dear Land of Hope, thy hope is crowned.
God make thee mightier yet!
On Sov'ran brows, beloved, renowned,
Once more thy crown is set.
Thine equal laws, by Freedom gained,
Have ruled thee well and long;
By Freedom gained, by Truth maintained,
Thine Empire shall be strong.

Land of Hope and Glory, Mother of the Free,
How shall we extol thee, who are born of thee?
Wider still and wider shall thy bounds be set;
God, who made thee mighty, make thee mightier yet.
God, who made thee mighty, make thee mightier yet.

Thy fame is ancient as the days,
As Ocean large and wide:
A pride that dares, and heeds not praise,
A stern and silent pride:
Not that false joy that dreams content
With what our sires have won;
The blood a hero sire hath spent
Still nerves a hero son.

The 'wider still and wider' line celebrated the huge sum the recently deceased Cecil Rhodes left for the expansion of the Empire. So, the 'contentious' words of 'Land of Hope and Glory' derive from re-written lines which had nothing to do with Elgar's original production, and over which he had no control. Yet this is the one piece with which Elgar is now so universally known, and so unfavourably bonded with notions of jingoism and nationalism. Ironically, Benson, author of the words of perhaps the best-known English ballad, is today almost totally forgotten, and even at the time many never knew Elgar had written the tune.

Perhaps that is why in later life, he came to hate it.

THE APOSTLES

'The Apostles' was commissioned by the 1903 Birmingham Festival. Press rumours started appearing early in the year, including this one in the Musical Times: 'A certain newspaper gravely states that Dr Edward Elgar is at present occupied in the composition of a new 'coral work'! What next? Perchance a 'Coral Highland Symphony'!'

The Echo of January 31st commented: 'It is an open secret that there has been considerable competition among the leading publishers to secure the publishing rights of this novelty. The matter has now been settled, Dr Elgar having given Messrs Novello his authority to issue the work. According to the Daily Chronicle the sum paid by this firm for the rights is the largest that has ever been given to any composer for an oratorio, and rumour quotes the amount as being represented by four figures, in addition to a substantial royalty on the sale of every copy.' This was repeated verbatim by several papers.

Times had changed for Elgar. Boosey and Co had published 'Cockaigne' and the Pomp and Circumstance marches to great success. Now they wanted 'The Apostles'. But the Festival Committee preferred Novello's and Chairman G H Johnson negotiated on Elgar's behalf - securing £500 on the receipt of the manuscript, a further £500 after 10,000 vocal score sales, plus a royalty of 6d per copy for everyone sold after 10,000. In modern money this amounted to a contract payment of about £80,000 with the royalty element being about £2 per copy.

The Birmingham Post reported in February: 'Immediately about their appointment the Orchestral Committee took into consideration the question of new compositions for 1903 and were glad to report that arrangements had been made for the production of a new work by Dr Elgar to be entitled 'The Apostles'. It was expected to occupy about two hours in performance and having regard to the great repute in which Dr Elgar's music was held, not only in this country but on the Continent it could not fail to be of the highest interest.

'Dr Elgar, the most original if not also the most scholarly of English composers will be afforded an opportunity of repeating or possibly eclipsing the success he achieved at our festival with the 'Dream of Gerontius'.

'The production of even one really great new work would doubtless satisfy the ambition of the Festival Committee. It would certainly suffice to uphold the reputation of the Festival and place the musical world under a lasting obligation for the number of original compositions answering to this description which have seen the light in Birmingham since the production of Mendelssohn's 'Elijah' more than half a century ago, may be counted upon one's fingers.

'Of Dr Elgar's new work, all that we are told at present is that it is an oratorio set to a text of the composer's own selection and that it will occupy about a couple of hours in performance. On the occasion of the first performance of 'The Dream of Gerontius' it may be remembered the performance suffered somewhat from inadequate preparation, more especially in the choral parts which are of exceptional difficulty.

'It is to be hoped that no such criticism will be possible in regard to the first rendering of 'The Apostles' and this hope is fortified by the information given by the Committee that parts are already in the hands of the publishers and that the work is secure which affords practical assurance that it will not suffer for want of due rehearsal.'

By the spring expectation increased though Elgar would doubtless not have welcomed this one, from the Piano Journal which appeared in April: 'Our contemporary is pleased to learn that Dr Elgar is to compose another oratorio. Such joy is misplaced until such time Dr Elgar succeeds in writing music of a more worthy nature.'

The Musical Times, in a two-column examination of what the work was to offer concluded: 'The foregoing is but a very brief outline of what may be regarded as an epoch-making work, full of suggestiveness and reverential artistry.'

As the Musical Times was published by Novello's, and considering that by April the work was hardly complete, these comments might be considered in the 'press release' category, but nevertheless they served to add to the expectation that 'The Apostles' was going to be worth their publishers' investment.

The Morning Post, following a comment contained in the Musical Times article that Elgar had been inspired to write the work by Handel's 'Messiah' warned: 'That Dr Elgar admires 'The Messiah' is natural enough. It is to be hoped, though, that he has not adopted it as a model, for there is no greater mistake than to attempt to revive old musical forms. A masterpiece remains a masterpiece and is impervious to the caprices of fashion. It is great partly because it revealed something new at the time of its production. Many oratorios have been written on the pattern of 'The Messiah' and these have all long since disappeared into oblivion. Dr Elgar is, however, not likely to commit so deplorable an error.'

The Pall Mall Gazette – conspicuously dropping the 'Dr' title - thought: 'Mr Elgar is without question the most spiritual, the most thoughtful musician of modern times. Richard Strauss has his own magnificent gifts; but for these assigned qualities Mr Elgar reigns at present supreme. He is remote from anything that is even to be suspected, from the most distant point of view, of being cheap. In 'The Apostles' the libretto of which he has chosen for himself, he deals with the details of his subject both before and after the Passion.

'It is a subject which we have reason to think, Mr Elgar has been inclined to treat in no conventional way. He brings in this monumental work the history of the Apostles down to their dispersal to preach leaving what may be called his heroes at the edge of their conquest of the Western World. We return to that point that you can nearly always find in the writings of the genuine musical genius some touch of the spiritual if not its essence. The links that run in a sure chain from Bach to Elgar are most certainly forged in a common spirit of workmanship and in these two instances the touch is essential.

'In these notes we have often inadvertently turned to Elgar as an example; but seriously we put these two great exponents of this overwhelming truth very near together in the hierarchy of musical achievement.'

But this appeared in the Morning Advertiser in early August: 'We are now close upon what is known as the provincial festival season. This year there are only two, the Three Choirs at Hereford and that at Birmingham and judging by their programmes the West Country celebration is by far the most important. It is surprising to find a small city such as Hereford more enterprising and doing more for native art than a rich commercial centre such as Birmingham. But so it is and we congratulate Hereford upon the fact.'

The article based its judgement on the fact that Hereford was to stage new works by Coleridge Taylor, Parry, Percy Pitt, Cowen and Bantock, and continued: 'Against this satisfactory announcement, Birmingham cuts a very poor figure with only one novelty, Dr Elgar's cantata, 'The Apostles' which is not a whole programme work.'

'Dr Elgar who is considered by many excellent judges to be our foremost man, is a child of the Worcester Festival. Leeds produced his 'Caractacus' and Birmingham his 'Dream of Gerontius'. With the exception of the variations for orchestra and a few minor pieces he owes his present position entirely to provincial enterprise. For more than a generation past our composers have had, metaphorically speaking, to live in the country. It has nourished them, fed them and made them the men that they are.

'For the time being the eyes of musical England are fixed on those festival towns where new works are to be performed. Next month amateurs will be turning to their papers to see if Mr Coleridge Taylor has improved the position he won with his 'Hiawatha' and the month after still more eagerly will they look for the verdict on Dr Elgar's 'Apostles'. We have no such musical interest in London. Seldom does anything happen here which marks a fresh departure in native art. The Royal Choral Society goes on in its old hereditary way at the Albert Hall. The Philharmonic Society lies low on the bedrock of sameness. The Queen's Hall Orchestra, with Mr Wood at its head, labours faithfully to instil a love for third-rate Scandinavian composers in our unresponsive bosoms and enterprising concert agents boom festivals for foreign orchestras and composers.

'A Happy Place is London for the English composer! If he is ingenious enough to write up to the level of musical comedy he may count his income by thousands of pounds per annum. But the man who has greatness in his mind's eye might just as well betake himself to the Sahara Desert and tune his lyre for the benefit of wandering Bedouins.'

A generous scene setter, and pen-portrait of the composer, which contrasted his status at this time to what it had been only a few years earlier was delivered by Robert Buckley in the Daily Dispatch:

'Walking through the high town of Hereford the other day, my eye caught a side-face that seemed familiar. The possessor thereof was looking in a shop window. He wore a very light suit and a straw hat and was well groomed despite his careless holiday dress. There was a slight student-stoop in the shoulders and in movement some suggestion of stiffness and fragility.

'It was Dr Elgar whose rise and progress is perhaps the most phenomenal circumstance in the whole history of English musical literature.

'A little further I came upon windows wherein were displayed Elgar post-cards, Elgar photographs, the work of Dr Grindrod of Malvern. The composer is represented as leaning his head on his hand and looking upward as though in a moment of inspiration. A day or two afterwards, Dr Elgar told me that the portrait was a photograph taken through silk and otherwise cleverly manipulated by the distinguished amateur above-named.

'The windows of the Hereford shops were lavish in their portraits of the composer, but nothing came within measurable distance of this amateur work of art, which conveyed the effect of a rapt monk looking out of his cloister-window about five hundred years ago.

'It seems but yesterday that in passing along the corridor of the Birmingham Town Hall I stopped to chat with a nervous looking man whose dress suit was the only festivity about him. We fell into conversation: the 'Black Knight' was in process of performance: I was talking to the composer: a soprano lead had just gone wrong: he was bearing the mishap as best he might, something anxious, however, about the reception of the cantata.

'Returning to the hall I there found a number of musical people who were pooh-poohing the work, their depreciation mainly based on the fact that the composer had been a member of Mr Stockley's orchestra in that very hall but a few years before.'

The report then cited various other examples of great artists who were not appreciated in their homelands, mainly because they were seen as locals. It added: During the Worcester Festival of 1896, when Mr Elgar's short oratorio 'The Light of Life', was to be produced, the writer was unable to procure a photograph or any other portrait of the composer throughout the length and breadth of Worcester, his native town.

'The Bishop, the Dean, the conductor, the man who had built the organ, anybody and everybody else was pictured all over the place. There was no portrait of him to whom Worcester had most reason to be proud. But everybody knew everything about Edward Elgar, whose octogenarian father, Mr W H Elgar, long was organist at St George's Roman Catholic Church in the Faithful City. Indeed, one of Edward Elgar's old associates was rather indignant concerning the composer's presumption. *'He, write an oratorio?'* he exclaimed, *'why, I went to school with him!'* There was no disputing the conclusiveness of this argument.

'It is seventeen years since the young Elgar published a pianoforte arrangement of a piece written for violin and orchestra, and about the same period since Mr W C Stockley of Birmingham thought 'Sevillana' good enough for production at one of his orchestral concerts. But nobody expected to hear more of the composer. Most young musicians compose a little; if lucky they get their production performed once – twice if they have influence with the press; and that is all.

'When Mr Elgar gave up the piano and organ and took to the violin they reckoned it was all over with him; he had chosen the lot of an orchestral player and was finally disposed of. But somehow the overture 'Froissart' was heard at the Worcester Festival of 1890 and the composer was encouraged.'

The feature then mentioned 'The Apostles' was due for its first performance later in the year at the Birmingham Festival. Elgar however was not interested in talking about it.

'Asked what he had been doing lately, he said *'Very little but hard work. The summer has been too wet for bicycling.'* He golfs a little, but his heart is not there. He has given some attention to the scientific aspect of kite-flying, but once upon a time a huge kite got the better of him and he had to engage a powerful navvy to bring down the refractory thing from mid-heaven. All he has achieved in this line, he regretfully remarks, is the destruction of his neighbour's spouting, and in future he is determined to fly kites only for the pleasure of his friends and not with the object of inventing a self-compensating kite that might be scientifically useful.

'Possibly Dr Elgar has been stolen by music from his proper station in the scientific world. Be that as it may, his career, we repeat, has been phenomenal and the same term may be used to describe the breaking down of prejudice against British composers which everywhere existed until the touring by Dr Richter of the 'Enigma' Variations, by means of which the great conductor converted England to Elgar, just as thirty years before, with the 'Tannhauser' Overture, he had converted England to Wagner.'

Another piece under the title 'Elgar at Home - by one who knows him' (probably Buckley again) - appeared in the Pall Mall Gazette: 'You are prone to imagine that there are several Dr Elgar's according to the clothes and the circumstances in which you see him. There is one in a dress suit, pacing the corridor of a concert-room in which a conductor is taking Elgarian works at unauthorised tempi. There is another in rough tweed and leggings, who frequents unfrequented lanes with chosen friends who, armed with a spirit lamp and other impedimenta, take tea under hedges 'like tramps'.

'A third, wearing a fancy waistcoat with silver buttons, hand-carved in the Bavarian Tyrol, smokes genially in front of his own poker-work 'fire-music' from Wagner, burnt on the panel over the study grate. A fourth walks slowly along Worcester High-Street, buried in a battered Panama pulled down to his chin. A fifth attired in the customary suit of solemn black, ambulates *lento* as though very tired in the precincts of a cathedral during a Three Choirs festival. This one wears a tall silk hat, crushed down on the forehead and gives the impression of a distinguished colonel home from India for a year's holiday and at present attending a funeral. Dr Edward Elgar is tall, spare, angular, grave and courteous. But no man can be more crushing.'

The author then gave a picture of Elgar at work: 'I found a sixth Edward Elgar the other day bent over a large table, hard at work – this one without coat or waistcoat, an ancient briar in his mouth. A huge fountain-pen, a Brobdingnagian, a Titanic pen, lay by the music-paper; a pen to write whole oratorio scores without a fresh drink. *'Holds about half a pint'*, he said *scherzando.*'

The article continued: 'The learned Doctor here took large gloves from a drawer. *'Not boxing gloves,'* he ejaculated. *'Golf. Splendid game. The best thing about it is this: When playing golf you can't think of anything else.'* He put on a cap to match the suit and together we strode towards the links.'

Such was Elgar's growing status in anticipation of 'The Apostles' that the press even indulged in a spat along the lines of 'we discovered him first'. This piece, for instance, appeared in The Birmingham Gazette: 'Worcester has the pride of being the birthplace of Dr Elgar whose talent we declared to them a good seven years ago. It was as far back as 1895 that we ventured to speak of Dr Elgar as our contemporaries spoke of him five years later. And here a situation of amusing character may be cited for the entertainment of the amateurs of the Worcester district and elsewhere.

'It was in 1895 that we left our beaten track to call repeated attention to Dr Elgar's capabilities. It was in 1900 that the Musical Standard attacked us on account of our supposed non-appreciation of Dr Elgar, that is, five years later.

'It was in 1897, two full years after our appreciation of Dr Elgar that the Musical Standard published a series of Victorian composers, bit and little, (75 or 100 the precise number escapes us). One thing we remember. Dr Elgar was not included. No portrait, no biographical sketch, no mention at all. Such is the irony of history.'

'Apostles' rehearsals began in early August. The Worcester Daily Times reported: 'The composer had a good reception and at the close he thanked the choir for their attention and spoke in favourable terms of the manner in which they had interpreted his music. Undoubtedly 'The Apostles' will form the greatest attraction of the Festival and the secrecy with which the work has so carefully been surrounded considerably adds to the interest centred in its first performance. The composer's motive as avowed to the choir on Monday night does not tend to lessen that interest. *'When you sing this work,'* he said, *'I don't want it to be a performance nor an entertainment. I want it to help people or do them good.'* Again: *'It is not merely a piece of music; it is much more than that.'*

'Dr Elgar said he hoped to conduct another rehearsal before the Festival when he would devote more time to certain passages. *'Everything was so nearly what I wanted,'* he explained, *'that I didn't stop.'*'

However, The Birmingham Gazette complained: 'The composer had a good reception and a most interesting evening ensued, which, however, would have been still more pleasant had there been anything like adequate ventilation of the room. The Hall was so heated by the large number of persons present that one feared the singers incurred liability to the colds which so seriously militate against good singing.'

Novello's refused to release any details of the music to the critics until a week before the performance and banned any discussion of the music derived from the rehearsals. This created a clamour for seats for the premier from an intrigued public. Applications for tickets were subject to a ballot and, as the Worcester Daily Times reported: 'For many hours on Wednesday the Strangers' and Place-Setting Committees were engaged allocating seats for next week's Birmingham Festival. For Dr Elgar's new oratorio 'The Apostles', there were 1,152 applications (972 coming through the Strangers' Committee), and has resulted in the rejection of 361applications, that being the number in excess of the Town Hall's accommodation.'

Such was the demand, that, according to reports, the Festival Committee were even considering an extra performance of the work at the end of the Festival week. Then came the performance.

Such had been the expectation that the press devoted considerable coverage to it – with nationals such as the Daily Mail and the Morning Leader, even printing passages taken from the work written out especially for them by Elgar.

The Birmingham Post indulged in scene setting: 'There are degrees of fashion even at a musical festival. All the performances at Birmingham are of course, fashionable, but that which took place this morning was regarded as the most distinguished of the series. Dr Elgar's new work 'The Apostles' was to be performed and so great the desire in society circles to hear this novelty that all the seats were applied for twice over, and those who managed to secure tickets had good reason to count themselves fortunate.

'The oratorio was not timed to commence until 11.30 but the ticket holders commenced to arrive a long time before that hour. The President, Earl Howe and Countess Howe arrived about a quarter past eleven and they were followed soon after by members of their house party at 'West Grove', the beautiful Lady Cynthia Graham attired in a dove grey dress with large feather ruffle and black hat, who arrived in the city last evening, being escorted by Mr Schuster. A large party again came from Highbury. Mrs Chamberlain who was wearing a red costume with black hat being accompanied by the Misses Chamberlain and several other ladies, and Mr Neville Chamberlain. The Lord Mayor (Alderman Hallowell Rogers) and the Lady Mayoress were accompanied by a number of friends from Greville Lodge.

'So fashionable was the assembly this morning that comparatively few of the visitors arrived on foot. The ladies were most handsomely attired. The majority of them wore black hats whilst some of the fur capes and necklaces were of the most exquisite character. Unfortunately, the weather was not so favourable as yesterday, rain falling during the time the distinguished audience was arriving and consequently as the ladies had taken precaution to come provided with cloaks, the spectacular effect of the scene suffered, so far as concerned the public who again crowded the barriers in Paradise Street opposite the main entrance to the hall.

'When Dr Elgar took his seat shortly before half past eleven every inch of the interior of the vast building was occupied by an audience which will undoubtedly rank as one of the most brilliant of the many distinguished companies seen within the walls of the historic hall. A conspicuous figure in the front row of the great gallery was Madame Clara Butt who had as her companion Mrs Elgar. There was also present an unusually large contingent of London pressmen including Mr Joseph Bennett.'

The six soloists for the performance were: Emma Albani, Muriel Foster, John Coates, Robert Kennerly Rumford, Andrew Black and David Ffrangcon-Davis.

The Birmingham Evening Dispatch described the two female soloists as they took to the stage: 'Madame Albani wore a white silk dress with just a touch of heliotrope on the waist, while Miss Muriel Foster was simply, though charmingly gowned in white, her toilette being completed with a large hat of purple velvet. Yesterday it was noted none of the lady principals wore head gear.'

Critics were divided on the music, possibly because the preceding secrecy created difficulties for critical assessment based on one hearing. Elgar had also originally planned 'The Apostles' having three parts, but ran out of time, the third part emerging as 'The Kingdom' in 1906. Some critics were not pleased.

The Morning Leader commented: 'I feel a quite exceptional difficulty in sorting my ideas as to 'The Apostles'. The one impression uppermost is that one has listened to something too big to be dismissed in one article, something which it is impossible to label and docket at once, something for which the right formula will not be found for many a day.

'To this difficulty is added another which is possibly more serious. The work is not complete and we have heard only the first two parts; and the third which is yet to come will probably be the most important in that we shall see the Apostles fulfilling their mission among the Gentiles and that is the main theme of the work.

'Dr Elgar has been his own librettist and has avowedly striven to arrive at the purely human significance of his subject using the word somewhat in its ardent sense. It is the only course possible for a composer of Dr Elgar's temperament and it is the course most in accordance with what we call the spirit of the time, to which, in passing, I proffer my complete adherence. But it is a course which has obvious perils and one of which not everybody can be expected to approve.

'Opinions will no doubt differ very widely with regard to the level of success achieved by Dr Elgar in avoiding these perils. It will be said, no doubt, that in trying to be human he has forgotten to be devotional. Others will say that in his realist moments he had attained variety only by occasional crudity. Others taking an opposite view, will accuse the work of want of variety and will say that this is due to excessive use of leit-motifs. I can only say now that while realising that such criticisms are possible, there is a perfect defence to all of them.

'The words are all taken from scripture and Dr Elgar has shown the greatest boldness in arranging his words in the most dramatic manner possible. In his view of the subject it is natural that the figure of Mary Magdalen assumes great importance; and his treatment of Judas whom he represents as betraying Christ with a view to forcing him to declare himself in his true nature is specially interesting.

'The music is fuller of leit-motifs even than that of 'The Dream of Gerontius' and the polyphony is in many places even more elaborate. The subtleties of orchestration are still more remarkable and triumphantly skilful, but still there is a greater simplicity and directness of speech in critical moments, though there is much brilliant realism. Yet the chief note of the music is one of devoted mysticism which we have come to regard as characteristically Elgarish.'

Joseph Bennet, in the Daily Telegraph believed the production 'was in some respects unique. It was so in my own personal experience for through all the years I have known the Birmingham Festival it has never happened that the whole musical world, not only in this country, but also abroad, has gathered more or less closely around the production of an Englishman. I recall compositions by Sterndale Bennett, Sullivan and others. These works excised attention each in its measure, but never in that respect were they serious rivals of such occasions as the production of Mendelssohn's 'Elijah', Costa's 'Eli' and 'Naaman' - we thought much of Costa then – and Gounod's 'Redemption'. It is a good omen that at last a man of our own race and nation has come to the extreme front and drawn to himself the wondering admiration of all who profess and call themselves musicians and lovers of the art.

'There is something impressive in the position now occupied by Elgar. He is not an intriguer. He does not compare heaven and earth making proselytes to believe in his own powers, neither does he trim his sails to catch the varying breezes of popular opinion. Having something to say in the fashion which appears to him best, he says it straight out and leaves the issue to the Fates. Yet, though sturdily independent, courting nobody, he now occupies the position of a man with whom most people are determined to be pleased.

'There must be something in him – much more than common – to bring about this result. But what that is cannot now be discussed. Elgar's latest work is one for calm consideration and deliberate judgement. It cannot safely be written, I speak for myself only, while the excitement of a first performance is still seething and there has been no time to analyse sensations and form conclusions.

'Besides, this remarkable oratorio is worth any amount of care in the handling. It is not the work of a mere trafficker in musical goods. Its sincerity is unquestionable, the loftiness of its aim cannot be denied and its strength must be taken into account whatever may be thought of its methods.'

Bennett continued describing the scene at the performance: 'What a crowd of musicians from many parts of the country and abroad flocked to the historic Town Hall ! Among those who came under my own observation, were Sir Frederick Bridge, Dr Cowen, Sir C Stanford, Dr Sinclair, Mr Lee Williams, Mr Herbert Brewer, Mr Gaul and Mr Benton, late chorus master of the Leeds Festival. These names, samples of a mass, show how deeply the musical mind of the country was moved by the production of a successor to 'St Gerontius'.

'Of course, there was not a vacant seat in the building. Equally of course the appearance of Dr Elgar in the conductor's place evoked loud applause, capped by the volleys of the chorus as the hero of the day turned to face them.

'No sooner had Dr Elgar brought his forces into action than it became evident that, accidents apart, the performance would be a good one. The close of the oratorio was followed by the boisterous compliments which on such occasions, no musician escapes. Dr Elgar doubly deserved them, first as a safe conductor, and yet more, as the composer of, perhaps, the most remarkable work of the present century.'

The Daily Graphic however felt: 'The new work was received with the utmost respect and the composer, who conducted, was much applauded at the close. But in spite of many beauties, 'The Apostles' as a whole, unquestionably proved a disappointment. It is ambitious and clever and in many respects even brilliant, but it lacks the unity of feeling and expression that should characterise a great work of art.

'Dr Elgar's music, it is needless to say, is founded upon the now inevitable system of leading motives; in-fact for intimacy and technical elaboration the score of 'The Apostles' surpassed anything that he has previously produced. It must be admitted too, that Dr Elgar handles his material with practiced skill. He has a natural genius for orchestration and his new work is to the full as picturesque and as rich in colour as it is possible for a new work to be. But when we pass beyond the questions of mere dexterity to discuss the value of the actual musical ideas employed it is not possible to be equally eulogistic and this is the test by which every musical work must stand or fall.

'Form in music as in everything else is fluid and liable to change. The qualities that give immortality to a work of art are independent of structure and design. Nothing could be more antiquated from a modern point of view than a mass of F Palestrina, an oratorio of Handel or a symphony of Mozart. Yet in spite of all recent developments in music these retain their power to charm and strengthen while what is merely clever and expert passes away. It is necessary to remember this because we are apt to be blinded by the dazzle and glitter of modern music and to forget that profound musical science and glowing orchestration are means to an end, not an end in themselves. In what we may call the accidents of his art, Dr Elgar is a master, but in 'The Apostles' it is my misfortune often to find the essential musical ideas arid and jejune.

'Yet there are many noble pages in the work, notably the closing chorus which strikes a note of true fervour and brings the story of Christ's life on earth to an august and even a sublime conclusion. Very beautiful too is the passage in which the remorse of Peter is told in a chorus of simple yet heartfelt pathos and another chorus 'Turn you to the Stronghold' has a noble breadth and dignity.

'It is possible that a second hearing may reveal beauties in much that today seemed to fail of its effect and that I may find pathos and sincerity in such passages as the elaborate monologues of Mary Magdalene and Judas Iscariot, which were treated, it must be frankly admitted, with extraordinary knowledge of musical effect, but which appeared at a first hearing, to have little to recommend them, save a somewhat superficial sensationalism. Criticism that is founded upon a single hearing of a work so elaborate as 'The Apostles' must of necessity be somewhat impressionistic and I shall be prepared to revise my conclusions at a later opportunity.'

After this, Elgar returned to orchestral music and a new milestone awaited – a festival devoted entirely to him.

THE ELGAR FESTIVAL AND
'IN THE SOUTH'

'In the South' premiered at the 1904 three-day Elgar Festival at the Royal Opera House, Covent Garden - the first ever devoted exclusively to the work of a single British composer. Also featured were 'Gerontius', 'The Apostles', 'Froissart', a 'Caractacus' selection, the two 'Pomp and Circumstance' Marches, the funeral march from 'Grania and Diarmid' and 'Sea Pictures'.

The importance of the occasion was marked by the first night attendance of the King and Queen, Princess Victoria and the Prince and Princess of Denmark - and tickets cost as high as £500 (in today's money).

The unusual venue amused one correspondent: 'Dr Elgar is the man of the hour in the musical world. It is not too much to say of the three days festival now drawing all smart society to Covent Garden that it is the most remarkable tribute which has ever been paid in this country to a composer of native birth. Just think of it! Fashionable opera-goers flocking in their hundreds to hear 'The Apostles'. Diamonds and duchesses in attendance on 'The Dream of Gerontius'! The conjunction is passing strange, but no less to the credit of all concerned. London has discovered Elgar at last.'

The Sunday Times commented: 'The Festival will probably contain quite enough new music for most of those who will be present. Dr Elgar is generally regarded as our most remarkable living composer, but it is singular how little London has heard of his music hitherto.'

The St James's Gazette carried a preview interview with Neil Forsyth, the Opera House's General Manager: 'The scene was the historic green room at Covent Garden and the walls around us glared red and green with the name of Dr Elgar, the greatest of living British composers. From the theatre itself came the strains of a violin; a skilful hand was playing with rare delicacy the music from 'The Dream of Gerontius'

'This Elgar festival is a bold experiment ?'

'Yes; such a thing has never been done before in the history of British music,' answered Mr Forsyth. *'It would not be possible now were it not for the intense enthusiasm of Dr Richter and the hearty cooperation of the Halle orchestra and Manchester chorus who had made such special studies of Dr Elgar's works.'*

'The popularity of Elgar is somewhat remarkable. We are said to prefer our musicians with foreign names.'

'An unjust charge against us,' said Mr Forsyth. *'We are a musical nation but not a nation of composers, and we are ready to listen to the best from any source. Our policy here, as you know, has been to offer every possible encouragement to British talent and I need not enumerate the operas by native composers which we have produced. The English people have an exceptionally high standard of taste, and hence a composer must have something new and worthy to say if he desires a hearing.*

'There is the secret of Dr Elgar's popularity, which dates from the production of 'The Dream of Gerontius'. It was a work which took him eight years to compose. Others had ventured in the same field and failed; he brought to the task boundless sympathy with the aims of the poet, deep conviction, and a rare mastery of the highest principles of his art. The nation is always ready to listen to such a man, whatever his nationality – in fact he compels attention.'

'A new work is to be produced during the festival ?'

'Yes, one of exceptional merit, a new orchestral composition.'

'Bookings ?'

'Splendid up to date, amply justifying our venture. Her Majesty the Queen has taken a box, and applications for seats are arriving from all parts of the Kingdom. The festival has been enthusiastically received.'

E A Baughan in the Daily News commented: 'To Elgar belongs the distinction of being the only British composer of serious music who has attracted the public, if we except Sullivan. The others are respected by musicians and amateurs of special knowledge. There is a reason for this of course – a very simple reason, but not easy to explain. While other composers have thought that all great music must be austere and such appeal to the intellect rather than to the feelings, Elgar has been content with an artist's great content to write according to his temperament. He has never been a musical doctrinaire.

'There have been strong influences in his musical life – Mendelssohn, Wagner and of late Richard Strauss – but these influences have been assimilated by his own individuality. In writing his oratorios Elgar has never set himself to copy the hard and fast models of Bach and Brahms. On the contrary in 'Caractacus' 'The Dream of Gerontius' and 'The Apostles' he has successfully employed all the weapons of modern music. Wagnerian declamation, the use of the leit-motif, the endless vocal melody, the orchestral commentary of intrinsic interest and all the modern orchestral colours are to be found in these works.

'That alone would not suffice to explain the popularity of his later choral works in England, America and Germany. There are many skilled musical workmen in existence; composers who know how to be interesting in their manner if their matter lacks originality. Indeed, the note of much modern composition is a fatal fluency of technical skill. Elgar has much more than this.

'How shall I analyse the qualities that make the speech of one artist touching, when that of another, quite as skilful in workmanship, and perhaps even higher in aim, falls on unheeding ears? Originality, inspiration, individuality – these are mere phrases. I am not even sure that Elgar's music is so very original; certainly, if Wagner had not written his 'Parsifal' a good deal of 'The Dream of Gerontius' would have been different in its style.

'It is rather, I think, that Elgar has a genuine nature capable of first-hand feeling. His moods are his own. The very weakness of his melodic style – a curious sensitiveness and almost feminine sentiment – is characteristic of the man. He is not a Prometheus of music; he does not dwell among the storms on the mountain tops. But he is a dreamer of dreams; his moods are very real. Above all, he has brought to the composition of 'The Dream of Gerontius' and 'The Apostles' a genuinely religious mind. Religion is not to him the mere subject for artistic treatment, nor does he deal with it in a conventional mood. It is as much part of his life as his love of the open air and the healthy sports of the Englishman.

'Except for this dreamy sensitive strain in his nature, Elgar is typically English. He does not attempt to imitate the solid reflectiveness of the Teutonic mind, which is really antipathetic to the Englishman. I think his audiences recognise the manly quality of his outlook which is so strangely in contrast to his nervous sensitiveness. But then Elgar as a man is a curious mixture of brooding mysticism and healthy sanity. I remember he once told me that if he had not been a musician he would have chosen the career of a soldier.

'His inner life is no doubt expressed in 'The Dream of Gerontius' and 'The Apostles'; his outer life is all for action. I do not think it far fetched to suppose that this cast of mind has had much to do with the position he has taken as the foremost English composer of the day.'

Frank Merry in the Daily Mail commented: 'A musical festival – at Covent Garden – in honour of a young English composer – is enough to take one's breath away. Wagner festivals we know, but Elgar festivals are a new portent. Let us open our eyes and see. The Renaissance of English music is coming, and this is one of the first fruits.

'The test of a musical nation is not the music it absorbs but the amount it can produce. England in the past has had her productive musical epochs, whence we get out old ballads, our glees and madrigals, our fine church music. Yet for the last hundred years and more we have had to sit at the feet of Italy, France and Germany, listening to their strains and trying to understand and assimilate their culture.

'But time brings its revenges. Then we were barbarians dwelling on the suburbs of an artistic continent; but now the old centres of music are becoming exhausted and the turn of the barbarians has come. Italian music has come to an end. Richard Strauss is the last expiring ghost of the once mighty German School. On the other-hand Russia has come to the front with Tchaikovsky, Norway with Grieg and England with Elgar.

'It is such men as these who form the real forces of the world's music. And who is this prophet who is to be honoured in his own country, whose music has seized upon the popular imagination with such irresistible force? Edward Elgar is a thorough Englishman, looking not so much like a musician as a soldier. He sets a new fashion in hair, for he wears it short. No charlatan, the immense scientific grasp of his art, comparing with that of the great masters, has been largely the result of sheer hard work. The same may be said of his position in the musical world.

'Elgar began on the lowest round of the ladder – as conductor of the attendants' orchestra which played weekly in a lunatic asylum. But if it was the bottom rung, it was yet the musical ladder, and up that Elgar stormed till he reached the top.

'The born composer must have a style. What is the Elgar style ? Frankly it is the English style. Take half a dozen works by representative English composers, Sullivan, German, Sterndale Bennett, Purcell – what do we find ? Music of a breezy healthiness of type, its characteristics opposed to morbidity or sickliness. And coupled with this we get pure tunefulness. While smaller composers have sought originality in dishing up the dregs of morbid Continental sentiment, Elgar has stuck to the sweetness, vigour and tunefulness in which the originality of English music must always lie.

'True the Elgar cult is not without its passive resisters. *'What'*, they ask impatiently *'is all this fuss about Elgar's music? We can see nothing in it'* They are the people who have not listened well. The reply is: *'Go and hear it: it grows on you. It is popular, even in Germany. Would you deny that the Germans are a musical people?'* And passive resistance subsides.

'The revival of English music is at hand and the personalities who are to take part in it are appearing one by one: here a violinist, there a composer. And when the tale has grown complete the event will happen and musical England will find herself.'

The Times commented: 'Four or five years ago if anyone had predicted that the opera-house would be full, from floor to ceiling, for the performance of an oratorio by an English composer he would probably have been supposed to have been out of his mind. At that time, concerts in theatres were unknown in the modern generation in England and oratorios and English composers seemed alike powerless to attract the general public. It is impossible to guess what has caused the transformation, but there it is, and it reflects credit on the enterprise of those who foresaw that the attempt would be worth making.'

The Daily Telegraph also observed: 'A great assemblage, including the King and Queen and other members of the Royal Family witnessed what must have seemed to many the apotheosis of British music. Who could have imagined such a scene thirty years ago, or believed it to be within the compass of a generation? Here was the temple of opera turned into a house of oratorio; its stage filled with singers and instruments brought specially all the way from Manchester while the auditorium was filled with one of those mighty and distinguished gatherings which only London can show. And all this in honour of a composer, who a few years since, was an unknown provincial musician.

'The revolution which has been effected and of which last night's proceedings were a demonstrative proof, needed a man – the man, and he came in due time from the depths of the country. Now he is the best known and the most conspicuous creator of music that England has produced for many years past. He came, if it may be said, out of the Nazareth of music from which one did not expect great things, and he came speaking with authority, not from the schools to which he never went but from his own musical instinct and taste.

'It was this aspect of the case which made the opening of the Elgar Festival last night so impressive and encouraging. Young musicians now know that if they only wait patiently the prize may come; at any rate they are not to be depressed by delay in its coming but should hope and work.'

The second night, also attended by the King and Queen, featured the London premier of 'The Apostles'. Reaction was mixed.

The Westminster Gazette commented: 'Elgar has fine themes in 'The Apostles', but too often he seems afraid of using these simply and effectively. The extreme elaboration of his music – the astonishing manner in which he combines and interweaves and transforms his innumerable themes and motifs – speaks volumes for his skill and ingenuity; but it is too often sadly ineffective in the result.'

E A Baughan, in the Daily News agreed: 'When 'The Apostles' was produced at the last Birmingham Festival opinions as to its merits were divided. Some stoutly held that it was a great masterpiece; others thought that, interesting as its workmanship is, Elgar has shown the limitations of his gifts. I myself inclined to this view. At the same time, I reserved the right of altering my opinion on a second hearing of the work, for it is not a composition I could well believe that showed all its facets to a passing glance. I cannot say that a second hearing removed this impression. The work seemed to me to lack the cohesiveness which a great work of art should possess. The scrappiness of which I complained when the work was produced at Birmingham was again very patent and I also noticed that the composer's melodic and harmonic style is by no means homogeneous throughout.

'Apart from any question of consistency of view in the work, it suffers to a great extent from a want of interest in the vocal writing for the principals. So much in 'The Apostles' is carried on by declamation that this weakness makes itself seriously felt and produces a sense of monotony, which ought not to be when one considers the wealth of ideas and imagination in the orchestra. And it certainly seems to me that the composer would have made more effect if he had written in a simpler style, for many of the complexities which look so interesting on paper are not effective in interpretation.'

'In the South' appeared on the third night, with Elgar himself conducting.

The Globe reviewed: 'This overture is perhaps as delightful an example of sane healthy music as even Dr Elgar himself has ever penned. The feelings depicted in it are those depicted on a sunny day in the Vale of Andora. The sheer joy of living forms the themes of a great part of the work but here and there comes a contrast such for example as the song of the shepherd or a reminiscence of the wars that Italy has seen or a movement of that thoughtful introspection which is seldom long absent from Dr Elgar's music. The themes which represent these varying moods are not only very beautiful in themselves but they are also woven together with consummate skill and the new overture is one of the finest of all Dr Elgar's works.'

The Times agreed, but with reservations: 'The contrast is admirably pointed, the themes are delightfully fresh and gracious and their treatment masterly, although the work would bear a slight curtailment notably in the passage where a part of the military music is textually repeated. This undue length is, however, but a very slight blemish on a remarkably beautiful work which affords an interesting parallel with Berlioz's 'Harold in Italy' at a point where a traditional tune is given out in a very attractive way on a solo viola.'

The Daily News commented: 'We account 'In the South' to be a really great and beautiful creation. Much was of course to be expected from such a composer when paying a first visit to fascinating Italy but it was not certain that the outcome of contact with such a land would also be fascinating. Yet so it is. The fresh feeling of gladness, the gentle and musing melancholy which comes from contemplating exquisite scenes of nature; the energy which thoughts of a great heroic past develop. All are here in rich abundance and the best of all is the artistic restraint that controlled the musician's thick-coming fantasies and made his whole powers minister to the beauty without which music is no better than a tinkling cymbal. Dr Elgar himself conducted the new work and at its close had again and again to acknowledge the warm applause of his brilliant audience.'

The Standard drew attention to the Tennyson quotation at the head of the work:

'…what hours were thine and mine

In lands of palm and Southern pine

In lands of palm and orange blossom

Of olive, aloe, and maize and vine'

and found that: 'the personal element indicated in the above is very prominent in the music, which indeed may be said to be more typical of the composer than of the sunny south. The contrapuntal writing is masterly and the scoring is most picturesque and in its entirety the overture fully sustains the reputation of its composer.'

'The impression left by the performances of the last three nights at Covent Garden is that in Dr Edward Elgar we possess a rarely gifted composer whose intellectuality is as strong as his imagination is vivid and fertile; a man who approaches his work from its spiritual side who believes in the heroic in the force of nobility and has the power to use with ease and sureness all the resources of his art to give convincing expression of that which is in him.

'The Elgar Festival is a unique event in the history of British musical art. The test was severe, the circumstance not wholly propitious but Dr Elgar has come out of the ordeal triumphant. The audiences have been large, the attentiveness remarkable and in the success of the scheme the valuable assistance of the Royal Opera syndicate should not be forgotten.'

The Pall Mall Gazette saw it this way: 'We are convinced that the gradual process which has been taking place in Elgar's mind leading him first from a somewhat primitive emotion into a very rarefied atmosphere of the same quality, and then onwards to a point where he allows his intellectual sympathies with the mysteries of life almost entirely to dominate him, has been one which is only comparable to the life-experience of the greatest masters. Elgar's latest edition to the treasury of the world's music, his Italian Overture, seems to show that he is now beginning to mingle these two ideas into a kind of unity which, in its final accomplishment, must assuredly develop into yet more extraordinary results.

'That Elgar, by the sheer force of his musical genius, and by a peculiar persistence of character, has been able to devote himself so wholeheartedly to the realisation of the talents entrusted to his care is a fact which is now beyond dispute.'

A KNIGHTHOOD, FEATURE ARTICLES AND A BIOGRAPHY

Elgar received his knighthood in the birthday honours which followed the Elgar Festival in June 1904.

The Daily Telegraph reported: 'The knighthood which has been conferred on Dr Elgar will be warmly welcomed by all musicians in the Empire as an honour to one who is now their acknowledged chief. This position he has attained through his own skill and indomitable perseverance, and without any of those meretricious accompaniments which often attend true genius.'

The Birmingham Post noted that the honours list 'contains very few names, indeed, of commanding interest.' But as far as Elgar was concerned: 'Here at least the public will recognise that the honour is one which will be worthily held by one of the men of whom any country may well be proud.'

The Daily News went further: 'Probably none of the birthday honours will be more popular than the knighthood conferred on Dr Edward Elgar, for no composer of native birth has more surely won the admiration of the public. It may not be generally known that Sir Edward Elgar is the first composer who has been knighted for some time purely as a composer. Sir Villiers Stanford had long occupied a prominent position as a professor at the Royal College of Music before he received his knighthood. Sir Hubert Parry and Sir Alexander Mackenzie were also more honoured as the heads of their respective teaching institutions than as composers.

'Indeed, one has to go far back to find a musician who has been knighted as a private individual. Until the King recognised the good work done by August Manns in the cause of the art, there had not been an instance for many years, of a musician being thus honoured who had not been connected with the Court or with one of the big teaching institutions. Sir Michael Costa and Sir Julius Benedict are the only exceptions that occur to the mind.'

Such was Elgar's newly elevated prestige that in-depth articles began to appear in popular magazines. It was time the public at large got to learn about this hitherto little-known genius from the provinces.

Perhaps the most interesting of these appeared in 'The Strand'– where an eight-page illustrated interview with the actor and screenwriter Rudolph de Cordova featured alongside a wealth of popular literature and fiction, including the first appearance of 'The Return of Sherlock Holmes'.

Many of Elgar's comments and biographical details contained in the piece have provided information for subsequent biographies, and it gave a particularly good insight into Elgar's life and character –especially as the style of the feature was to give full vent to Elgar's personal reminiscences and comments:

'Was not Herr Steinbach, the conductor of the Meiningen Orchestra, among the others who said that you have something different from anybody else in the tone of your orchestra ?' I asked Dr Elgar as we sat in his study at Malvern, with a great expanse of country visible through the wide windows.

'I believe so,' he replied; *'and that remark has been one from which I naturally derived great pleasure.*

'You know,' said Dr Elgar, as he settled down to talk for the purpose of this interview, in accordance with a long-standing promise made in what he came to regard as an unguarded moment – *'you know, since you compel me to begin at the beginning, that I 'began' in Broadheath, a little village three miles from Worcester in which city my father was organist of St George's Catholic Church, a post he held for thirty-seven years.*

'I was a very little boy indeed when I began to show some aptitude for music and used to extemporize on the piano. When I was quite small I received a few lessons on the piano. The organ-loft then attracted me, and from the time I was about seven or eight I used to go and sit by my father and watch him play.

'After a time I began to try to play myself. At first the only thing I succeeded in producing was noise, but gradually, out of the chaos, harmony began to evolve itself. In those days, too, an English opera company used to visit the old Worcester Theatre and I was taken into the orchestra which consisted of only eight or ten performers and so heard old operas like 'Norma', 'Trovatore', and, above all 'Don Giovanni'.

'My general education was not neglected. I went to Littleton House School until I was about fifteen. At the same time I saw and learnt a great deal about music from the stream of music that passed through my father's establishment.

'My hope was that I should be able to get a musical education and I worked hard at German on the chance that I should go to Leipsic [sic], but my father discovered that he could not afford to send me away and anything in that direction seemed to be at an end.

'Then a friend, a solicitor, suggested that I should go to him for a year and see how I liked the law. I went for a year but came to the conclusion that the law was not for me and I determine to returned to music.

'There appeared to be an opening for a violinist in Worcester, and as it occurred to me that it would be a good thing to try to take advantage of the opening, I had been teaching myself to play the violin.

'Then I began to teach on my own account and spent much leisure as I had in writing music. It was music of a sort – bad, very bad – but my juvenile efforts are, I hope, destroyed.

'Although I was teaching the violin, I wanted to improve my playing, so I began to save up in order to go to London to get some lessons from Herr Pollitzer.

'On one occasion I was working the first violin part of the Haydn quartet. There was a rest, and I suddenly began to play the 'cello part. Pollitzer looked up. 'You know the whole thing?' he said.

'Of course,' I replied

'He looked up curiously. 'Do you compose yourself?' he asked.

'I try' I replied again.

'Show me something of yours,' he said.

'I did so with the result that he gave me an introduction to Mr., now Sir, August Manns, who, later on, played many of my things at the daily concerts at the Crystal Palace.

'When I resolved to become a musician and found that the exigencies of life would prevent me from getting any tuition, the only thing to do was to teach myself. I read everything, played everything and heard everything I possibly could. As I have told you, I used to play the organ and the violin. I attended as many of the cathedral services as I could to hear the anthems and to get to know what they were so as to become thoroughly acquainted with the English church style.

'The putting of the fine new organ into the cathedral at Worcester was a great event and brought many organists to play there at various times. I went to hear them all.

'The services were over later on Sunday than those at the Catholic church and as soon as the voluntary was finished at the church I used to rush over to the cathedral to hear the concluding voluntary. Eventually I succeeded my father as organist at St George's.'

The interview moved on to explore Elgar's wider musical education.

'You ask me to go into greater details about my musical education. I am constantly receiving letters on this point from all over the world, for it is well known that I am self-taught in the matter of harmony, counterpoint, form, and, in short, the whole of the 'mystery' of music, and people want to know what books I used.

'Today, there are all sorts of books to make the study of harmony and orchestration pleasant. In my young days they were repellent. But I read them and I still exist.

'The first was Catel [Charles-Simon Catel, A Treatise on Harmony, 1802], *and that was followed by Cherubini* [Luigi Cherubini – A course in Counterpoint and Fugue 1835]. *The first real sort of friendly leaning I had, however, was from 'Mozart's Thorough-bass School'. There was something in that to go upon - something human. It is a small book – a collection of papers beautifully and clearly expressed – which he wrote on harmony for the niece of a friend of his. I still treasure the old volume.*

'[Sir Frederick] *Ouseley and* [Walter] *Macfarren followed, but the articles which have since helped me the most are those of Sir Hubert Parry in 'Grove's Dictionary.'*

De Cordova then asked how the various authorities on music which Elgar had studied had mixed in his mind.

'They didn't mix, and it appears it is necessary for anyone who has to be self-taught to read everything and – pick out the best. How to forget the rubbish and remember the good I can't tell you, but perhaps that is where his brains come in.

'It would be affectation were I to pretend that my work is not recognised as modern and I hate affectation, yet it would probably surprise you to know the amount of work I did in studying musical form. Only those can safely disregard form who ignore it with a full knowledge and do not evade it through ignorance.

'Mozart is the musician from whom everyone should learn form. I once ruled a score for the same instruments and with the same number of bars as Mozart's G Minor Symphony and in that framework I wrote a symphony following as far as possible the same outline in the themes and the same modulation. I did this on my own initiative as I was groping in the dark after light but looking back after thirty-years I don't know any discipline from which I learned so much.

'I was interested in many other things besides music and I had the good fortune to be thrown among an unsorted collection of old books. There were books of all kinds and all distinguished by the characteristic that they were for the most part incomplete. I busied myself for days and weeks arranging them. I picked out the theological books of which there were a good many and put them on one side.

Then I made a place for the Elizabethan dramatists, the chronicles including Baker's and Hollinshead's, besides a tolerable collection of old poets and translations of Voltaire and all sorts of things up to the eighteenth century.

'Then I began to read. I used to get up at four or five o'clock in the summer and read – every available opportunity found me reading. I read till dark. I finished by reading every one of those books, including the theology. The result of that reading has been that people tell me I know more of life up to the eighteenth century than I do of my own time, and it is probably true.

'In studying scores the first which came into my hands were the Beethoven symphonies. Anyone can have them now, but they were difficult for a boy to get in Worcester thirty years ago.

'I, however, managed to get two or three and I remember distinctly the day I was able to buy the Pastoral Symphony. I stuffed my pockets with bread and cheese and went out into the fields to study it. That was what I always did. Even when I began to teach, when a new score came into my hands I went off for a long day with it out of doors and when my unfortunate – or fortunate ? – pupils went for their lessons I was not at home to give them.

'By the way, talking about scores, it will probably surprise you to know that I never possessed a score of Wagner until one was given to me in 1900.'

Elgar then went on to reminisce on his early life, playing with the Worcester Glee Club.

'I first played second fiddle and afterwards became leader, as, after a time, I used to do the accompanying. It was an enjoyable and artistic gathering and the programmes were principally drawn from the splendid English compositions for men's voices. The younger generation seemed to prefer ordinary part-songs and ballads also were introduced and the tone of the thing changed.

'It was in 1877 [when he was 20] that I first went to take lessons of Pollitzer. He suggested that I should stay in London and devote myself to violin playing, but I had become enamoured of a country life and would not give up the prospect of a certain living by playing and teaching in Worcester on the chance of only a possible success which I might make as a soloist in London.

'The thing which brought me before a larger public as a composer was the production of several things of mine at Birmingham by Mr W C Stockley to whom my music was introduced by Dr [Herbert]*Wareing, himself a composer and resident in Birmingham.

'Don't suppose, however, that after that recognition as a composer, things were easy for me.'

Elgar then related the often-quoted anecdote about being given an opportunity to rehearse his work in London – and losing out to Sir Arthur Sullivan.

The popular version of this story –as portrayed in the famous 1962 BBC biopic by Ken Russell - is that it happened during the months of struggle Elgar endured after moving to London in 1889 - the one opportunity given to him to prove his worth before a London audience, which was then, by fate, denied him. But the version he gave to Cordova was slightly different.

'The directors of the old Promenade Concerts at Covent Garden Theatre were good enough to write that they thought sufficiently of my things to devote a morning to rehearsing them. I went on the appointed day to London to conduct the rehearsal. When I arrived it was explained to me that a few songs had to be taken before I could begin. Before the songs were finished Sir Arthur Sullivan unexpectedly arrived, bringing with him a selection from one of his operas. It was the only chance he had of going through it with the orchestra, so they determined to take advantage of the opportunity. He consumed all my time in rehearsing this, and when he had finished the director came out and said to me, 'There will be no chance of your going through your music today.' I went back to Worcester to my teaching and that was the last of my chance of an appearance at the Promenade Concerts.

'Two similar occurrences took place at the Crystal Palace: rehearsals were planned which never came off, so I was no nearer to getting a hearing for big orchestral works.'

There then followed a passage which has become the origin of one of Elgar's most famous quotations:

'Dr Elgar has a delightful and most acute sense of humour so that I was sure I should not be misunderstood if I ventured to ask a question about his 'musical crimes'. He smiled.

'But which of my musical crimes do you mean ? From the point of view of one person or another I understand all my music has been a crime', he replied lightly.

'Then he added, *'Oh you mean 'The Cockaigne' 'The Coronation Ode' and 'The Imperial March' especially. Yes, I believe there are a good many people who have objected to them. But I like to look on the composer's vocation as the old troubadours or bards did. In those days it was no disgrace for a man to be turned on to step in front of an army and inspire the people with a song. For my own part, I know that there are a lot of people who like to celebrate events with music. To these people I have given tunes. Is that wrong? Why should I write a fugue or something which won't appeal to anyone, when the people yearn for things which can sir them'.*

'Such as Pomp and Circumstance,' I interpolated'

'Ah, I don't know anything about that', replied Dr Elgar, *' but I do know we are a nation with real military proclivities and I did not see why the ordinary quick march should not be treated on a large scale in the way that the waltz, the old fashioned slow march and even the polka have been treated by the great composers; yet all marches on the symphonic scale are so slow that people can't march to them. I have some of the soldier instinct in me and so I have written two marches of which, so far from being ashamed, I am proud.'*

The article finished with an insight into Elgar's working and his influences in his surroundings – he was living at Craeg Lea on the Wyche Road near Great Malvern at the time. The large, detached house, which still stands, commands a fine view from a high vantage point on the Worcestershire side of the Malvern Hills, across the wide plane of the River Severn towards the Cotswolds and beyond.

'How and when do I do my music? I can tell you very easily. I come into my study at nine o'clock in the morning and I work till a quarter to one. I don't do any inventing then, for that comes anywhere and everywhere. It may be when I am walking, golfing or cycling, or the ideas may come in the evening and then I sit up until any hour in order to get them down.

'The morning is devoted to revising and orchestration of which I have as much to do as I can manage.

'As soon as lunch is over I go out for exercise and return about four or later, after which I sometimes do two hours' work before dinner.

'A country life I find absolutely essential to me and here the conditions are exactly what I require.

'As you see,' and Dr Elgar moved over to the large window which takes up the whole of one side of his study, *'I get a wonderful view of the surrounding country. I can see across Worcestershire, to Edgehill, the Cathedral of Worcester, the Abbeys of Pershore and Tewkesbury and even the smoke round Birmingham. It is delightfully quiet, and yet in contrast with it there is a constant stream of communication from the outside world in the shape of cables from America and Australia and letters innumerable from all over the world.'*

With Elgar reaching a much wider public, the commercial viability of books about him also became a possibility, and the first of these appeared soon afterwards.

It was written by his friend and tireless champion, the Birmingham Gazette correspondent, Robert Buckley. In correspondence, Elgar thought the book was 'a little premature', but it was published as part of a 'Living Masters of Music' series which also included biographies of Debussy, Joachim, Richard Strauss and Puccini. It is still available today.

The book covered Elgar's story from his beginnings up to the period of 'The Apostles', and in a rather trenchant declaration in his introduction, Buckley states: 'Whatever this book states as fact may be accepted as such. The sayings of Elgar are recorded in the actual words addressed directly to the writer and upon these I rely to give to the book an interest it would not otherwise possess.'

Buckley waxed lyrical in his monograph, never hiding his admiration for his composer friend: 'It was in the 'Black Knight' period that I first visited the composer at 'Forli', a charming cottage under the shadow of the Malvern Hills, meet situation for the dreamy ton-poet, the creator of ravishing harmonies.'

But his enthusiasm hardly struck accord with the more hard-headed London critics.

The Westminster Gazette thought: 'Mr Buckley writes frankly as a worshipper, and now a few of his critical, or uncritical observations in regard to the compositions of his hero might well have been omitted. To talk of Elgar as 'the greatest musician since Beethoven, possibly the greatest since Bach' considered as a matter of expression in music, is emphatically, to adopt a colloquialism, 'coming it rather strong'; while many other observations scattered up and down Mr Buckley's exuberant but brightly written pages are hardly less open to criticism.'

The Pall Mall Gazette agreed: 'The biography of a man like Sir Edward Elgar, who has been for years a recluse, and suddenly become a great public figure is usually a 'sort of book' and nothing more. The author is too often in a hurry to get through what he calls the 'antecedents' and after a chapter or so, you stumble on the celebrity full grown. It is all too familiar, too cold, too palpable; and the dip into the past makes the picture obscure and everyone uncomfortable. The material comes at first hand. Every Elgarian dictum here has been addressed to his Boswell either in conversation or correspondence and the friendly association seems to date back a dozen years or so. The result is a vivid and personal study, for which the composer's admirers, and the world outside of music will be grateful in nearly equal measure.'

John F Runciman in The Saturday Review went further: 'Mr Buckley squandered his pages on repeating many times things that were not worth saying in the first instance: so we may perhaps presume that he has not left himself room enough to give us the heart of the matter. We are told at least fifty times that Elgar was his own teacher and a hundred times that it was by his own perseverance and energy that he won his present position. Granting all that – and I would have been willing to grant it without reading this book – what are the essential qualities in Elgar's music that entitle us to call it great?

'Mr Buckley compares Elgar with Richard Strauss as an orchestral colourist, which may well be; he places him with Bach and Wagner as a polyphonist which it is a trifle early in the day to say. There is nothing young and fresh in 'The Dream of Gerontius' nor 'The Apostles', and the Coronation [Ode] was a beggarly production. In truth Elgar seems no more an original composer than a dozen other men who had their hour and were knighted; he is vainly trying to galvanise that obsolete form the Oratorio; and in proclaiming him the English musical messiah, Mr Buckley is simply playing the reactionary's game.

'And finally Sir Edward Elgar should pray to be preserved from the friends who repeat on his behalf the same old lie, told about every musician who has no dramatic ability, that only his fastidiousness prevents him finding an opera libretto. Nonsense, it is not fastidiousness but lack of dramatic power that prevents composers finding librettos. If Sir Edward Elgar felt the inner need to write an opera he would have found a subject ere now. Besides, a musician who is content with such threadbare themes as 'The Black Knight', 'King Olaf', 'Lux Christi' and 'The Apostles' cannot justly be accused of over-fastidiousness.'

THE PROFESSOR

Shortly after Elgar received his knighthood, local businessman Richard Peyton, offered £10,000 – about £800,000 in today's money – to endow a chair of music at Birmingham University. But only if Elgar would accept the post as its first Professor.

Friends urged Elgar not to accept. He ignored their advice, telling one that: 'I am not going to teach. I can't for one thing & won't try for another.' Thus, the self-taught composer, without a single qualification to his name, became a Professor of Music at a leading provincial University – and embarked on a course which he would come to regret.

Sir Oliver Lodge, Birmingham University's Principle, negotiated the appointment, commenting the University had decided not to 'blossom forth immediately with a faculty of music, conferring degrees' adding he would not be surprised if that differed in some respects from ordinary lines.

Robert Buckley in the Birmingham Gazette, seized on the comments attacking the conventional use of degrees in music and their champions, the academics: 'as conferring distinction for mere book-learning and proficiency in a sort of mechanical composition without much reference to the inspiration without which is no enduring art. Sir Frederick Ouseley at Oxford University introduced many desirable innovations and yet his opinions and his music are hopelessly obsolete. His successor, Sir John Stainer, who in his time was accounted a rabid revolutionary can by no means be regarded as of the modern school, and even Sir Hubert Parry, the present holder of the office and undoubtedly one of the best equipped musicians England ever possessed is so far in the rear of the most advanced of the progressive school as to be regarded by them as almost out of sight, a mere dot, as it were on the horizon.

'Among the most progressive of the modern school, Sir Edward Elgar holds a conspicuous place and it may therefore be inferred that his teaching will point to the future rather than the past. He believes that music, like everything else, is subject to evolutionary law; that progression is essential to life, that to stand still is to perish, that the old mines are practically worked out, and above all, that new mines of surpassing richness exist for the capable and adventurous explorer.

'The old style of study and examination has over and over evoked satire more or less good-humoured, but always tending to show, that while the degree proved the holder to be an excellent theoretical musician, well acquainted with the forms and rules of the art, and conversant with its history the distinction has no weight in determining his quality as an artist – even as a clever imitator of what had gone before, much less as a creator.

'A leaning to warm colouring was held to be rank heresy, if not flat blasphemy. Critics and examiners were severe on departures from the solid diatonic style of the old English school. Young composers were exhorted to flee from harmonies intended to be expressive and to rely on their effects on the contrapuntal contrivances and 'learned devices' which unhappily the studious tyro was inclined to regard as having been exploited ad nauseam, in addition to the disadvantage incurred by speaking to modern ears in the idiom of an age long past.

'Yet the Universities for so many centuries regarded as unique plenipotentiaries of the musical muse and chartered conferrers of immortality held to the old lines. In their examination papers the aspirant to musical honours saw what was understood to be oratorio on the rough. There was the canto formo or subject which was to be the foundation of your exercises. On it you built with a sort of cabinet making ingenuity all sorts of counterpoint and all sorts of mixtures of counterpoint.

'Not a syllable was said about art, or inspiration, or the emotional aspect of music which is the principal aspects. Candidates congregated for the examinations talked only of 'learned devices' and the fads and special theories of the examiners. To 'let yourself go' was considered a fatal error, while to excel in problem like contrivances which were without a spark of divine fire but which broke no rule, was reckoned a certain passport to the coveted hood.

'Sir Edward Elgar, we believe, may be relied upon to 'change all that'. Inspiration will count for something. Not for everything. No musician has a more profound sense of the value of solid theoretical knowledge. He holds that the rules must be the point of departure. You must know and assimilate the opinions of the theorists before you can begin to become a law unto yourself. Sir Edward Elgar's musical experience in extent and quality differs widely from that of the average University professor. He has never been drilled in the systems of the schools. He has never been 'cribbed, cabined and confined' by the exigences of a learned mentor.

'On the other-hand he began at the beginning, and having no help, had to think ten times the harder. From the first he took the advance view of music, and also from the first surrounded and nourished his musical studies with all the great literature within his reach. Much has been alleged concerning the illiteracy of musicians and most of what has been said is too true. Music is so absorbing that many musicians become one-sided and therefore lop-sided men, apparently unaware that by their exclusive devotion to one art they lose much more than they gain.

'On this point we can be sure of outspoken deliverances from the new Professor. There are other matters on which plain speaking is required and concerning these too, we may be sure that Sir Edward, at the proper time, will not be backward in liberating his soul.'

E A Baughan felt Elgar's appointment 'fell as a thunderbolt on the world of music.' The news was more surprising because Sir Edward Elgar has always been an independent musician in the sense that he did not receive his musical education from any institution and has not been connected with any of the Universities, except as the recipient of the honorary degrees of Doctor of Music at Cambridge and Durham.'

However, Baughan felt the appointment was 'exciting' and might lead to new developments in music: 'It is not difficult to conceive the broad lines of the tuition which would be given at Birmingham if Sir Edward Elgar were head of the musical side of the university. He would do his best to bring all branches of music within the scope of the faculty. Oratorio as well as comic opera, the string quartet as well as orchestral composition, would receive attention.

'Pupils would not be warned off the field of modern music, nor would they be given foreign models to copy which are inimical to the British spirit. As far as it is possible the formation of a true British style in music would be the chief aim of the Birmingham University. The course of study would be practical. The student would be taught the use of the orchestra as he is now taught the use of the piano. Possibly there would also be a chance of teaching him how to conduct in a practical way, for it may be imagined that Sir Edward Elgar would do his best to form an orchestra in connection with the university.'

'The old degrees are no doubt an excellent passport for an organist, a professor of theory, or a church musician. In the case of Cambridge it also means now that the holder has been generally educated at the university. But no one in the musical world views an Oxford or Cambridge degree as proof of the holder's knowledge of modern music or of his practical musicianship in an artistic sense.'

Elgar indicated his intended approach at a Birmingham Clef Club meeting also attended by Richard Strauss. The Star reported: 'he was fully conscious of the responsibilities he had incurred and assured his hearers that he had no intention of shirking them, but would do his best to give his new office all the dignity of which he was capable and he would never leave out of sight his main object which would be to found on English soil a truly English school of music.

'We in England could not hope for immediate success such as had attended Dr Strauss in the breaking open of new paths but there was a good proverb which taught us that a cat may look at a queen, the application of which to the matter in hand was that modest ambition was lawful for everybody. But even in this matter we cannot compete with Germany because in Germany both cat and queen are spelt with capital letters.

'He had, he continued, received much advice as to his methods of procedure and the sum total of it was that he should begin at once to demolish everything that is existing. But he said that he had no wish to be disrespectful to the musical equators and he would proceed slowly with the work of building up without giving offence to any one of the equators.'

The first lecture, 'A Future for English Music' was given on March 16th 1905 in Birmingham's City centre Midland Institute. Elgar wore his Cambridge honorary doctorate robes. University staff filled the platform while public and press crowded the hall.

The Manchester Guardian thought it was 'admirably delivered and marked throughout by verbal felicity no less than by originality of thought and breadth of view.' Lady Elgar, in her diary commented: 'E looked most beautiful in his gown and hood, then to lecture. Crowded hall. E. lectured splendidly, held his audience breathless.'

E A Baughan, in The Outlook commented: 'It will be very surprising if the inaugural speech of the Birmingham Professor of Music does not bring a storm of dissent about his ears. He said nothing really new – nothing which has been said over and over again by critics and others – but the world is so constituted that it pays no attention to ideas unless they are expressed by someone in authority.

'The peculiarity of the British musical world is that it is impossible to speak out without some composer or other taking your remarks as directed maliciously against himself and for that reason it will not be surprising if the columns of the Times shriek with protests; indeed rumour states that this will happen, but at the time of writing the battle has not begun.'

Baughan commented that Elgar had been 'careful – too careful I think' – to exempt from criticism any of his fellow living composers, by taking the year 1880 as the starting point of a renaissance of British music.

'Now the year 1880 was chosen with diplomatic skill, for from that year practically dates all our post Mendelssohn and Sterndale Bennett composition. The last twenty-five years includes the activity of Sir Charles Stanford, Sir Hubert Parry, Sir Alexander Mackenzie, and Dr F H Cowen, as well as that of Sir Edward himself. So, all these composers may have the satisfaction of thinking that they are in the movement.

'At the same time, the Birmingham Professor gave a back handed hit or two to the British composers of the last twenty-five years. He admitted that some of those who were accustomed to playing the works of Beethoven, Weber, and the most modern man of that date, Wagner, could not help feeling that the music given them to play was, not to put too fine a point on it, rather dry, although they were anxious to believe all that a friendly Press told them about the glories of the new English school.

'That is one of the passages in his lecture that I expect will raise a deal of correspondence. The opinion was diplomatically expressed; but if it means anything, it means of course, that much of the work of the composers since 1880 has been too dry.

'I cannot help feeling that Sir Edward Elgar might have couched his opinions in a less ambiguous manner. In tracing the history of British music and the causes of why it had not been popular with Englishmen, a distinction should be made. There have been practically two schools. One of which Sir Charles Stanford and Sir Hubert Parry have been the leaders, worked against the mamby-pamby sentimentality of the Mendelssohn-Sterndale Bennett influence. The other, which includes Sir Alexander Mackenzie, Dr F H Cowen, Edward German and Sir Edward Elgar himself, has worked more or less on open lines.

'The Stanford-Parry school took Brahms as its model, for Brahms was supposed to be the corrective of a tendency to sensationalism. The second school has shown the influence of no particular composer, but in the earlier eighties there was still some connection with the Mendelssohn-worship which had its last exponent in Sullivan. The initial mistake made by the Stanford-Parry school was in the imitation of Brahms. The composer of the 'German Requiem', was a very great musician, a man of lofty thought and originality. As a contrast to Wagner and the emotionalists, Brahms was predestined to be the standard-bearer round whom certain classes of mind would rally. In the meantime the growth of orchestral music in Germany itself had been far from anything which Brahms had to say. Wagner's influence on music-drama had not made much way, but in purely orchestral music it was gradually gaining force year by year, whereas Brahms was practically a reactionist as far as the orchestra was concerned. The orchestral movement found a new voice in Germany as far back as 1889, when Richard Strauss came forward with his 'Don Juan' symphonic poem.

'It was not extraordinary that certain of our British composers should have stood still, for until lately we had but little orchestral music in England and the choral works which our composers wrote for provincial festivals were more or less conventional in character. No one dared to depart from what was considered to be effective choral writing. The pre-occupation really retarded British composition while the public of amateurs was becoming more and more familiar with the works of Wagner. Those of our composers who did not belong to the Brahms set had not the courage and perhaps had not the originality to be completely in the Wagner movement and consequently their works lacked distinction. The public in consequence would have nothing to do with British music of any kind.

'Sir Edward Elgar pleaded for a real British school of composition; that the younger men should draw their inspiration more from their own country, from their own literature and from their own climate. Then, it should be inferred we should not be so imitative. But I rather fancy he hit the mark more surely in his complaint that so much of British music is white and commonplace.

'What does this mean after all, but there have been no great British composers? I make bold to say that since Sullivan hardly any composer of our nation has had anything approaching genius. Even so their music might have been more popular in the best sense if the models copied had been more sympathetic to the British temperament. It is difficult to say what that temperament precisely is, and I notice that Sir Edward Elgar did not attempt to define it. But one can at least gain some idea of it by a process of elision. The English mind, then, is not given to abstract reflection; it is not essentially philosophic; it is imaginative but not fantastic; it is not precise in the Gallic sense; it is not subtle; although practical it is not logical; it is sentimental but not passionate.

'The Birmingham professor on the other hand, protested against the idea that a heavy robustness was characteristic of the Englishman in his art. Neither that kind of heaviness nor the heaviness of German reflectiveness should be our musical expression. What are we to deduce from the fact that the most popular composers in England have been, in modern days, Chopin, Mendelssohn, Sullivan, Wagner, Tchaikovsky, and to some extent Richard Strauss?

'Finally, Sir Edward Elgar might have pointed out a material and simple cause for our want of pre-eminence in the art of composition. It is that all our best composers, with the exception of himself have had to earn their livings as professors at the music schools. They are the grave of talent.'

The Birmingham Post described Elgar's appearance: 'At first he was manifestly not at ease in his new position, and after a criticism of musical festival arrangements he remarked: *'It is quite in accordance with this upside-down condition of things that a man without the proper notion of addressing an assembly is now speaking to you. How funny!'*

'After the first shyness was over, however, Sir Edward got on the best of terms with his audience and his face was wreathed in smiles as he elaborated his principal witticisms. In view of his extremely spruce, well-groomed and smart appearance, it was a surprise to many people to find that he was really such a careless, good fellow, with the keenest possible sense of humour, and a hearty relish for a joke.

'The daring professor gave a little shock to the be-capped and be-gowned girl students. He reminded them in one of his delicious though extravagant asides of an old theory of the ancients – that the world was made to revolve by the eternal climbing of the damned up the bars of their prison house, as rats make their cage revolve by their treadmill exercise on the wires. A little involuntary 'Oh!' escaped from the sweet-girl students.'

'Next to this', it added, 'was the emphatic repudiation of Continental criticism, respecting which he said – *'I have had the advantage or disadvantage of having my works played abroad and have mixed with foreign musicians and can therefore speak with some authority – and more feeling – as to the attitude of foreigners generally. I am not continually wondering what the intelligent foreigner thinks or says of English music: in-fact I'm like the very bad boy, I don't care!'*

'For the simpering class of critics Sir Edward expressed hearty contempt; and casting aside for the moment professorial dignity, tilting his head to one side and assuming a smile of schoolgirlish simplicity, he said: *'You know – they simper like this'*. Of course, the audience laughed though some of the dons looked rather more solemn than ever.'

The World commented: 'The first appearance of Sir Edward Elgar as Professor of Music at Birmingham was very interesting and must have been a little disappointing to those who had painted in their imaginations a picture of Sir Edward defying the lightnings amid the ruins of all existing reputations and institutions, his hands imbrued with the gore of all previous professors. He did not go about looking for heads to break. On the contrary he spoke with reverence and affection of many things which are not commonly supposed to be modern. Very modern, however, in the best sense of the word was his exposition of the view that music should not be for musicians only but was meant for an ideal audience consisting of all the intellectual men and women of the day.'

After this first lecture, Elgar embarked on his first concert tour of America, where he received an honorary Doctorate of Music from Yale University. While there he was accused of attacking the National Anthem in an interview with the Dayton Herald in Ohio, allegedly claiming it was *'stolen from the German'*, and that: *'the words are stupid, some of the lines won't rhyme and the man who sings it and thinks of what he is saying can't respect himself.'*

The Worcestershire Echo reported the incident: 'At the present moment he seems to have expressed himself in an interview with no uncertain voice. He is obviously an enemy of the conventional National Anthems, a matter which one might have guessed from the fact that he put so much national feeling into his now famous 'Land of Hope and Glory'.

'For example, though he is not exactly hostile towards our own anthem (*'because'*, he says, *it was stolen from the German'*) he nevertheless considers that *'the words are stupid some of the lines won't rhyme and the man who sings it and thinks of what he is saying can't respect himself.'*

'Elgar continues by saying to his American interviewer: *'Your national hymn is even worse than England's. You haven't got any regular legitimate song. There is 'Yanky Doodle' which has words that are stark idiocy, while the music would set the teeth of a buzz-saw on edge. Then there is 'Hail Columbia' which is nearly as bad in every way as 'Yanky Doodle'.*

'Whether Sir Edward really said these things or whether these things are attributed to him it is impossible for us to say. We simply go by cold print; but not since the performance of Elgar's 'Variations' have we known him so explicitly frank as he was when he wrote that score. We trust that the conversation was authentic, if only to prove once more that it is just possible for a great English musician to have a sense of humour.'

The London press were quick to publish Elgar's denials. The Pall Mall Gazette reported: 'From Sir Edward himself we have received this communication by wire: *'Interview never took place; am contradicting it in toto'.* We have elaborated Sir Edward's contradiction by quoting these words because the repudiation should be made all the more emphatic. But beyond this there is the question of journalistic morality against which this is a deplorable offence.'

The Musical World commiserated: 'During his recent visit to America he was not immune any more than any other good people who preceded him from the imaginative interviews of that land. These gentry if they do not succeed in culling words of wisdom from the lips of their victims do not hesitate to publish what in their opinion they ought to have said. In view of extraordinary statements going round as the result of such an interview, Sir Edward Elgar has found it necessary to publish the fact that he knows nothing of the alleged interview, the whole thing being *'an ignorant and absurd fabrication'*

The Sunday Times however said this: 'If one may place faith in an American interviewer, which is somewhat doubtful, Sir Edward Elgar has been speaking very disrespectfully of 'God Save the King' dubbing it *'the silliest thing imaginable*. That is rather a 'whole-hogger' phrase, but one cannot well quarrel with it as it must be admitted that the words of what Mr W S Gilbert called our 'illiterate National Anthem' are little more than doggerel.'

J S Van Cleve in the New York Tribune thought: 'Sir Edward's remarks were scarcely worth so much bother. It is an old thing for Englishmen to ridicule the grammar and the rhymes of 'God Save the King' but only ignorance at this late date asserts that its melody was 'stolen from the Germans' or find it unsatisfactory for that or any other reason. Its adoption by several of the German countries as well as the United States is a tribute to it, in the face of which, Sir Edward's sneer only serves to make him more ridiculous. After all, musicians of Sir Edward's type ought to be permitted to criticise national hymns – they cannot write one.'

Back home, the socialist publication The Clarion published a discussion between Music Critic Georgia Pearce, and co-founder of the paper Montague Blatchford, over how much Elgar's music could be considered 'English'.

Pearce had acclaimed Elgar as the 'leader of the English renaissance in music'. Blatchford wondered whether 'his influence on English music and English musicians may be actually harmful. I have only heard some few examples of his work; but what I heard was not English in subject nor in sentiment, so far as I am able to judge.

'I don't say that Elgar is not a composer of English music, only that he doesn't seem so to me. And so Mrs Pearce might be quite right, but I shall have to go and talk to her on the subject and then if she can play me any of Elgar's music that is as characteristically English as any Shakespeare's songs, and Thackeray's stories are or even as English as Scott and Dickens, I will admit I was mistaken and will withdraw all my heretical opinions with cheerful alacrity.'

Sir Walter Scott was Scottish.

Attitudes towards Elgar were now beginning to develop tones of criticism. The honeymoon with the critics who had hailed him as a Messiah during the previous decade was coming to an end.

An American Critic, Laurence Gilman, declared that Elgar had 'no individuality' – a view echoed by the English critic J F Runciman who felt that 'The Apostles' 'has a mastery of musical mechanics and that its best inspirations are, in essence, a dilution of Wagner, and is in the main, dull, unleavened and inexpressive.'

Letters also started to appear from those now feeling empowered to offer dissenting views on Elgar's music.

One, from an anonymous author, calling himself 'An Amateur Musician' appeared in the Worcester Echo, and condemned 'The Apostles' as 'almost entirely devoid of what may be termed 'musical thought', that the work contains 'no ideas' and that it is 'peppery, theatrical and cheap'.

Elgar gave his second Birmingham lecture, 'English Composers' on November 1st 1905. He was typically forthright: *'Quartets, symphonies, operas, symphonic poems are put forward in increasing numbers and the authors are anxious to get a hearing. But even amongst all the concerts now organised it is impossible for a tithe of the works to be heard. How do I know this? Well, since I have held the Professorship I have been consulted in, I fear to say, how many cases and the vast numbers of MSS sent to me! I sometimes look round my heaped-up study and say: 'I could make seven shillings a day of th' paper; yet I learn nothing from all these save a little skill in comparing of styles.'*

The Birmingham Post approved: 'Sir Edward wished to see English composers encouraged and he was in favour of the programme at, say, an orchestral concert consisting of English works only. It would be possible to make dozens of programmes by Englishmen, but where were the audiences? There must be something wrong, some wane of interest. In France, they had concert after concert without a German, English or Italian name in the programme; in Germany, programme after programme with nothing but German names, except, perhaps, Scandinavian: but in England we had not arrived at that yet.

'The popular apathy was such that if English music only were performed the programme would not, as a rule, be commercially successful – in other words, the audience would not care to go.'

Musical Opinion thought this: 'In a few spare moments I took the trouble to draw up a series of programmes for orchestral concerts in which nothing but British compositions were included. It would be possible to give a series of about three concerts, of which the music would be well worth hearing for its own sake; and there the repertoire ends.

'And (how shall one put it?) the programmes of these concerts did not contain a single work of undoubted genius, if you omit Elgar's own 'Enigma' Variations and 'In the South' overture. We are, I was forced to recognise, singularly lacking in the big forms of composition. In their early days, both Parry and Stanford wrote symphonies of promise, of which even now, some of the movements are worth hearing. But the compositions as a whole are not of the very first rank.

'I am not at all sure that the fuss made about British music is altogether advisable. For many years we neglected it entirely, mainly because the British school of the period had nothing to say to the amateur which he wished to hear. Then came a kind of renaissance and concert goers – thanks largely to Elgar's own compositions - began to see that it was possible for an Englishman to write music which was not an imitation of Brahms. With that discovery a kind of madness has come over the musical world. Every day the press publishes letters deploring the neglect of British compositions and the composers themselves – especially the younger men – have joined in the fray.

'Now the public does not care a brass farthing who writes the music to which it listens, so long as the music is worth hearing. The public had some experience of the average British composition at the Promenade Concerts and elsewhere and it is by no means keen on hearing too much of it. Exaggerated championship always does harm; and I am inclined to think that the protests made against Sir Edward Elgar's lecture are proofs that the admirers of British music have already gone too far in their enthusiasm.'

Stanford, sneered in a letter to The Times: 'If Sir Edward Elgar is correctly reported as saying from the professorial chair at Birmingham that 'English music is held in no respect abroad – that was to say, the serious compositions which up to the present time had been turned out'- he is stating what a little investigation at such musical centres as Berlin, Vienna, Leipzig, Hamburg, Amsterdam and the Rhineland will prove to be an undeserved aspersion upon the taste, judgement and perspicacity of foreigners and an unjust disparagement of the influence which has long been exerted by the music of his own country. In fairness to foreign taste, to my colleagues at home and to the reputation for accuracy which our universities have so deservedly earned, I traverse a statement – which Sir Edward himself, even, within the radius of his own experience could hardly endorse – in loyalty to his friends abroad.'

The third lecture, 'Brahms Symphony Number 3' took place in November 1905.

Elgar was reported to have said the form of the symphony was strictly orthodox and it was a piece of *'absolute music'* there was no clue as to what was meant, but *'as Sir Hubert Parry said, it was a piece of music which called up certain sets of emotions in each individual hearer. That was the height of music.'*

The Manchester Guardian reacted: 'Some of us might well sit up and rub our eyes in astonishment at his championship of 'absolute music'. He protests first of all against people when they hear a Beethoven symphony *'calling up all sorts of pictures which might or might not have existed in the composer's mind'*. But did not Beethoven himself tell Neate on one occasion that whenever he wrote he had a picture in his mind ? And if we set that aside as an exaggeration is it not beyond dispute that Beethoven very frequently worked upon a picture?

'Sir Edward Elgar lays it down that music is at its height when it merely *'calls up a set of emotions in each individual hearer'*, and that when music is *'simply a description of something else it is carrying a large art somewhat further than he cared for'*. Music *'as a simple art'* being at its best *'when it was simple without description'* as in the case of Brahms' Third Symphony.'

'If this means anything at all it means that 'absolute music' – in which themes that are purely self-existent, not springing from the desire to 'describe something else', are taken and woven into a total pattern – is by far the highest form of musical art. That much of the greatest music of the world is of this kind no one can deny. But does not Sir Edward Elgar blunder when he denies the rank of first-rate to music in which the composer gives us a *'clue to what was meant'*, as he expresses it?

'Did not Beethoven give us a clue to what he meant when he called his Sixth Symphony 'The Pastoral'; when he called the Third, the 'Eroica' and bade us see it in his own reflections upon Napoleon; when he said of the opening theme of the Fifth, 'Thus fate knocks at the door', when he calls one great overture 'Leonora Number 3' and shows us in it Florestan and Leonora, and 'paints' by means of a trumpet call the arrival of the governor; when he calls another overture 'Coriolanus' and 'describes' therein the various characters so clearly that any ordinary attentive reader of Shakespeare can pick them out at once ?

'If all this is not *'giving us a clue as to what was meant'*, if this is not making music *'a description of something else'* by what appropriate name shall we call it?

'But the case against Sir Edward Elgar may be pressed still further. Look once more at the sentence: *'He thought music as a simple art was at its best when it was simple without description'* as in the case of Brahms' Third Symphony.

'Well in the first place it does not do to assume that even the most 'absolute' of musicians has not been 'descriptive' merely because he himself has not told us so at once. Brahms, for example, probably worked upon 'pictures' a great deal oftener than we imagine.

'It is quite to enumerate compositions of his, ostensibly non-descriptive, that are now known – from Kalbeck's 'Life' – to have had a poetic or pictorial basis. These works do 'mean' something external to the notes themselves and if the composer did not give the 'clue as to what was meant' to every purchaser of a copy, he certainly gave the clue to private friends.

'But if Sir Edward Elgar's thesis is rickety here what are we to say when we apply it to his own case? How many pages has he himself written that are frankly descriptive? What is the prelude to 'Gerontius', for example or the 'Cockaigne' Overture, or 'In the South' but a series of 'musical descriptions'?

'If he really believes now that music is at its height only when it concerns itself with nothing but purely tonal pattern-weaving, he is condemning all his own best work *en masse*.'

Comments from the next lecture - 'English Executants' were reported in The Birmingham Gazette: *'Solo singers were the pets of the public, liable to high, perhaps misguided, praise, and also to reviling if they failed to come quite up to what was expected of unthinking, enthusiastic, educated savages.*

'Our chorus singers had long been our insular wonder and pride. But it was possible to pick the voices and so to train or over train them that they turned out music with the regularity of a steam engine – and were sometimes just as explosive. There was something wanted – a better ability to understand the subject.'

Under the headline 'Brainless Singers', the Daily Telegraph reported: 'Sir Edward Elgar said we had certainly too many brainless singers. Our chorus singing was our insular wonder and pride but one thing these great choruses needed was more understanding of the subjects they sang. In this respect we were far behind a good German chorus whose power of voice was subordinated to real musical knowledge.'

The report continued that while admitting that British orchestral players were *'the finest in the world'* he then said that England was *'especially weak in solo wind instruments'* and England was *'very badly off'*, for conductors *'apart from Henry Wood'*.

It added: *'We had, however, too many mere pedantic mechanics, who, if they must keep time at all, would do it more successfully in a factory yard – people who conducted without any love, hate, or any feeling at all. Our solo singing lacked much in dramatic force as distinguished from theatrical singing, and that, he considered arose largely from the fact that we had no real dramatic stage art in England.'*

He then commented on the Acting profession: *'We have no drama in England. That is to say we have no dramatic (stage) art; we have in the ranks of the theatrical profession enough good actors to properly cast one play – and NO MORE: dressed up dolls and dummies fill the stage at most of our theatres and the public seem more of less satisfied. These people cannot act – as acting is an art – they only dress up and pretend to be somebody else – which is a very different thing.'*

The Birmingham Post commented: 'Let us for a moment try, at all events, to listen. Sir Edward Elgar went out of his way to fling a stone, not merely at musical executants concerning whom perhaps he has a right to speak but at English actors and actresses. *'They are mostly,'* he cries, *'dressed-up dolls and dummies who fill our stage – there are only enough actors and actresses in the ranks of the profession properly to cast one drama and no more'.* We wonder how many recent dramas he has seen in London or elsewhere before he ventures on so sweeping a generalisation.'

A letter to The Standard from a Mr F T Grien, 'a very close observer of English acting and drama' added: 'In my admiration of the great composer whose name is a credit to the art of England, I am second to none. But the very fact that one so highly placed should pronounce in public the sweeping condemnation of a profession which is sister to his own renders it imperative that somebody should enter a protest lest the opinion should gain ground that our drama ranks even lower than it does. In all my experience I cannot find any justification for the cruel and, I regret to say, unjust verdict which Sir Edward Elgar has passed.'

The lecture also inspired doggerel verse in one unnamed publication:

A case of Oblique Vision

When Edward the Elgar condemns without stint

Our actors, 'tis vain to reply

That he looks at the stage with a prejudiced squint

When he has but a 'cast' in his eye

The Star quoted actor-manager Beerbohm Tree: 'I think if Sir Edward paid a visit to an English theatre, he might modify his opinion.'

In the face of this, Robert Buckley of the Birmingham Gazette, realising the difficulties Elgar was getting himself into by such blatantly ill-considered remarks, took it upon himself to travel down to his Hereford home and run a damage-limitations exercise under the guise of a 'special interview' subtitled: 'Sir Edward Elgar explains his lecture'. The report described him as: 'genial, cheery, at peace with all the world and apparently unconscious of the storm of adverse criticism evoked by his last lecture.

'Too busy to read the newspapers, my casual reference to the treatment of the matter rather tended to his mystification. When the situation developed he said: *'The newspapers have evidently printed certain portions of my lecture without context. This may be inevitable but it is nonetheless misleading, though I blame nobody and am quite content to let the matter stand where it is.'*

'Now, concerning conductors,' he said. *'There was no reflection on English conductors. On the contrary I paid a tribute to Dr Cowen who has done splendid work all over the country. When I said we had but one conductor who devoted himself entirely to conducting I differentiated him from the composer-conductors and the organist-conductors who do not make a speciality of conducting. What I wanted to convey was the need for a school of conducting, the lack in England of the opportunity the study and practice the difficult art of conducting.*

'How can men become conductors without opportunity? There is Richter, Seidl, Nikisch, Lamoureux and the rest.

'Why should we in England not have more specialist conductors: men who give their whole attention to conducting, and who do not, let us say, rely on some other branch of the musical art and only practice the art of conductor occasionally?

'Then as to the epithet 'brainless singers'. To quote this without the context is egregiously unfair. I paid a gorgeous tribute to English singers. I never want anything better than English singers – of the right kind. I mentioned Mr Plunket Greene. Take him as a type – a gentleman, an artist by temperament, a man of genuine culture. That is the kind of singer we want nowadays. Mere voice is not enough. We must have a high intelligence.

'The schools of music have pulled us up splendidly and they continue to do capital work. But we are not perfect yet. And – as you know – as everybody knows – we still have amongst us 'brainless singers'.

'The same may be said of English executants. I am immensely indebted to them. We may have not attained the highest standard. But we are progressing. There are English performers who completely satisfy me. The real trouble is that we have in England at the moment no great dominant mind. We have no Goethe. And this want makes itself felt through all the arts.

'Then we have no school of dramatic art. That means that our artists are more or less deficient in dramatic sentiment. By the word dramatic I intend to cover a wide area.

'I wish performers to have a correct perception of the dramatic meaning of things. For instance I could wish them to be, not sentimental, but romantic, which is nobler, but not theatrical, but dramatic, which again, is the better part.

'How can singers (let us say) attain the requisite mastery of all the subtleties of the dramatic art without the facilities for study

But I see no reason for going into these matters at length. If people want to know what I say in my lectures, let them go and hear them. I can't be held responsible for the unavoidable omissions of the sub-editors - I believe the poor sub-editor is always blamed for these things. All I aim at is to point at what defects still remain to us, in the hope of getting them remedied if possible.

'It seems what I said about English choruses has occasioned some surprise. But the portion to which I refer was given as the opinion of foreign critics, not as my own. I said that foreign critics were inclined to the opinion that the tone of English choirs was heavy and that they were liable to flatness. And I mentioned these views of others in order that attention might be given to them. It is the faithful criticism that is helpful.'

Buckley then added: 'At this juncture, Sir Edward was disposed to waive further discussion and make a break for the laboratory where he makes all sorts of things that smell strong and go off in explosions like those which the foreign critics attribute to English choral bodies.'

But he continued: 'But there was one more point, to wit, Sir Edward's opinion concerning actors. *'Only a sufficiency of persons who can fairly be called actors and actresses to form the cast of one drama,'* I think you said. How about that Sir Edward?

'It's perfectly true. Moreover, I am not the only one to say it. The decadence of the stage seems to be admitted by all the dramatic critics. What do we see in the London theatres? One or perhaps two real actors or actresses in a play. The rest too often are what I said, in the main but dolls and dummies. They do not act, they could not act, in the true sense of the term. They merely dress up and pretend to be someone else.

'We have no school of dramatic art like that of France. That is why real actors are so few. I have a long acquaintance with the London theatres and I am also acquainted with the theatres of three other countries. And I cannot help feeling the difference. There is little or no acting in England, as the term is understood in France and Germany, where the minor parts, which in England would be given to inferior artists, are mostly exquisitely done.

'No drama worthy of the name can produce its legitimate impression by means of one actor's good work in the leading part. All the parts require to be well done. And this is precisely what we do not get in England.

Yes, I repeat it – but it is really a matter of common knowledge – we have in England enough actors to properly cast one drama and no more. And in my opinion, we have no school of dramatic art, as in France.'

At this point, Elgar once again diverted Buckley's attention: *'But come and see my laboratory – stay, here's a recently discovered portrait of Bach. Volbach, who made the discovery, gave me this copy, published by the Bach Society. There's strength ! Something like Bach ! That's much better than the portraits we have seen up to now. There's power !'*

'Five minutes later,' wrote Buckley, ' we were in the laboratory. Years ago, Sir Edward, then unknown to fame was experimenting with scientific kites. During the 'Apostles' period he took a deep interest in all sorts of weird snails and such like which he kept in an aquarium in the drawing-room, and which he kindly fished from their native lair for my especial delectation.

'Now we went downwards towards the chemicals.

'That's nitrate of silver' he said. *'I made it myself. It's a good sample.'*

'What did you make it for?'

'To show it to you. Mind that bottle. It's mercurous chloride.'

'What's mercurous chloride?'

'Why – mercurous chloride – what else?'

'He took some colourless liquids and threw them together into a glass bottle. A reddish liquid resulted. *'That's a precipitate of so-and-so,'* he said.

'When I left, my impression of Sir Edward was as troubled as it had been fifty times before, with a difference. This time he seemed to be a country gentleman with a taste for chemistry who composed a little music between times.'

The fifth lecture was 'The Critics'. The Birmingham Post reported: 'The critics of music in this country,' he said, had a difficult task to perform in as much as their work had to be hurriedly displayed or in the opinion of newspaper editors it was worthless. The editor, of course, wanted news and he wanted that news quickly. Whether he wanted it correct of course was a matter of his own conscience (laughter) – as he had regretfully noticed in the past week (renewed laughter).

'It would appear that the English people did not read much about music, except in snippets of serio-comic lectures or perhaps telegraphed reports of isolated sentences from serious ones (laughter). Except in rare cases – there were one or two editors who knew something about music – the articles only referred to some sensation of the moment, or some special event, which was practically the same thing.

'It was this combination with journalism which occasionally made criticism fall somewhat lower than the critic's own ideal. It was the natural outcome of a hurried daily press and a want of sufficient musical appreciation amongst editors generally. But the journalistic side had been the mainstay of such critics who, inadequately equipped on the musical side had to report matters musical.

''It is so much easier' remarked the speaker amid laughter *'to write of a definite object such as the number of the audience, or the amount of applause, or the dress and so forth than to describe such an intangible thing as music.'*

'Sir Edward proceeded to point out the difficulty which was presented to the critic who heard a work for the first time but who had plenty of time allowed him in which to prepare his article and remarked that it must be infinitely more difficult to the hurried journalistic critic. In journalistic work sometimes details were given which might be necessary but which in no way added to the dignity of musical criticism. Information was given for instance as to the numbers of the audience which was often quite unintentionally misleading.

'For instance, they read of 2,000 people in Worcester Cathedral as a 'small audience' while 1,900 people gathered in Birmingham or Leeds Town Hall was described as an 'enormous audience'. (Laughter). This might be a trivial point', Sir Edward went on; *'it was in one way, but not in another.*

'That sort of thing was to be deprecated on account of the effect it had on the prospects of new works. Subsequent performances depended very much on the reports in the papers among conductors and committees who were unable to be present at the first performance.'

Elgar also referred to *'the shady side of musical criticism'* commenting: *'We have still articles purposely written for the annoyance of anyone in particular and one of our reviewers prefers to use trigonomic ink in preference to other fluid.'*

The next lecture provided a summary of what he had said before. As the Birmingham Post commented: 'It had been said – not by him – that the multiplicity of our music schools up and down the country tended to produce mediocrity. He would not contest that statement now; for the moment it was beside the point because it was not only mediocrity that suffered from an excess of numbers.

'Many good and capable artists were sorrowfully waiting for the time of recognition which came so slowly, or not at all. If we did take infinite pains with our education and yet produced mediocrity in music we must bear the responsibility somehow.

'He had no wish to attempt to dictate or desire to prophesy in the sense of prediction when he delivered the inaugural address, and he had no desire now. The object of that address was to show what might be and he touched incidentally on the past and the present

'He divided the active musical world into three sections and had devoted a lecture to each. His remarks were intended primarily for young musicians. And through the musical world they had travelled, those who had accompanied him had noted the living and, it might be, blossoming things and they were hoping to reach the fruit in due time; but they had not sat down to admire the milestones. They had learned from much reading and criticism that they wished to see in this country a school of composition which should have some hold on the affections of the people and be held in respect abroad.

'He asked young men to draw their inspiration from their own country and their own literature, and, in spite of what many would say, from their own climate. That suggestion had been the subject of some shallow remark.

'Confusion had been caused by some of our young spirits complaining violently of the laws of harmony and crying out against pedantic tyranny. To an open mind that would seem an unnecessary outcry, seeing that the complainants did not see themselves bound to follow the rules.

'It was a mistaken view to say they were held down by pedants and academic tyranny. If they wanted to know their destiny they must learn it not from the law, but from the temper of the times – not the unreasoning and unquestioning temper, but the temper of the best, the educated, the reasonable and artistic few.

'Turning to the question of absolute music which had also been raised, he said he still looked upon music which existed without any poetic or literary basis as the true foundation of their art. No argument he had read, had altered that view. Symphony without programme was the highest development of the art. Views to the contrary were often held.'

But the paper added 'It had been said that his views with respect to Brahms's Symphony were astounding considering what he had written himself. He had never referred in his lectures to his own compositions save once. He had written overtures and things with titles more or less poetic and suggestive but was he so narrow as to admire his own music because he had written it himself? No, certainly not.

'When he saw one of his own works by the side, say, of the Fifth Symphony, he felt as a tinker might do when he saw the Forth Bridge, or as amazing when he saw the campanile of the new University. He looked on Strauss as the greatest living composer. Absolute music, if necessary to have a basis at all, as a basis must be logical.'

One aspect of Elgar's lectures was, however, too much even for the papers.

Elgar's remarks on performers had deeply hurt the composer and conductor Sir Frederic Cowen, his sense of betrayal heightened by history. When the unknown Elgar had struggled to establish himself in London in 1890, he had written to all the musical luminaries of the time in the hope of advancement. Cowen had been the only one to reply, giving advice and encouragement. Subsequently he had been an indefatigable Elgar champion.

He was so hurt by Elgar's reported remarks that he sent him a cutting from one of the papers – then published Elgar's reply: *'I am very much distressed by the absurd cutting you sent me. The telegraphed reports of my lecture are, as far as I know, wholly misleading and perhaps made so purposely. In the meantime, you know me, I hope, better than to think I should say the senseless nonsense imputed to me...'*

The Birmingham Post was amongst others which, with undeniable condemnation, commented tersely: 'On the subject of the press we must express our regret that Sir Edward should have employed an expression in his letter to Dr Cowen that is open to grave objection. To say that telegraphed reports were 'wholly misleading and perhaps made so purposely', is to charge the press with a deliberate attempt to mislead the public and injure the lecturer without any obvious motive – a charge that Sir Edward would have considerable difficulty in establishing'

The Musical News of December 9th 1905 summed up: 'Sir Edward Elgar must really be beginning to feel sorry that he accepted that Birmingham professorship seeing that now, he cannot open his mouth apparently without finding himself embroiled in some more or less lively controversy.'

INTRODUCTION AND ALLEGRO FOR STRINGS
AND THE FREEDOM OF THE CITY OF WORCESTER

At the end of 1905 The Westminster Gazette reviewed the new music produced during the year, concluding that there had not been that much. As far as Elgar was concerned it said: 'Sir Edward Elgar has himself been disappointingly unproductive. True he has, in his capacity of Professor of Music at Birmingham University delivered several addresses which created no little stir; but even appraising those remarkable utterances at their highest possible valuation they represent but a sorry substitute for the new music which one would sooner have had from their author's pen instead.

'Sir Edward Elgar is now forty-eight and the works he has produced number over fifty including therein works of such magnitude as 'The Dream of Gerontius' and 'The Apostles', representing each, half a dozen ordinary symphonies. Nevertheless, it is a pleasing belief on the part of many that he still has his best work to do and those holding this view are naturally anxious to see its accuracy verified. One acceptable new work Sir Edward did, however, give us in the course of the past twelve months in the shape of the delightful 'Introduction and Allegro' for Strings.'

Elgar had said that the foundation of the piece had been an episode when on a short holiday at Llangranog on the Welsh Coast, where he had heard a group of people in the distance, singing what he described as a 'Welsh tune'. The tune had been indistinct but stuck in his memory and some time later he built the work around his interpretation of what he had heard.

The Daily Telegraph thought the piece: 'A fine specimen of the composer's remarkable skill and ingenuity. The resourcefulness of the composer is shown by the series of striking contrasts obtained, and the merry fugato section is very cleverly developed. One of the chief themes was developed from reminiscences of a little Welsh melody and this is developed with superb effect, especially in the climax near the end.'

For The Times: 'What is really a remarkably poor little Welsh tune is turned to noble purposes in the two movements, and never has the composer given us work of finer or more individual quality, in spite of the tenuity of its theme. When it is as familiar as the spirited 'Cockaigne' and the beautiful Variations there is little doubt that it will rank as high as they.'

The Yorkshire Post: 'The work, indeed, is distinctly original in conception and treatment and doubtless will become popular for on a first hearing the naïve little Welsh tune sticks in the memory and the entire composition is of that kind which excites greater esteem with familiarity.'

These were carefully chosen, even 'polite' words, and despite the popularity of the piece today, regarded by many as one of Elgar's best crafted works, criticism was scant.

It premiered, along with the Third Pomp and Circumstance March in a large programme, spread over two concerts which also included, 'Sea Pictures', 'Cockaigne', selections from 'Caractacus' and 'The Apostles'.

E A Baughan considered The Pomp and Circumstance march: 'a good symphonic poem spoilt. The opening theme muttered by the lower woodwind and horns strikes a sullen and angry note as if the dogs of war straining at the leash. The gradual treatment promises much but then comes to an inevitable trio, very clever in rhythm, but not broad enough to be popular. It might have been developed into something big had the march-form permitted the composer a free hand, but as it is you feel that the music is limited by its aim of popularity. Still, the March is a vigorous piece of work.

'Introduction and Allegro' was relegated to the final few words of Baughan's piece: *'the work is a tribute'* the composer tells us *'to that sweet borderland where I have chosen to make my home'*.

Even the Birmingham Gazette, in a long article about Elgar's move to Hereford, only mentioned it in passing and audiences did not appear to warm to it. When Richter introduced it to the Manchester public later in the year, he was so surprised at the public reaction that he played it again, without explanation.

As late as 1916, the Pall Mall Gazette mentioned that a Promenade Concert programme included 'Introduction and Allegro' – 'a work that after lying fallow for many seasons has now taken the rank it deserves.'

Appreciation of the Introduction and Allegro changed, but only after repeated performances. It is now one of Elgar's most admired productions. Ironically it is also one of the few Elgar works appreciated by those who profess to dislike much of his output.

In the same year Elgar produce the 'Introduction and Allegro for Strings', Musical World provided a vivid pen-portrait of what he was like at this time: 'I met him in one of the great hotels of Europe. The vast entrance all white and gold, fairy like with flowers and beautiful women was full of the indefinable air of romance; from an orchestra in some secret place floated the languorous music of Saint-Saens's 'Samson and Delilah' and men and women came and went as in a well-ordered procession.

'He walked towards me with head slightly bent, his tall spare frame attracting attention by its aristocratic aloofness. He looked what very few eminent men do look – distinguished. It was not his face, though that was fine; it was not his head, though that was well poised: it was something, I know not what – a way of holding himself, a manner of walking as though even here he had dreams and visions.

'He entered into conversation with an air somewhat cold and distant; but in a minute the frostiness had disappeared and he talked with the hesitating, interrupted eagerness of a nervous man who has something important to say.

'That Sir Edward Elgar is nervous and exceedingly sensitive no man who has spoken with him can deny; and they say that when he conducts, his face twitches, and the tears come streaming down. But this nervousness, so evident and unmistakable, is not for one moment permitted to interfere with the free expression of his thoughts and opinions; it is held absolutely under control by his iron will and by the spiritual intensity of his nature. To speak to a man of the potent individuality of Elgar is to receive vivid impressions that oust in a flash the irritating insistence upon the consciousness of one's surroundings.

'This fairy palace of subtle scents and amorous sounds faded; and the banqueting hall before me, gleaming with the white arms of women and glistening with silver plate, was no longer there; the little trills of feminine laughter, the rustle of silk, the delicious hum of happy life around me – all this died away, and my personality, swept from its normal path, was aware of nothing but a pair of eager eyes that probed, of an astonishing brain that questioned.

'When you are in the company of a person of average intelligence it never occurs to you to think that inside that undistinguished head there is a brain working, functioning and carrying out its mysterious processes; but with Elgar the thought strikes one that within that brain are being born unimaginable thoughts that in *there* is hurry and nervous bustle – sensations being rapidly garnered, to be fused together some day and delivered to the world in sound. The impression is one of intensity, of great powers of assimilation, of greater powers of creation.

'It was only on leaving him that it occurred to me to analyse his 'manner', the superficial characteristic of the inner man. Allowing myself then to dwell upon the thought of him, there came into my mind the vision of a man who was more than kind, and of a musician who was something more even than a composer of music.'

In 1905 Elgar was also recognised by his native Worcester when he was made a Freeman of the City – an honour which had its origins in Medieval times, recognising people who were of especial merit in their home towns and cities, and bestowing certain privileges. By the early 20th century, however, the title was purely ceremonial.

After receiving the honour, Elgar gave a speech which provided an insight into his boyhood in the City. The Worcester Journal in its extensive coverage of the event reported: 'Someone had recently written that unfortunately he knew nothing of English Church Music. The writer of that sort of paragraph must have thought that as a boy he did not notice what was going on around him. At the first chance he had, he went to the Cathedral – they would know he attended another place – and he was there at every possible service.

'His dear old friend Dr [Alfred] Done [Organist at Worcester Cathedral] lent him books and often as a small boy might have been seen staggering under a large folio book of ten clefs trying to make them out. He really thought he knew a little about English Church Music and after he had spent years and years in the Cathedral that seemed to him an unnecessary reproach.

'He had many opportunities in the City. In addition to Dr Done he had the help of Mr Alfred Caldicott [conductor of Worcester Music Society and Professor of Harmony at the Royal College of Music] who brought with him from Leipzig new ideas and modern thought. He could not go through the list of names but he must mention Mr [Arthur] Quarterman [conductor of the Worcester Glee Club]. There were a number of people who were masters of music and from whom he had been privileged to learn something. Amongst them were those who used to sing. There was an education for a man in the old English part music.

'He supposed that that sort of thing was gone. Amongst those who sang really well, although they never took a prominent place in the world were the late Mr William Tyers and Mr Oliver Milward. The latter was now an old man and some of them did not remember him singing.

'Although he could not admit that he deserved the honour, he admitted that he had worked hard. His first word as a freeman might be impertinent. What were they doing for any other boys ? If they had any boys or girls who were musical were the musical conditions for their training any better now than they were 40 years ago ? They might think of that some time, build a large hall where performances might be given equal to those in other towns.

'There were plenty of chorus singers in Worcester. Everyone was supposed to talk about the influence of music and the good it did, but he would like to see the 50,000 inhabitants – the workpeople of the factories – given an opportunity of hearing works like 'The Messiah' and 'The Elijah' in a hall for the charge of sixpence. They had no place in which it could be done at present – but they could think of that sometime – the sooner the better.'

He ended by paying tribute to his parents. His octogenarian father was too ill to attend the ceremony and his mother had died in 1900, but, as the report concluded: 'She brought a knowledge of literature which was quite unusual in the days in which he was brought up, and many of the things she said to him he had tried to carry out in his music.'

THE KINGDOM

The following year – 1906- opened with reports of Elgar's health. The Staffordshire Sentinel in February said: 'A report has been gaining ground to the effect that the health of Sir Edward Elgar is such as to cause his closest friends anxiety. Of a highly nervous disposition, and of a constitution which can hardly be classed as robust, Sir Edward is devoting himself with his accustomed self-absorption to the composition of the latest part of 'The Apostles'.

'The strain on the nervous forces of the man must be enormous under any conceivable circumstances, and it is therefore a matter for universal regret to hear it suggested that a nervous breakdown is likely to cause even a temporary cessation of his activities. Sir Edward is however said to be anxious to complete 'The Apostles' in order that the work may be produced at the Birmingham musical festival in October next.'

The source is not clear, but the local paper in Hereford gave further detail which could only have come from someone close – maybe even Elgar himself: 'Sir Edward is coming up to town to stay with his friend Mr Leo Schuster for a few days, and he will probably take a short rest elsewhere before resuming work.'

Alice Elgar's diary made a number of remarks on the same theme. Elgar had felt the strain of the work involved with what was to become 'The Kingdom', and his health was suffering, resulting in a number of visits from doctors. But by the time news reached the papers her diary noted that his health had improved, though he still seemed to be suffering from headaches. The general improvements allowed him to resume work on 'The Kingdom', and by March the Birmingham Post reported the new work would debut on the Wednesday morning at the Festival, with 'The Apostles' performed the previous evening.

In early April he and Alice went on tour to America again, visiting Cincinnati where, under the headline 'Sir Edward Waves Off Interviewers' and the sub-heading 'Lady Elgar, is, however more gracious', the Cincinnati Post remarked: 'A tall spare figure in ice-cream clothes, with drawn brows and a worried expression, that's Sir Edward Elgar. Lady Elgar, small, plump, with laughing blue eyes and the prettiest manners imaginable, accompanied him.

'Sir Edward Elgar is the typical Englishman, silent, reserved, and unsocial – until after dinner. He pulled at his drooping moustache nervously and waved the interviewers away with a thin but firm hand. His horse-blanket-checked great coat struck the bystanders dumb with admiration. It was so English, you know.

'Lady Elgar was enveloped in a long red cloak with a white fur boa about her throat. She wore a small travelling hat. Her voice is low and sweet and her laugh is as full of fun as that of a girl… *'I have met so many nice people in America that I can have nothing but the pleasantest impressions of your country,'* she said. *'And the young American girls – they are so sweet and charming that I never will believe the writers who say they are anything but delightful.'*

The New York Times quoted Elgar: *'I am not a stranger to America. I have been here before and have so many good friends that it seems like coming home. In-fact I am more at home here than anywhere else. I am in thorough sympathy with the modern life here, the hustle and briskness of your life.'*

The New York Tribune asked him 'about the progress of music as an art in England, and he said meaningly: *'We live on an island and some of us never get off it.'*

The comment was amplified in the New York World: 'Sir Edward's lectures on 'Modern English Music', created a sensation, inasmuch as England has insular prejudices and has not gone outside for musical ideas, scorning all innovations.'

On returning home he completed 'The Kingdom' but little appeared in the press, until rehearsals began.

Robert Buckley in the Birmingham Gazette mused: 'As he came on with the baton, I remembered his first public appearance on that platform some twenty-three years before. He had written a piece, which he had scored for the orchestra, and Dr Waring having spoken well of it, to Mr W C Stockley, the latter, with his never-failing good nature, proposed to give it at one of his orchestral concerts. Young Elgar played among the fiddles having come up from Worcester for the purpose and making haste to return on the same evening; worrying the railway folks to that end, until they gave way and the thing was done.

'Mr Stockley wished the composer to conduct his piece, but Edward Elgar shied at the thought of leaving the fiddles and assuming the baton.

'No, no, you'll do it much better,' he said.

'Then leave the orchestra and go into a side-gallery and hear your own music,' proposed Mr Stockley.

'No, no,' again responded the timid young man. *'I'd rather play with the fiddlers'.*

'Which he did, coming forward at the close in response to a determined call for the composer. He appeared shy, and, perhaps, a little awkward, as he stood there with his fiddle under his arm, bowing hurriedly and retreating to the cover of the fiddle-desk with electric speed.

'The audience of Saturday morning last sat out 'The Kingdom' with undoubted satisfaction. No startling incidents occurred. All hearers were impressed with their privilege in being allowed to hear the very first complete performance of any chorus of the work whatever. And Sir Edward, unusually placid and comfortable, succeeded in holding himself down. The nervous irritability which once pursued him and which worried the orchestra into a like frame of mind, seems to have largely if not altogether disappeared.

'Sir Edward has arrived. He is in the centre of the ring: on the crest of the wave. His reputation is at its highest. His fame is assured. He knows that every mother's son of the band, every mother's daughter of the choir, and everybody else, will strain every nerve to do him justice. With Sir Edward holding the reins, the team never wants the whip. When Edward Elgar comes in front of the festival performers everybody is geared up in a moment. Such is the effect of prestige. The man of less celebrity may be well served, but still he falls far short of the service accorded to fame.'

As expected, seats had been snapped up for the performance long before, with only a few remaining tickets for standing at the back being available, costing one guinea, which in today's money is more than £80.

The Worcester Journal captured the atmosphere: 'We found the usual throng of eager, expectant, gorgeously attired people, all trying to look as if they had written the work themselves, and some of them almost succeeding. After all, people do not, as a rule, pay one guinea and costs merely to say 'I was there' so I expect there is something genuine in a festival audience with their devout attention to their vocal scores and their charming air of detachment from all worldly matters.

'The whole scene was elevating; the whole atmosphere was charged with electricity. One noted so many well-known types. The old Festival Stager, quiet, composed, absorbed, score in hand, ostentatiously familiar. The ardent amateur, busy with pencil notes and ready with a 'Jaeger' label for every tune. The diffident but earnest novice, who strives to emulate the old stager and the ardent amateur, and very much wishes that he knew what that clever Mr Jaeger means by his charming analysis. The opulent night-seer and lion-hunter, who goes to a festival as he goes to Madam Tussaud's and who is quite aware that both are dependent on him for their very existence. The critic with a well-chosen manner indicative in being engaged in assimilating every subject under the sun, except music. The great musician, oblivious of all other types, and cognisant only of a very small and very select coterie surrounded by a sort of mental halo, only to be approached upon bended knees.

'They were all there, all apparently enjoying themselves, and each, I think, in his own way, conscious that he was making one of a really privileged band – privileged to assist at the production of a great work of national art, to be present at the apotheosis of a great national creative genius.'

As to the performance itself, the Morning Leader concluded: 'The Prelude is without doubt among Sir Edward's noblest inspirations. At the same time it is in contrast to the mystic darkness of 'The Apostles'. It is immensely strong in the best scene, and makes the hearer know that conflicts await the new born Church. Indeed 'The Kingdom' throughout moves more on an earthly plane than 'The Apostles' and thus is more easily grasped at a first hearing.

'There was a time that a novelty at a festival meant an empty house. But when Sir Edward Elgar appeared to conduct 'The Kingdom' this morning there was not a vacant seat in the Town Hall.

'That no outward sign of great success was lacking goes without saying. That 'The Kingdom' is an artistic triumph in many ways is also certain, but it is too early yet to say whether it surpasses either 'The Dream of Gerontius' or 'The Apostles' and the end leaves us almost in greater doubt than the close of 'The Apostles' as to the ultimate shape of the Sacred Trilogy which is the second part. The third part, the very title of which has not yet been decided on alone can solve these problems. And all criticism must, of course, be subject to this important reservation.'

Joseph Bennett wrote this in the Daily Telegraph: 'Sir Edward Elgar is the man of the hour here and now. His 'Apostles' was performed last evening and its successor 'The Kingdom' had a first hearing this morning. Both were conducted by the composer, each appealed to a crowded hall, and the audience seemed very pleased, as assuredly they were very patient. These repeated successes of the English composer who has come to bulk most largely in the eye of the world are in aspect the more astonishing the closer they are looked at.

'They upset a good many previous conclusions and I confess that had my opinion been asked of 'Gerontius' or 'The Apostles' before either were tested publicly, I should have declared that such music stood no present chance of acceptance by our good English folk, by the nation which, in art matters, and especially in this art, loves the simple and direct. But Sir Edward Elgar, by a happy stroke of fortune, captured his countrymen just as they had become in sufficient measure sensible of the modern spirit and had begun to show signs of a movement en masse.

'Whether the composer drew a bow at a venture or saw a chink in the armour opposed to him, matters not. He hit the mark, and now the British public as though given up to the charms of mystic music, to the convolutions and involutions, the permutations and combinations which not long since they would have wondered at and in their bewilderment rejected. How has this come about?

'The question is not to be answered off-hand, and I certainly, though having an opinion, shall not here venture upon a reply. The matter of the moment is that the Elgar charm seems as strong as ever, that a hypnotised public responds meekly to the suggestions of a gifted and daring operator and that the movement rolls on with sustained if not increasing force.

'What more convincing proof of this could be desired than that which has struck every observant man at the present festival? The two enormous audiences, the patient attention given to the music, and the response elicited by every tour de force, a response nonetheless obvious to experienced observers for being soundless – these things are not to be explained away by flippant tongues, nor lightly treated as indications of what is going on the recesses where are the springs of musical feeling and taste. Even the sternest champion of orthodoxy must take Elgar in a serious spirit. He is tremendously in earnest.

'As for 'The Kingdom', it must, like all important works be heard till familiarity in some measure takes the place of its opposite, till the crooked has been made straight and the rough places are made smooth. But impressions are worth giving. They may be wrong and they may be right; in any case they have a passing interest.

'The dominant impression brought away from the Town Hall by me was that Sir Edward Elgar has given us nothing better adapted to gratify the average taste and judgement than his latest work. Saying this, I must guard against the possible conclusion that the composer has gone back from the principles and practice with which he is identified. He has done nothing of the kind and as a matter of fact that which is fundamental in 'Gerontius' and 'The Apostles' is found at the base of 'The Kingdom' also. But in his new work, Sir Edward has chosen to modify his method for reasons to be found perhaps in his subject, or in some sense of expediency adequate to the result.

'Speaking generally and without reference to particular pages, 'The Kingdom' is built on broader lines than its predecessors. The choral sections are more developed, even in some cases as though to the end of the musical effect, a point to which more attention should be directed in these days of exaggerated regard for the 'word'.

'At any rate, musical effect is there and that in a measure which no doubt will surprise many who expected to find the art 'cribbed, cabined and confined' by the theory which denies it independence and individuality when within hailing distance of omnipotent speech. That theory carried to a fanatical extreme is doing infinite harm to vocal music and there is reason to thank any composer be he eminent or of low degree who indicates a reasonable compromise.

'In the present work I find also enlarged development of the individual utterance. Our composer has too often shown an inclination to be scrappy and set music to conversations, in which each person concerned thinks himself bound to interject something as often as possible. The new oratorio is not free from this, but, on the other hand, we have more or less extended solos, the most important of which, given to the Mother, fills nine pages of the pianoforte score.

'Here is a distinct gain to musical interest, another being an appreciation of the value of beauty in music, beauty of melodic phrase, of harmony, and for all that makes for artistic euphony. In point of melody, Sir Edward seems with difficulty to reconcile beauty and the exigencies enforced by his ever-shifting harmonies and continuously-changing tonality. This is also a matter for compromise. There should be a way out of the impasse as the composer has partially indicated in the present work.

'The continuous interest of Elgar's orchestration, a point upon which amateurs do not need instruction, is in 'The Kingdom' as manifest as elsewhere. So, with the sense of and skill of climax, save at the close, where climax called imperatively for its rights and did not get them, and so especially with tonal transitions, many of which are extraordinarily successful in rousing attention.

'To sum up this record of first impressions, it is no more than that the new oratorio is in various commanding respects the most acceptable work which Sir Edward Elgar has yet given us. It has not the morbidity of 'Gerontius', and, as an art creation, it stands on a higher plane than 'The Apostles'. At the close of the performance, the composer-conductor was again and again greatly acclaimed. This honour he had fairly won.'

The Tribune thought 'The Kingdom' an advance on 'The Apostles' but criticised various sections: 'The scene of the Pentecost itself is disappointing but the chorus of the people in Solomon's Porch, which follows it, can hardly be too much praised for vigour and actuality. The succeeding scene between Peter and the multitude, noble and affecting throughout and rising to a superb climax, is, I think, as fine as anything Sir Edward Elgar's sacred music can show since the 'Proficisere' of 'Gerontius'.

'What follows is of less interest, though there are many beautiful passages here and there. The long solo given to the soprano ['The Sun Goeth Down'] which balances the contralto scena for Mary Magdalen in 'The Apostles', however much it may retard the movement of the story is not devoid of interesting points.

'Very simple and touching is the scene of the Breaking of the Bread, but it is permissible to regret that the composer felt it necessary to set music to the Lord's Prayer, for though this is also simply and reverently done one hardly feels that the setting justifies the introduction of those special words.'

The Globe, concluded: 'The chief impressions left by 'The Kingdom' are threefold. First the directness which characterises the Prelude as compared with 'The Apostles', is maintained throughout; secondly it is richer in contrasts than 'The Apostles', and lastly, though it is really as full of detail as its predecessor, it seems simpler because of the more logical subordination of detail to the whole scheme. It is certainly more likely to obtain a hold on the hearers, at first acquaintance at any rate, than 'The Apostles', because of this very quality.'

The Star thought that most people had come away from the performance with a much clearer grasp of the work then either 'Gerontius' or 'The Apostles': 'Personally I think the impression is largely due to a very welcome characteristic in the work itself. It is not so much that the actual design of the other works was less intelligible, but that Sir Edward Elgar's art has progressed with rapid strides in the direction of stripping away unessential details and leaving the main things more sharply outlined.'

However, the Morning Post felt: 'much of the music seems to have been hurriedly conceived with the result that the design of a great part of it lacks constructive finish, though the individuality of the composer invariably asserts itself with distinction.'

The Birmingham Post, had this to say: 'It is rather doubtful whether it was quite the wisest thing to give 'The Kingdom' immediately after 'The Apostles'. The literary scheme of the one being a sequel to that of the other, no doubt the juxtaposition of the two enabled us to see the complete picture much more clearly; but on the other hand the music of the new work is so similar in idiom and in phraseology to the music of 'The Apostles' that we could not fight off a perpetual feeling this morning that we were hearing comparatively little that had not been told us before.

'Elgar's individuality has hitherto been very pronounced; barring a little Wagnerism in 'Gerontius' there is nothing in his music as a whole to remind us of other men. That being so, it is a pity that he should not begin reminding us of himself as he undoubtedly does very often in 'The Kingdom''

The critic then considered the characters portrayed in 'The Kingdom', pointing out that it: 'was bound to start with one big disadvantage; Judas and Jesus are dead and there is no definite dramatic personality to take their places. We are left with John and Peter – who can never be much more than vague abstractions in music – and the Virgin and Mary Magdalene, neither of whom now happens to be placed in circumstances that can make well defined personages of them. The inevitable result is monotony of mood; all the characters are so much alike that we can scarcely distinguish them from each other. The fault does not lie with the librettist – who is in this case the composer – but in the subject, though having selected such a subject, the composer must, of course, dree his weird [submit to his destiny].

'If we ask why such a subject was selected we are plunged once more into a question that has already caused some difference of opinion in connection with 'The Apostles' – the question as to how far Elgar's religious prepossessions stand in his way as a musician. In his anxiety that is to bring home to audiences the significance of certain events in the religious history of the world that happened some nineteen centuries ago, does he not tie his hands at times, fettering his musical imagination with a lot of matter that cannot be bent to really musical purposes?'

The critic added he had received from 'my good friend Canon Gorton – who had had a strong influence on Elgar in the preparation of the whole theological theme of both 'The Apostles' and 'The Kingdom' – a copy of his interpretation of the libretto. The consistency of it is all is as undeniable as the theology of it is unimpeachable. But a text may be an admirable summary of church history, and still be in many ways, unsuitable for music.

'Put theological prepossessions aside, forget the high theme on which the oratorio is based, look at it purely from the point of view of musical art, and we are tempted to remark 'Beshrew the Holy Women!' One woman with the savour of the humanity we know about her – one Carmen or Isolde – is worth a vestryful of them.

'A fascinating sinner is better than a tiresome saint; and that Elgar's saints are sometimes tiresome will hardly be seriously disputed. There is only one test of a work of art – the quantity and the quality of art there is in it. It may be full of the wisest philosophy and inculcate the noblest moral sentiments, but if the art in it – in this case the music – does not appeal to us the rest is naught.

'Many people I know go to 'The Apostles' and 'The Kingdom' as they would to church, to be morally edified. No artist can look at them from that point of view. The point is not what edifying texts the scissors have snipped out of the Bible, but the kind of music to which the text has been set.

'It is no doubt true that the lame man asks Peter for an alms or that 'to him that is afflicted pity should be showed'; but the statements in themselves will no more draw us to the concert room that the statement that Queen Anne is dead or that the 'buses run along Corporation Street'. The only thing that will draw us there is a setting of the words to fine music.

'The point then is this: Is the music of 'The Kingdom' in itself great enough to satisfy those who go to art for the art there is in it, not the theology? Now in the first place, Elgar's prepossession with his literary scheme obviously gets in his way very often. He forgets the very fact on which Wagner insisted, that since music needs plenty of space in which to unfold itself, a text for music should be as simple as possible – containing plenty of opportunities for emotion but little incident.

'Elgar's need to keep moving from incident to incident in order to tell his story often leads to musical scrappiness; one labelled theme treads on the heels of another, but there is little chance for broad development. When two men sit on the same horse, one must ride behind; Elgar the story-teller has his way, and Elgar the musician is put in the background.

'The beautiful opening chorus for example, that promises so well for a great musical picture does not get past its fifth bar before Peter cuts in an interrupts it. And frequently after that one cries out in despair for some long sweep of melody, some two minutes of continuous thinking, in place of this perpetual pasting together of a scrap of this theme and a scrap of that in order to drive some lesson home to us, or to remind us of other situations in which the same themes have meant this or that. It is the leit-motif system exploited to death; the continuity of the music is sacrificed to the supposed necessity of telling the same story over and over again.

'In 'The Kingdom' in fact, Elgar exhibits in an even exaggerated form the two vices of style that one hoped to have seen the last of in 'The Apostles'. One is the practice of putting page after page together by merely pinning one piece of music-type, forming a leading theme, on to another piece of music-type that forms another main theme.

'Besides this mannerism there is another that now seems ineradicable from Elgar's style – his practice of making the second bar of a phrase either an exact repetition of the first or a sequential imitation of it. Examine the first thirty pages of 'The Apostles' and you will find at least sixty cases of this kind. In 'The Kingdom' there must be, including the old and new themes and their repetitions, at least 300 examples of them.

'The fatal mannerism has long been a characteristic of Elgar. It will be found in practically all the themes of 'In the South', in 'Cockaigne', in the 'Pomp and Circumstance' marches and in 'Gerontius'. When once you become conscious of it, it goes a long way towards killing your interest in the music; the melodies seem so mechanically made that they almost cease to draw blood. That, at any rate, is my own experience.

'And yet, in spite of all these flaws, 'The Kingdom' is in some respects a fine work. It has fine scenes, that is, though they are overweighted by the scenes that are not fine, and though the general level of inspiration is, in my opinion, below that of 'Gerontius' and 'The Apostles'. Some of the choral portions are so obvious in sentiment that one can hardly believe they came from the delicately spiritual brain that conceived 'Gerontius'; but much of the choral writing is highly effective, and the laying out of parts for the voices is as expert as ever.

'A good deal of the music must frankly be called dull in itself but Elgar is now so consummate a master of effect, particularly of orchestral and choral effect, that he can often almost persuade us against our own judgement that the actual tissue of the music is better than it really is. The constant similarity of the music to that of 'The Apostles' is a serious flaw that will ultimately tell very much against the new work.

'To sum up, in spite of the undoubted beauties of many parts of it, the questions one must ask with regard to 'The Kingdom' are these – Does it say anything that Elgar has not already said in 'Gerontius' and 'The Apostles'? Does it show any advance either in technique or imagination? Does it show any recovery from the mannerisms of style that have been steadily growing upon Elgar during the last ten years?

'The answer to all these questions, I think, must be 'No'. I cannot believe that the work will add much to its composer's reputation, or that it has as long a life before it as its two immediate predecessors. If the future proves me to be wrong no one will be more pleased than I.'

The Festival also featured 'Omar Khayyam' by Granville Bantock. The Post critic perceived: 'The few fervent eulogists that could see no flaw in 'The Kingdom' like the equally fervent detractors who could see no good at all in 'Omar Khayyam' can both be dismissed with a tolerant smile. Mr Bantock's name is anathema to some people just as Sir Edward Elgar's is like the blessed word 'Mesopotamia' to others. Mr Bantock, however is in the happier case; he will easily survive the assaults of his enemies, while Elgar will be fortunate if he survives the advocacy of some of his friends.

'Speaking broadly the best critics are at one as regards 'The Kingdom'. They recognise the great beauty of many episodes in it and the general air of mastery that Elgar now imparts to all his work. On the other hand objection is taken in several quarters to the tame ending to the *'singularly dull, characterless and unemotional setting of the Lord's Prayer'*, as the 'Daily News' puts it and the scrappiness of much of the thematic texture.

The 'Times' dwells upon that last-named defect; the 'Atheneum' also speaks of the sometimes 'mechanical' treatment of the leading themes. The 'Manchester Courier' thinks 'The Kingdom' *'decidedly inferior in expressive power and general conception' to 'The Apostles'*

'Altogether, the public verdict is most concisely expressed in a sentence from Mr Baughan's careful article in the 'Daily News': '*My first impression, then, of 'The Kingdom' is not of the vital type. Much of the music is beautiful; some of it even grand and big; but there is a good deal that is mere tone painting; much that is laboured, dull and mephitic,*' while in other respects the score shows increasing *'mastership of the composer's means.'*

This drew protest in a letter from Arthur Troyte Griffith - 'Troyte' of the 'Enigma Variations': 'Since the first introduction of 'The Apostles' certain critics have continuously reiterated that the oratorio was dull, disjointed, scrappy and all the rest of it. Now your critic repeats in your columns the same doleful strain over 'The Kingdom'. How is it that those that crowd these uninteresting performances take such a different view from their mentors?'

Elgar's health problems and his American trip had robbed him of enough time to complete 'The Kingdom' adequately. As biographer Percy Young later commented: 'Writing against the clock is not always the best incentive.'

After this, he abandoned oratorios for good, made no significant utterance for two years – and when he did, turned to purely orchestral music.

THREE AMERICAN INTERVIEWS AND THE WAND OF YOUTH

Elgar toured America again in 1907. On April 7th he gave an interview to Miller Ular of the Chicago Sunday Examiner: 'I asked why he said he was a *'musician by accident'*

''Why,' he answered *'I was never intended to be a musician. I taught myself to be a 'cellist, a violinist, an organist, a pianist. I learned, practically unassisted all I know about the art of music.*

''I was interested in many things – chemistry as much as any – and it was really an accident I became a musician. I think it was the incident of the bassoon that partly decided me to become a musician.

''I was interested in amateur music making with several friends and wrote some compositions for the crowd of us. I played the bassoon and often went serenading, playing some of my little compositions, and some others.

''So, one night we made full preparations to serenade a young lady. We were tuning up and making ready. I held my bassoon up to my eye and sighted through it at the sky to make sure it was alright.

''Suddenly I felt a strong hand grip on my shoulder. 'It's worth 40 shillings if you fire it off, young man.' I heard a voice say. 'You mustn't discharge firearms near the public highways.'

''Well, he was a crestfallen constable when I showed him it was nothing but a harmless musical instrument and played a tune for him and sent him off very much cast down.''

Ular then gave the conversation a 'violent wrench and asked him two questions at once, two questions any musician would feel interested in asking him: what is your favourite of your own works and what do you think is going to be the music of the future ?'

''It's hard to say,' he answered, *'hard to reply to both of your questions. Really I believe my overture 'Cockaigne' realizes about as near to what I had in mind as any. The 'In the South' overture, I actually composed in a single moment. It was in the Compagna on a pleasant afternoon, by the side of an old Roman way. A peasant shepherd stood by an old ruin. In a flash it all came to me – the conflict of the armies on that very spot long ago, where now I stood – the contrast of the ruin and the shepherd – and then all of a sudden, I came back to reality. In that time I had composed the overture – the rest was really writing it down.*

''As to the music of the future, I don't know anything about it. I simply write what I want and go ahead with it and pay no attention to criticism. Why, since I wrote 'The Dream of Gerontius' I have not read a single paragraph in a newspaper or a magazine about myself – not a word of criticism. They might influence me in my work – I will not let them influence me.

"As to my ideas and ideals of music writing – I simply write what I wish, when I wish it and how I wish it – you see I am quite independent – and pay no attention to any man or what they think about my music. As to fame I care nothing for it. When I conduct or play, I never see my audience – never am conscious of its existence. I try to be no more self-conscious than the novelist, or poet or painter, who knows nothing and thinks nothing about those who may read or see his works.

"I will never write 'programme music', never limit my musical ideas by forcing them to express what they cannot express. It is true that in my Symphonic Variations, I tried to depict musically, in one variation after another, the character and temperament of various of my friends – but that is not musical realism, and in the 'Pomp and Circumstance' I have intended simply to depict the military idea in tone – the idea of a big splendid army marching – a display of soldiery."

The Chicago Inter Ocean also interviewed him: 'In the opinion of Sir Edward Elgar, the great need of the musical world at present is intelligent musical criticism. At the same time he protests that he has not read a criticism of his own compositions since 1893. If there is an inconsistency or an apparent contradiction here, Sir Edward did not explain it, possibly because there was no time.

'We sat on a gorgeous but uncomfortable red plush divan in the corridors of the Auditorium Annexe, and nearby stood Sir Edward's man servant with his master's coat and hat, respectful but impatient.

"*There are a great many writers upon musical subjects today,*' said Sir Edward, abruptly turning the conversation from a carefully rehearsed lead as to his ideas upon modern tendencies of composition, '*who possess admirable literary ability, but no musical knowledge. A review of a new composition usually comprises three-quarters of a column in which the critic attempts to supply the composer with a programme for his work, or comments upon the poetic and artistic values of the theme he may have chosen.*

"Then follows a short and entirely adequate paragraph devoted to an attempt at a musical analysis of the work. In-fact it seems that people are no longer able to listen to music as absolute music. They must be supplied with a programme, or, lacking that, with a detailed thematic analysis, in which the passing moods and emotions of the work are carefully labelled and listed.

"Even so, representative and universally respected a critic as Hansilk of Vienna found himself embarrassed when asked to review the D minor symphony of Brahms without the aid of a previously prepared analysis, and after declaring his purpose to estimate it purely as absolute music, he is unable to do so without employing the familiar figures of speech that have become so prominent and misleading a part of the critic's somewhat limited vocabulary.

"He had to write the old stock phrases about 'storm and stress' 'thunderous utterance' etc etc and of the technical analysis on absolute musical lines he proved himself entirely incapable.

"This inability to listen and appreciate music musically is not limited to the likes of those who attempt to write about it. It is characteristic of our entire so-called musical public. People are interested in the artist rather than in his art. In society it is always the personality of the musician that I hear discussed. 'I had lunch with Nikisch yesterday' someone says proudly. But who Nikisch really is, what he stands for in the musical world, this person probably knows nothing of."

The correspondent then asked 'Is the programme music of the present due to the effort on the part of the composers to cater to this attitude of the public and the critics? Is this attitude the logical result of descriptive and symbolic music.'

"Rather it is the logical result of musical ignorance. Programme music is a natural phase of our development but whither this development is leading us it is quite impossible to say. Musical progress at present is a working out in all directions. Each man is going his own way perfecting the resources of the orchestra and adapting them to his special needs, enlarging the possibilities of harmonic colour, creating new forms, or modifying old ones.'

'As you have done in the oratorio?'

"But not with the intention of modifying the oratorio. I have never written a work for an especial purpose or for a particular occasion. My oratorios were the result of an ideal long cherished and slowly realised – the outcome of an artistic impulse, not of a calculated plan. That they have been produced for the most part at the Birmingham Festivals is an entirely natural coincidence, nothing more.

"Our more important musical event is this annual [sic] festival, and after my first success, the management expressed the desire to produce each of my important novelties. As the works were finished I therefore saved them for these events."

The interviewer summed up: 'Sir Edward is entirely logical in his attitude on the programme question and protests that he has never supplied or edited a detailed programme or analysis of any of his works. Like Strauss, however, he has a good Man Friday in the person of Mr A J Jaeger who supplies the public with the hints and guides it so habitually demands. The impression was gained that Sir Edward did not entirely approve of this gentleman's efforts on his behalf. He certainly expressed in no uncertain terms his desire that the public judge his music as absolute rather than descriptive and in this position he has the support of so eminent a man as Felix Weingartner, who protests that the man with the programme book is usually too busy reading to find time to listen to the music.'

Elgar was then given free rein to air his views by the New York Times: *"In America an extravagant curiosity as to musical personages usurps the interest in music itself. A generation ago among those who gave any attention whatever to music one might hear the enquiries 'Have you heard this symphony or that sonata? Let us discuss it.' Today we hear 'Have you heard Campanini conduct 'Aida' or Farrar sing 'Juliette'? Let us talk about them.*

"It is by no means certain that the widely prevalent curiosity about conductors and singers may not ripen into legitimate interest in music itself but it is absurd to pretend that New York, for instance, is musical, because, excited by the rivalries of two opera houses supporting rival artists, you spend your time furiously discussing their merits. Music is above personality and it is a mere impertinence to discuss the merits of the interpreters in the presence of the art itself.

"Is there anything in the world less worthwhile than these eternal personalities? What a pity that music cannot be separated from them. Music is the purest of the arts and it ought to be the most impersonal. A painter paints a picture and hangs it on the wall. There it is. An author writes a book and it circulates throughout a continent. In neither case need the artist appear, though I admit that latterly the public has dragged them to some extent out of the privacy which ought to be allowed them.

"But in the case of music everybody concerned is obliged to live night and day in the eye of the public. Not only is this true as to those who sing and play; it applies to composers as well. The apparent interest of the public in music is, I fear, largely nothing more than a manifestation of exaggerated and morbid curiosity as to other people. The talk which is supposed to be about music – I mean among the best classes and in the most exclusive drawing rooms – is the idlest, silliest chatter. One doesn't hear an intelligent word on the subject.

"The extraordinary compositions foisted upon the public by so-called music critics are a great handicap in the progress of musical knowledge. What could be more dreadful than those remarkable articles printed as literary interpretations of musical art! One goes to a symphony or an opera to hear, to listen to the achievements of an art whose fleeting appeal is to the ear. With what emotions does one read - if he is so unwise as to read – the fanciful translations of musical emotions which the critics pretend to embody in literary art – for I presume they are artists in their way. The most of this stuff is rubbish. It is not a criticism of the music at all, but a lot of words, which may read very fine, yet have no more connection with the subject they pretend to discuss than has the sporting article or the murder story in adjoining columns.

"You have in this country, three, or perhaps four, musical critics who know something about music; one of them in the Musical Editor of The New York Times [i.e the paper to whom he is speaking]. The office boy might write most published musical criticism, for all the knowledge and intelligence they evince. No, I am afraid you are not destined here to immediate musical pre-eminence. I have not heard enough of your work to judge whether you are in process of establishing a National School. I see no indication of it.

"I don't mean to say that America is alone in this matter of gossip supplanting real musical interest. The same is true in Europe, but to a much less degree. I am afraid Europe is still far ahead of you in understanding and appreciation of this art. Mr Carnegie was allowed to say that no English City had a permanent orchestra. We have at least four great permanent ones and the Continent is full of splendid permanent orchestral organisations.

"So incompetent is criticism even there, however, at least so devoid of helpfulness is it, that I have given up reading it. I have not read a criticism of my own work for, I suppose, fifteen years. Neither do I care anything for public opinion. I enjoy writing and I enjoy conducting. When I do the latter I look about on the orchestra and say to myself 'Oh what a lot of good fellows', and we have a splendid time together. When we are through, somebody is likely to pull my coat and tell me that there is an audience there, and I remember and turn around and bow. I fear I was not cut out for a popular musician.

"My idea of musical art does not separate it from common life. I have little sympathy with the class of men who live and move and have their being in music. I prefer to live a fuller life. I am busy with my affairs. I have some knowledge of the law. I am something of a chemist. I sometimes think on the great considerations of religion. The ideas that come to me in the course of an active life I am moved to express in musical terms.

"I decline to think music, dream music, eat, drink and sleep with music. I look with something akin to pity on men who read, read, read, nothing but music but know nothing but music. What have they to say in music? What do they know of life and the real emotions of men, living thus in the artificial atmosphere of their art? How may they hope to rise to the free and pure expression of human feeling which rose in the breast and escaped in the fingers of a Mozart of a Schubert, the world's great natural musicians.

"One never becomes a musician by reading about harmony or even listening to compositions. After all, the principals of music are easily learned; the rest is nature and the soul. If nature tends to express itself otherwise than in the terms of music it cannot be forced against itself. If the soul has nothing to utter, no gift of expression or musical knowledge will suffice to make a musician. How, then, is one to fill his soul except by living – by plunging into life and experiencing all that life has?

"I am known as a composer of religious music. I have been described as a monk, even. I do not pretend to be a 'religious' man in that sense. I live the free life of a man in the world. I knock about Europe. I do my appointed work in my own corner of the world. And then I am moved to express myself in music.

"I don't know rightly how others have done this. I am described as self-taught. I do it as best I know how.

"Religion is a much-misunderstood thing. There is so little of it. What we have today, what we see about us is religionism. Religion has become a profession, a political cult, a system. Religion itself is a very noble and beautiful thing. This is what I have tried to express in the works which the public is good enough to like – and to misunderstand."

When Elgar returned to England, he attended, once again, the Morcambe Festival in Lancashire.

Four years earlier, in a letter to Festival Chairman Cannon Gorton, he had written: *'I cannot well express what I feel as to the immense influence your Festival must exert in spreading the love of music: it is rather a shock to find Brahms's part-songs appreciated and among the daily fare of a district apparently unknown to the sleepy London Press: people who talk of the spread of music in England and the increasing love of it rarely seem to know where the growth of the art is really strong and properly fostered.*

'Someday the Press will awake to the fact, already known abroad and to some few of us in England, that the living centre of music in Great Britain is not London but somewhere farther north.'

The letter was published in the Musical Times, with the comment: 'What will the musical critics of 'the sleepy London Press', make of this?'

A typical reaction came from the Pall Mall Gazette: 'It is a letter which, to our thinking, is from one point of view deplorable, and from another irrational. Dr Elgar can never complain that he has been neglected, to take one instance in the columns of this paper. We have always been among the most outspoken and professed admirers of his later work – let us say, from 'Caractacus' onward. In general, in the London Press, too, his noble work has found the readiest recognition. When one of his greatest compositions was produced at Dusseldorf there were representatives present of the Press of London (including the present writer), who for the sheer enthusiasm of music, took the trouble to travel to Germany in order to be present at the performance.

'The London press has followed Dr Elgar round the provincial festivals – to Sheffield, to Leeds, to Birmingham and elsewhere. We venture to say that no living English musician, however well known, has in recent years attracted London critics so keenly as Dr Elgar.

'Dr Elgar's position seems to be that the London musical Press is so utterly, so brutally somnolent that it is actually unacquainted with the art-work of Morcambe. One may ask at the outset in reply to this extraordinarily unjust criticism: 'Are the musical doings of Morcambe intended to be criticised by the London Press?' Dr Elgar apparently thinks so; for disregarding the natural calls, in the course of a busy season, made upon the London Press by work given in London, he adds: 'Someday the Press will awake to the fact, *to some few of us* in England, that the living centre of music in Great Britain is not London but somewhere farther north.'

'If this be so, then why in the name of all that is serious, should London critics leave their 'provincial' centre in order to travel to a 'metropolitan' centre, like Morcambe, if indeed Morcambe be the place to which he refers, where he might be referring to York, Inverness, Aberdeen, Manchester or Birmingham? The fact is that Dr Elgar's scornful attitude towards London critics, because they know not either Morcambe, nor that mysterious musical centre 'somewhere North' is not only unkind; it is also uninformed. It is in that phrase 'the living centre of music in Great Britain' that any controversy which may be aroused with lie.

'The fact then remains and you cannot get away from its truth that the art of music is cosmopolitan. Therefore, that place that illustrates the cosmopolitan art of music most successfully in any country must necessarily be the musical centre of that country. To pursue the subject any further in any detail would be almost childish; but one or two observations may be fruitfully made. To London come some of our best provincial choirs; in London many of the principal English and Welsh musical competitions take place. Is there any single centre 'further north' of which the same may be said?

'From concert to concert always busily noting impressions and collating comparative merits, or from opera to opera – whether at Covent Garden or at the theatres that thrive on musical comedy – the London musical critics must fare in their daily work, taking a pride in their professional career, and allowing very little to pass them by. This, for London alone, as we have said, they will constantly, too, make excursions into the Provinces or to the Continent, as Dr Elgar well knows, to correct, appraise, commend, or rightly condemn. This is Dr Elgar's 'sleepy London Press'.

'He should have been the last man to make such an accusation as this, which is totally unjustified by the facts of the case. Anyway, when the new opera season which opens at the end of next month at Covent Garden, calls sleepy London critics back from an undeserved holiday, we shall look also for the invasion of the critics, who dwell in the musical centre of Great Britain, 'somewhere further North'.'

The Morning Post: 'It is indeed difficult to understand what could have induced Dr Elgar to commit himself to such unjustified assertions. No one has less reason than he to complain of the attitude of the London Press. In his journey towards fame his road has been made easy by the very journalists whom he now terms 'sleepy', seemingly because they have taken no notice of the performance of some part-songs by Brahms at Morcambe! The word 'sleepy' is about the most inappropriate that could have been employed. One may well wonder if Dr Elgar has the faintest idea of the amount of work a London musical critic gets through during a year.'

Elgar reacted in a letter to local resident Stanley Ridder, who had written to the papers supporting his comments: *'I have not followed the newspapers at all concerning the Morcambe letter: I think your letter is admirable, but the press invariably misquote & assume so much that is false that it is not worthwhile to attempt to put matters straight.'*

Now in 1907, in a speech during the Morcambe Festival Elgar said this: *'I read in the preface to the Festival book that Canon Gorton says that he has been unable hitherto to secure the presence of the London critics. Believe me, you want London reports, but you don't want London criticism. You must set a standard for yourselves. In London I know they have large choral societies, but this sort of thing they have not. In some ways the Londoner, superior as he is, is about 150 years behind in the matter of music.*

'Lord Chesterfield in his advice to his son, tells him not to fiddle himself, but to acquire fiddlers to amuse him. Well, most of the Londoners do that. They hire people to amuse them and they like music most when it is expensive. When I said three or four years ago that the living centre of music was not in London but somewhere further north, I meant it, and it is so still. My critics who grumbled at that expression did not notice until about four years afterwards that we were talking on two different things. They were talking about the music they paid for; I was talking about the amount of music you made in your own hearts and in your own homes. You have music and you make it. There is the difference and that difference remains still, and possibly will remain.

'I said last time – my remarks were infamously reported - that here the commercial element in the matter of prizes had never come in. I reported to say that I advised you to keep the commercial element out, which is quite another matter.

'I made a calculation last Festival and it seemed to me that the most anybody could win was 7s 6d [about £30 in modern money]. Well you know, if a critic is terrified that a man may become commercial in music for the sake of 7s 6d, I pity that critic, and I pity the man who reads his criticisms, because if you would sing music for 7s 6d, what would you criticise for 7s 6d?'

This time, there appears to have been scant reaction from the London Critics – after all, they apparently weren't there.

In the same year, Elgar produced his first Wand of Youth suite, based on material he had written for a family play when he was 12. Robert Buckley in the Birmingham Gazette, recalled Elgar's early life: 'His twelve voluntaries for the organ sold to a London publisher for five pounds, had certainly paid him better than the Enigma Variations, which having been given by all the orchestras of the world for five or six years, brought in considerably less [he was paid one guinea for the copyright]. The music he had given away, perhaps to see his name in print, had brought no recognition. His songs were not given to vocalists.

'His 'Salut d'Amour', which, after fame arrived, became popular enough for the barrel-organs, was so little known that somebody ventured to steal the melody and publish it in another form from which a curious and amusing critique resulted. When Elgar's celebrity brought the 'Salut d'Amour' into prominence, somebody discovered that Elgar had borrowed it from the plagiarist who had really borrowed it from Elgar.

'At what point Elgar began to compose is not ascertainable. Perhaps it is so early that he is unable to remember. But here he appears as the composer of a Suite called 'The Wand of Youth', seven pieces written for the entertainment of the composer's family in 1869, when he was only twelve.'

The Daily Telegraph thought of the work: 'Some of the music proved to be extremely quaint and attractive and all of it was marked by that sureness of touch which we expect from works from his pen,' though it found 'Slumber Scene' 'rather dull' and 'Fairies and Giants' 'verging on the commonplace'.

The Times found 'Slumber Scene': 'charming' ... 'we may be permitted to doubt whether any boy of 12 could have imagined the curious *basso ostinato* which is used with such fine skill as can only come from a mature brain. It is very easy to see a great many of the little devices by which the man has improved the boy's work; effective harp passages and points of imitation speak to every hearer of 1907 rather than of 1869, but the freshness of the main ideas, the vivacity of contrast in the last movement between the fairies and the giants and the pretty thought embodied in the section called 'Fairy Pipers' breathe of a boyish imagination.'

The Morning Post thought the Suite 'one of the most charming and graceful efforts imaginable. The Elgar of 1869 and the Elgar of today harmonise well together. With the adoption of a sane simplicity in the subject-matter and the same concentration of harmonic power upon such unassuming themes a perfect style would be provided for the setting to music of a purely child's story like that of 'Peter Pan'. [Eight years later Elgar used some of this in 'The Starlight Express' children's play.]

The Westminster Gazette thought 'the work is too slight, perhaps to add very greatly to Sir Edward's reputation, though a good deal of the music is pretty and pleasing enough and all of it is beautifully scored. It is interesting to notice, too, how early the characteristic Elgar idiom seems to have manifested itself, some of the melodies and phrases of the suite being remarkably similar to those which have long since become familiar with the composer's later works – and also how little of it is in any marked degree suggestive of other composers or in any way derivative. Elgar was apparently himself from the very beginning.'

The Daily News found the 'Sun Dance' 'Mendelssohnian' but thought 'Fairy Pipers' had a 'haunting beauty'. 'The little suite represents a side of the composer which is not to be detected in his very latest compositions. It rather suggests that he should have long since written a light opera.'

The Observer noted: 'these pleasing and graceful pieces show a melodic invention truly wonderful for a boy of 12. Indeed, with all due deference to the composer's art, as evidenced by his later works, there are few examples of Elgar's music which show such freshness of melody.'

However, it added: 'As music, the suite is undoubtedly pleasing, but, judged by modern standards, even when the fuller orchestration is taken into consideration it is not specially remarkable. It is, however, a proof of the genius of the composer in writing a melody that is at once tasteful and original, and a hearing of the music makes one think that in the domain of light opera, Sir Edward Elgar, had he chosen, might have exceeded the achievements of Sullivan. Perhaps it is not too late for him to make an essay in this sadly neglected phase of art.'

THE FIRST SYMPHONY

In 1908, Elgar finally delivered his long awaited First Symphony.

The Referee attended an early rehearsal: 'So much curiosity has been evinced in this work that I think the record of my impressions as the music became audible for the first time may be acceptable. At the request of Dr Richter, the composer took the orchestra through the work and it is doubtful if a symphony ever received a better reading at first sight.

"*Not a note has been heard,*' said Sir Edward in a few preliminary remarks expressive of his confidence in the abilities of the members of the London Symphony Orchestra, and that sentence was the keynote of the great interest that evidently animated the players. A sharp tap of the baton against the desk and there was heard from the double basses a low murmured A flat softly accompanied by a roll from the kettle-drums. Immediately afterwards there stole on my ear a long drawn out melody played by the violas and woodwind. Its lofty and noble character reminded me of the deeply impressive 'Judgement' theme from 'The Dream of Gerontius' so wondrously expressive of Divine love and infinite pity.

'Whatever idea in the composer's brain inspired this opening – which proved to be the dominating theme of the symphony – it can scarcely fail to suggest to earnest listeners the spiritual power of the love that conquers all things. This thought became conviction when the theme was repeated by the full orchestra, thereby acquiring a commanding and stately dignity.

'A rapid diminuendo and the Introduction obviously ended, for a new theme, the antithesis in sentiment to the foregoing came softly from the strings. It was restless, agitated over its own turbulence. Here was no charity rather selfish insistence. There were explosive fortissimo chords; demi-semiquaver scale passages rushed up the strings and were answered by the harp; and after one of these was heard from the highest register of the violins a new theme, which proved to be the second subject coming downwards with a calming power as of some angelic host.

'The spirit of unrest and rebellion became pacified; but only for a brief period. The first subject returned and with it a renewal of strenuous conflict which continued long and fiercely until exhaustion seemed to intervene. Then softly from the horns I heard the beautiful motif of the opening which appeared to show a better way. But the malign spirit came back and war was raged afresh; yet the first motif was irrepressible becoming more in evidence as the development proceeded, until at the close of the extended movement it prevailed and the end was peace.

'Only twice did the composer stop the orchestra and when the number was finished it was obvious the orchestra was impressed with the loftiness and virility of the music.

'A peculiar sensation of transference to another scene of action came to me with the opening of the second movement. It began in an exuberant manner as expressing the pride of life in early manhood and the music sped on its way with the impatience of youth; anon assuming an air of recklessness and almost fierce determination, passages from the woodwind hurling against the energy of the strings. Presently a quieter mood came with a new theme from the flutes, to be succeeded by another, treatment of these forming a central portion. The first part returned, as expected, but gradually its energy abated as though youthful ideals and aims were being subdued by the realities of life.

'The restrained influence increased, slowly but surely. I seemed to detect the presence of the motif at the opening of the Symphony and soon after the music became softer and softer until there only remained a single note, held pianissimo by the strings. From this, without pause, there presently uprose the chief melody of the slow movement, heartfelt music of beauty and solemnity, rousing memories of happiness and pain; now sobbing as in hopeless grief; anon seeming to find comfort in resignation and steadfast hope and finally ending in the peacefulness of faith.

'A brief pause and the composer raised his baton for the finale. What would this reveal? It would be difficult to place a worthy crown on what had been heard. Such were my thoughts as the music recommenced slowly, as though the composer were collecting his thoughts. Presently quotations and reminiscences of the principal theme were heard until expectation was keenly excited, and then with an exuberant rush up the scale the violins gave out what was evidently the principal subject of the last movement. Again, the note of vigorous manhood was struck, and the music became robust with sturdy life, the joy of which was increased by a second subject.

'Presently a march-like theme came, adding to the general elation and in this mood I was carried on until the opening motif returned to which the themes appeared to make obeisance; but the motif did not come to subdue but to strengthen, and the gloriousness of its mission seemed to find triumphant declaration in the final coda.

'Such were some of my fleeting impressions on first hearing Sir Edward Elgar's symphony. Doubtless the music will suggest other thoughts to many, for to quote the composer's words to me concerning its meaning' '*It has no poetic basis or programme. It is a symphony, a composer's outlook on life,*' and we each regard existence through our own spectacles. But whatever message the music conveys to the listeners, there can be no doubt of the composer's loftiness of conception, the sanity of his methods and the past-master craftsmanship of his resource. Personally, I have no hesitation in declaring that a truly great work has been added to British music.'

Robin Legge in the Daily Telegraph commented: 'I am confident that there was no exaggeration in Dr Hans Richter's brief, but pointed speech. In thanking Sir Edward for the symphony and for permitting him and his orchestra to produce it, Dr Richter declared, with hand on heart that the permission conferred and honour on the recipients. The words were simple, but they rang true. Moreover, Hans Richter is not one given to idle babbling. Therefore, after hearing the speech, if so the single sentence may be described, and after listening to the final – and very thorough – rehearsal and to the initial performance, I agree that the Halle orchestra, a fine body of players, enjoyed a distinctive honour.'

'It is no part of my intention to enter fully into details of this masterpiece now. Nevertheless it is well to record impression while that impression is white hot. First then, Elgar seems, in spite of much complex scoring to have returned to simpler ways and a simpler expression than he employed in his later oratorios. Here, we have much the language or rather the idiom of 'Caractacus' or 'The Dream of Gerontius' than of 'The Kingdom' or 'The Apostles'. He has, in fact, retired, as it were, in order to leap the farther.

'In this he has shown a fine mastery over himself, while his mastery over his means is amazing as ever before. The form employed is, roughly speaking, the conventional symphonic form, with a difference, of course, for the old classical style pure and simple has little enough in common with the moods and the feeling of today. There is here a central theme, as the analyst says, which in a sense purveys the whole structure but it expresses merely a mood and its variations and has nothing in common with Berlioz's 'idee fixe'.

'But thematic beauty is abundant. It is exquisite in the adagio, and in the first and second allegros, the latter a kind of scherzo; when the rhythmic impulse, the power and the passion are at their extreme height, when the music becomes almost frenzied in its superb energy, the sense of sheer beauty is still strong. That the mood of beauty never changes it would be absurd to say but the feeling is ever present that, whatever the poetic basis, whatever the mental foundation of the symphony the composer has maintained from the first setting-down of the central theme to its final exposition in the last pages of his score the sway of beauty.

'For the moment let us stop there, merely adding a few lines as to the reception of the work: There was an enormous audience whose attitude was interesting to watch. After the opening movement the applause was spasmodic, but thorough in parts of the auditorium. After the second it became more general, while after the extremely beautiful and poignantly expressive slow movement the composer was called onto the platform to bow several times by a crowd that was almost beside itself with enthusiasm. Again this scene was repeated at the close and from none was the applause more hearty than from the orchestral players themselves who rose as one man and cheered Elgar to the echo. Elgar has certainly added a masterwork to our national musical literature.'

He added the following day: 'Yesterday I endeavoured to give an idea, however small, of the important character of Elgar's last composition, and I pointed out how splendidly enthusiastic was its reception by the enormous audience, which, by the bye, was by no means purely local since many faces familiar in London musical life were visible in the Free Trade Hall. Precisely why the audience waxed so enthusiastic, why that great multitude 'let itself go' as the phrase has it, it is difficult to explain to a public that was not present – since the question is one of feeling rather than or arbitrary and conventional habit.

'But I have a shrewd suspicion that the intense humaneness of Elgar's unprogrammatic music had much to do with its ready acceptance, just as the public were immediately seized many years ago, by Tchaikovsky's Pathetic Symphony. Certainly, the classical symphonic form does not impel a public – we have many examples to prove the contrary. Nor do deviations from it have any other effect.

'In Manchester the rumour was rife that in some mysterious manner General Gordon's life was depicted by Elgar in terms of music, but this was emphatically denied by Elgar himself, and it may be added that neither Gordon nor any other concrete hero was called to mind by the music as it passed. The symphony bears no motto; it gives no indication whatever of a hidden meaning. For its title there stands these words and these only: 'Symphony by Edward Elgar. To Hans Richter, True Artist and True Friend' (Why in these circumstances, the 'inventor' of the Gordon myth did not suggest Hans Richter as the hero it is not easy to say.)

'It has been made public that Elgar denies having set out to illustrate any particular story or phase of life. He has written in the fulness of life's experience, and such 'poetic basis' as he has used is implied by the statement – I believe Elgar's own – there is expressed here the contrast between the actual and the ideal in life, the innumerable phases of joy and sorrow, struggle and conquest. Emphatically, joy is triumphant.

'It is difficult, I repeat, to give a clear idea of the manifold beauties of this truly astonishing composition to those who have not yet heard it. Possibly time may reveal lacunae in the work which were not discernible on the occasion of the production when one went out for to hear with ears expectant of beautiful and perhaps new things. Yet I must say that, writing many hours after the performance, when the glamour of the crowded and enthusiastic audience is dimmed, hence the sound of their applause no longer rings triumphantly in one's ears, I have still no hesitation in repeating my words of yesterday, that Elgar has given us a master-work.

'He has shunned the pitfalls in which many modern composers have been trapped. Though there is an abundance of sentiment, there is no trace of sentimentality or of weakness. And what is possibly of infinitely more value just now, there is a robustness, a sincerity, a power, a conviction and an individuality that while they give life to the music today, yet rightly lead one to anticipate a still further advance when Elgar shall elect to compose his second symphony.

'For Elgar himself has not previously attained to such heights, even in his most distinguished work; and while he is still in the prime of life, he must not overlook the noble example of Verdi – ever to rise higher.'

The Daily Mail commented: 'It is quite plain that here we have perhaps the finest masterpiece of its type that ever came from the pen of an English composer. I have always upheld the opinion that Elgar's truest medium of musical expression lay in the orchestra alone; and this, his latest work, goes far to confirm it.'

The Morning Post found the work profoundly sad and added: 'It is not intended to imply that the Symphony is monotonous; far from it; its contrasts are wonderful but they are contrasts in colour and not in spirit. Yet though that spirit is always one of either sadness or strife, his phrases are always conveyed to the ear, though a wonderful display of orchestral resource, by a command of tone colour, which in the clearness of its shades, the purity of its tints and the harmony of its hues has seldom been surpassed.'

The Birmingham Post thought: 'It is quite clear that Elgar has found a new vein. While the Symphony is in every way a personal work, reminding us of none of his predecessors in the same line, it exists in a different world from his oratorios and his previous orchestral works. The Symphony is genuinely new Elgar, new both in feeling, in idiom and in workmanship.'

But E A Baugham, in the Daily News wrote: 'The first hearing of this symphony did not make me feel that Elgar's ideas naturally get expressed in a big manner. The merit of the symphony is that the composer has expressed what sounds like genuine emotion. All through the work there is a curious unity of mood, even the allegro molto gradually merging into the adagio, as if the composer's energetic outlook were intermittent and he must perforce return to a mood of nervous and passionate sadness. The prevailing note of the symphony is a sensitive and sad acceptance of the inevitable. This homogeneity of mood should make for constructive strength, but the symphony did not give me that impression.'

Baughan thought the opening 'laboured' and the whole first movement 'lacked motive force and the music gave me the impression of standing still. To tell the truth, the development is scrappy. The little musical ideas are bandied about and not caught up in a swirl of a great emotion. I had the idea that the composer wished to portray the perplexities which beset a soul in its march towards an end appointed by the will, but an artist must make these perplexities clear, and Elgar has not done that.

'Perhaps he has tried to express too much or has not got what he wants to express into proper focus. Perhaps to be quite honest and frank this impression was due to some want of mental grasp in myself, and of this I can write more definitely when I have heard the symphony again.

'Still, my impression tonight was clear enough. In the second movement there is much that is highly interesting in a modern manner, and the composer's use of his material is masterful indeed. But again there is a want of genuine motive force. The slow movement on the other hand is by far the most successful section of the symphony. It is as genuine as 'The Dream of Gerontius', as lyrical and as fresh as the 'Enigma Variations', with a deeper note of passion.

'From here to the end of the symphony, which is by far the most powerful work the composer has done, we are carried along with irresistible force. No wonder the audience cheered Sir Edward Elgar, for his new symphony, whatever its weakness may be is certainly the most considerable composition which has yet been written by a British musician.'

The Westminster Gazette had not forgotten Elgar's 'sleepy London press' comments: 'Sir Edward should certainly feel gratified by the amount of curiosity which his work has excited, though London music-lovers may perhaps feel slightly aggrieved that he had accorded to Manchester the honour of hearing the actual first performance of the work. But then, Sir Edward has never had much respect for musical London and long ago informed the world that England's true commercial centre of gravity was to be found 'somewhere further north'. Hence doubtless his choice of Manchester for the first performance of the work.'

Perhaps the most remarkable review came from Robert Buckley in the Birmingham Gazette – remarkable because it *was* from Buckley. He said this: 'Manchester was shrouded in fog which penetrated the Free Trade Hall and made the lights burn blue. According to the authorities it had the further effect of reducing the attendance which, however, in the end, fell but little below the average.

'There was a great gathering of musicians and musical amateurs of the North but the rank and file of the population was sparsely represented, the galleries as well as the floor had many empty benches, a new symphony having but little drawing power compared with a new oratorio. Then we settled into hushed expectation for the new departure of Sir Edward Elgar, who, from the first has admittedly been a master of orchestration. Richter was to conduct though the composer was known to be present.'

Buckley thought the opening theme 'lucid and unaffected but has no special beauty, and indeed, is a melody which anybody might have written. After this hymn-like melody comes an agitated allegro, arousing expectation which its progress scarcely satisfied; there is a want of spontaneity, a laboriousness, a muddiness which make it almost unintelligible, with sudden hustlings of the brass and apparently meaningless crashes of the drums which seemed to be hastening to emphasise nothing.

'Here the attitude of the audience was one of deeply respectful boredom, accompanied by the usual signs, namely consultation of watches and immersion in the explanations of the analytical programme.'

And of the second and third movements: 'everywhere great skill is manifest, if nothing more, the most is made of the themes but the themes themselves are not arresting. There is more workmanship than invention; more technique than inspiration and the reminiscential bulks too largely: no composer can escape the influences of his compeers, but when those influences dominate long movements the impression is unsatisfactory.'

And as for the fourth movement: 'Once more the effect is of laboriousness without the inspiration which convinces, which lays hold of the listener and will not let him go. Yet the interest of the audience deepened towards the close and the composer was called on the platform and applauded in the middle of the symphony as well as at the end. It was however, largely a success of esteem and not a brilliant success even then. The band scarcely seemed at home with the music; the strings were rough, and other departments failed to exhibit the perfection we expect from an orchestra of such reputation. Succeeding hearings may modify one's opinion, and fortunately Elgar will be able to command such repetitions.

'We would prefer to welcome this first symphony as one of the immortals – perhaps the first immortal of its kind from the pen of a British composer – but with the merit that every work of Elgar must infallibly have there is a dreaminess and sense of over-elaboration which awaken fears that the composition was rather a taskwork than an outpouring of something which must be said, and that while the art of the decorator is everywhere admirable, the material decorated was neither rich, nor rare.'

Lady Elgar noted in her diary: 'Quite beautiful and after 3rd movement E. had to go up on platform & whole Orch. & nos. of audience stood up – Wonderful scene. also at end.'

Shortly after, the symphony received its London debut.

E A Baugham in the Daily News reviewed commenting that Elgar was 'popular because he has something to say, and there is a distinct individuality in his music. Those composers who complain of neglect and imagine that Elgar's vogue is due to all kinds of causes but the music itself, may rest assured that when they can write compositions which move an audience they also will be popular.'

But he said this of the music: 'The opening section was praised with the modification that in the working out the composer seemed to stand still and that the movement as a whole has not the epic grasp of a genuine symphony writer. Nor did I care very much for the allegro molto, original as it is in rhythm and workmanship.

'A second hearing has not given me a different impression. Indeed, I must confess I found much of the first movement laboured and wanting in inspiration. Apart from the fine opening, with its noble first subject, the interest is frittered away in a scrappiness which certainly has not the effect of being an expression of great imagination or inspired inventive powers.

'The composer seems to have wished to say something, which unfortunately has not got itself articulated. The most interesting feature of the allegro molto, which on the whole is hardly worthy of the rest of the symphony, is the manner in which the composer, towards the end of the section, gradually slackens its energy and pace until it merges almost imperceptibly into the adagio.

'The adagio may not be great music, but it is very sincere and real and in it all the tender and sensitive qualities of the composer are faithfully reflected. You cannot ask more of a musician than that he shall express himself. In this slow movement with its beautiful, serene and pathetic end, Elgar has found himself.

'The finale would be just as moving if it did not give an impression of labour in its development. It must be remembered, of course, that the composer's development sections are extremely complex and that he has tried to write in a more modern style than is usual in a symphony. On the whole, then, the symphony is a most interesting work. If it has long stretches of what seems to be arid music-making, there are also poignant and beautiful passages. The work is interesting, too, as conveying the impression of real thought and emotion. It is certainly the finest symphony a British composer has written, and more than that, no foreigner since Tchaikovsky has composed a work of such vitality and freshness.'

The work was performed almost 100 times in its first year alone. During that period the following appeared in Vanity Fair: 'Sir Edward Elgar, be his shortcomings what they may, has succeeded in achieving the almost impossible task of turning the British composer into a sound commercial asset.

'The composer of all ages and all countries has had to limit his gastronomical expectations to the proverbial loaf of bread and cup of water, but in England he has usually been forced to rest content with the cup of water alone, obtainable free, gratis, and for nothing at the nearest drinking fountain. His compensations have suffered accordingly. Grinding poverty and an utter lack of recognition are not by any means the incentives to good work that the rich and successful would have us believe.

'Sir Edward Elgar, however, has proved that this lamentable state of affairs is partly the composer's own fault and that the acquisition of modest competence is still possible – even to an English writer of music. Yet the secret of his success is obvious enough. He has not distained to write popular music. He is the one serious composer whose tunes have found their way to the barrel-organ and he has reaped his reward.'

The article commented that an audience for an Elgar concert was quite different from that normally encountered at places like the Queen's Hall: 'It is a 'promenade' audience, reinforced by a goodly number of recruits from the ballad concerts and the purlieus of the bandstands at the Earl's Court Exhibition. Perhaps they come because they feel flattered that a man whose music they really like should have been acclaimed by more competent judges as the greatest of English composers. Perhaps they come from curiosity; perhaps from snobbery. The fact remains that they do come – and pay for the privilege. Of course, the superiors are apt to sneer at Elgar on account of his very popularity; but then the superiors are usually relieved from the disagreeable necessity of earning their own living.

'Let me hasten to explain that I do not place Elgar on an equality with Wagner and Beethoven because he is occasionally vulgar. There are many things in his music which are extremely repugnant to me personally, but I protest that vulgarity is not one of them.'

THE JAEGER MEMORIAL CONCERT

August Jaeger, Elgar's champion at the publishers Novello's, died of TB on May 18th 1909. Jaeger had been a rock to Elgar's career from the very beginning and in return Elgar immortalised his friend as 'Nimrod' in the 'Enigma Variations'.

The Spectator devoted a page to his obituary: 'No one ever got to know him without admiring his simple, generous nature but the circle of his friends was never large. Even in the world of music, Mr Jaeger was by no means widely known. He was neither a composer nor a performer and though he wrote a good deal in the Musical Times and was responsible for the analyses of most of Sir Edward Elgar's principal compositions, his work was largely anonymous and this fact, coupled with his natural modesty and his delicate health withdrew him from public notice.'

E A Baughan in The Daily News thought: 'Jaeger held a curious position in the musical world by virtue of his enthusiasm. He drifted into Novello's where he made for himself a unique position by dint of his enthusiasm and 'flair' for discovering new composers. I met him almost every day at lunch and the long and heated argument we had remain as a vivid remembrance. The British school of composers owes much to this enthusiastic German.'

For their part Novello's sponsored a memorial concert in the Queen's Hall in January 1910. Parry, Walford Davies, and Coleridge Taylor conducted their own works. Richter conducted the 'Enigma Variations' as well as works by Wagner and Brahms. Elgar also appeared, conducting three elements of a new song cycle to the words of Sir Gilbert Parker, and sung by Muriel Foster.

In the programme, Elgar wrote: 'I regret that the whole work could not be prepared in time for this concert. It is necessary to say that the character of the complete cycle is 'narrative'; this explains the choice of the poems which, sung apart from the work, may appear more suited to a man's voice. It would have been an honour to me to have produced a large work in memory of my friend to whom I owe so much.'

The Morning Post considered: 'The trend of the cycle as far as could be gathered from such part of it as was given is in the nature of the lamentation over a lost love but speculation as to its character is in fact as futile as an attempt to judge the ultimate effect of Sir Edward Elgar's music since the work is admittedly incomplete. But a feature it is possible to comment upon is the wonderful human note sounded in the music. In its general style it is totally different from anything Sir Edward Elgar has written before; the manner is less restricted, broader and is invested with an extraordinary amount of appeal.

'The first number 'Was it Some Golden Star' which expresses a view that the lovers have met in some past age and are living again, is distinguished by its simplicity, but by the recurrence of a refrain of great plaintiveness and great depth. Between its reappearance there is varied but never inappropriate treatment in contrast.

'The second 'Oh Soft Was the Song' refers to a time of possession, again in the past, and is set by haunting music that has the calm dignity of Beethoven, but with a glow suggestive of smouldering fire which is particularly Sir Edward Elgar's conception.

'The third, although entitled 'Twilight' is an 'Adieu' and the repetition of the word expresses a wistful longing that provides a song of entirely new character and places the composer on a still higher plane of success in causing music to represent emotion. There is little doubt that the cycle, when complete, will prove as epoch-making in vocal writing as his symphony has proved in orchestral writing.'

But Elgar never completed it and the cycle remains an Elgarian enigma.

The Morning Post had recognised 'lamentation over lost love', particularly in such lines in the first number [5]

'Have you forgotten it

All that we said?

I still remember though

Ages have fled

Whisper the word of life –

'Love is not dead'

In the final song [6] there were these lines

'Sometime shall the veil between

The things that are and that might have been

Be folded back for our eyes to see

And the meaning of all be clear to me'

Elgar was careful in his programme note to refer to the nature of these words and how more appropriate they would have been for a man to sing – yet he chose a woman. Also the curious numbering of the cycle raises questions. These were merely three songs from an allegedly incomplete work. In the programme they were listed in order of performance numbers 5, 3 and 6 - yet they logically hang together as a complete work.

One is bound to speculate: if this cycle carried in its words a 'lamentation for a lost love' – for whom?

THE VIOLIN CONCERTO

In the autumn of 1910, the Cheltenham Chronicle, recording an anecdote concerning Fritz Kriezler, mentioned: 'It is known in musical circles that Sir Edward Elgar has been engaged for some time on the composition of a violin concerto. A select few were privileged to hear a rehearsal of it in a private house during the Gloucester Festival week; and according to all accounts, the work is one of the finest things the composer has yet done. One enthusiast ensures us it will simply take the musical world by storm.'

Robin Legge, writing as 'Musicus' in the Daily Telegraph commented: 'It is a matter of first-rate interest that his violin concerto is to be played by Fritz Kreisler at the first two – mark the two – concerts of our nonagenarian Philharmonic Society – the composer conducting at least on the occasion of the production.'

'I was privileged to hear a particularly thorough rehearsal of the concerto with pianoforte accompaniment only. This, however, occurred after a prolonged and most enthusiastic description of the work, its main points, its many beauties, and the rest, had been given to me by the eminent violinist who is to introduce the concerto to the world. Frankly, I have never seen a keener enthusiasm in one musician for the music of another as Kreisler showed for Elgar's concerto.'

'Frankly I believe that Elgar has succeeded in a very high degree in revivifying the once moribund concerto form and I believe that that will be the universal verdict. November 10th [date of first performance] then, is likely to prove to be a date of rare historic importance in modern British music, for we shall obtain then the reply to the question so often asked – Is this the long-awaited master-work, the fourth violin concerto in the literature of music?'

The Morning Leader commented: 'It is not too much to say that the musical world has been awaiting Sir Edward Elgar's new concerto for the violin for years. For many years he has been speaking about it to his friends; for many years he has been quietly working at it when the spirit was with him. When it was at last announced that the concerto had been actually finished, musicians were all agog the world over. For Sir Edward Elgar occupies a position which is somewhat different from that of the majority of our British composers – he is regarded in the light of an international asset and has a high place of honour on the Continent. The result is that there is almost what might be termed a concerto boom at the present time, and once again Sir Edward is the man of the moment. The great virtuoso is loud in his praises and has gone so far as to say openly that it is a greater violin concerto than even Beethoven's!'

Kreisler then gave an interview in the Christian Science Monitor to pianist Haddon Squire who had accompanied him in his concerto preparation:

'In your opinion, does it rank with the Brahms and Beethoven?'

'Yes; we have not yet had a romantic concerto of this value.'

'Has there been any really great concerto since the Brahms?'

'No'

'Taking into consideration the newer developments of musical art, how does this work stand?'

'In a way, quite outside; although from the player's point of view it is perhaps the most difficult of all concertos for endurance and it is the first to have all the intricacies of modern scoring. Elgar has told me he regards it as one of his finest works.

'He tells me that he has used many useful themes and that for emotional force it surpasses anything he has yet written. Although the writing is modern there is none of the cacophony we so often get nowadays. A continuous sense of almost poignant beauty runs through the whole work and it is built on tremendous lines, moreover it is easily understood.'

'Is there any new development of violin technique?'

'Yes, a good deal of new ground is broken, particularly in the use of double stopping. Had we not been educated by the Brahms, this concerto might have been thought unplayable.'

'Speaking generally, what do you personally find the most striking features of the work?'

'Perhaps the originality of the themes and the wonderful accompanied cadenza in the last movement, which is a summing up of the whole work.'

'Will you ever play this concerto with piano accompaniment?'

'No. The orchestra is such an integral part. In these days, the concerto is a sort of symphony with a violin obligato.'

'In comparison with living composers how do you regard Elgar?'

'As one of the greatest and I am particularly proud of the fact that he has dedicated this new work to me.'

But the Court Journal remarked: 'Thanks to the championship of those who have voluntarily become its sponsors the success of the work is assured for a time, be the music, good, bad, or indifferent and it is scarcely likely to be the second.

' Here are a few of the terms culled from an article in a contemporary by a well-known writer upon musical matters who has formed his judgement from reading the work on paper :
'Ravishing dialogue – one of the loveliest snatches Elgar has ever written – most arresting force – exquisite gentleness of appeal – brilliant enough to satisfy the most ardent virtuoso – splendid fire and energy.' Sir Edward will find it hard to live up to such a comprehensive eulogy.'

The Daily Mail described the premier: 'With rapturous applause such as might have greeted the victor of Trafalgar the great company gathered in Queen's Hall last night acclaimed Sir Edward Elgar and the triumph of his new concerto. There was an atmosphere of expectation in the hall as the audience assembled for the Philharmonic concert that marked beforehand a great occasion.

'The enthusiasm of those amateurs who had seen the score of the new work now to be first produced and the musicians who were to interpret it had prepared musical England for the revelation of a masterpiece, and music lovers crowded to the great hall palpitating with enthusiasm.

'So, when Sir Edward Elgar who was conducting the whole concert walked, a tall, military figure, baton in hand to the conductor's desk to direct the National Anthem and the preliminary items of the programme, he faced an audience as great and expectant, even if not so fashionable as the premier of a musical comedy might have attracted.

'When, after the preliminary numbers Herr Fritz Kreisler, the soloist of the concerto, stepped, violin in hand, upon the platform with the composer, a tense silence fell upon the crowded hall and was not broken until at the end of the first of the three movements of the concerto there burst out a hurricane of proud recognition of an English masterpiece.

'The storm of applause hushed itself for the assured delight of the second movement, to break out again when that was ended, and then to still itself once more, not to miss a note of the concluding and culminating phase of the composition. Then when the end came, the huge audience went wild with pride and delight. For a quarter of an hour they called and recalled the man who had achieved a triumph not only for himself but for England, and hailed him with wonder and submission, as master and hero.'

Lady Elgar noted in her diary: 'Crowd <u>enormous</u>. Excitement intense -performance wonderful. Enthusiasm unbounded – <u>Shouts.</u> E walked backwards & forwards bringing Kreisler but England wanted <u>him</u> & he had to come by his souse.'

For The Times, the work was: 'a masterpiece; serene, logical, sincere and most original, it shows an assured mastery in the handling of resources which has often been missed in the composer's former works, more particularly in those of later origin.'

But The Daily News thought: 'In criticising this new work one must not remember anything that has been said or written before about it. It is certainly a very remarkable one, and one that hardly any other living composer could have written. But it has one or two weaknesses, although the many beautiful passages it contains make one forget its faults.'

The critic found much of the music in the first movement 'sombre' and the opening theme of the concerto 'not of remarkable interest', but 'for sheer beauty, the slow movement has few equals in music, past or present.'

The Free Press commented: 'The new work proved to be more scholarly than emotional and by comparison with the composer's Enigma Variations and the symphony, it is less effective.'

The Westminster Gazette reflected that the concert included the 'Naides' Overture by William Sterndale Bennett. This was a 'rather curious choice. Was it intended possibly to fulfil the function of the skeleton at the feast and to remind Sir Edward in the heyday of his glory that other great English composers have been hailed before him whose works have subsequently gone the way of all things? I wonder. Certainly, Sterndale Bennett enjoyed in his time a reputation hardly less than that of Elgar today. Yet his music, beautiful as much as it is, belongs now emphatically to the 'dark, backward and abysm of time.''

The Standard commented: 'Englishmen are so jealous of Elgar's reputation, so proud for the place that he has won for himself and them in the annals of contemporary history, that possibly not a few will regret that he should have thought fit to cabin and confine his music by shutting it up in the prison-house of Concerto form, for we feel that it is still a prison-house, notwithstanding that the composer has extended its boundaries.

'Self-imposed limitations and the exigencies of the solo part not infrequently seem to restrict the spontaneous flow – the rugged sweep of the music's action. There is not quite the same sense of bigness and freedom of thought as manifested in the Symphony and the very eloquence of the advocacy leads to the suspicion that the composer is not convinced that his case is a strong one. Melodically it is by turns chaste and sensuous and emotional in feeling, but it does not tear at heartstrings; urgent it is too, if seldom passionate.'

The Observer said: 'Unfortunately in the development of his motives he has relied principally on persistent phrasial reiterations and help-over-the-style sequences to assist his work to a due length. As one of several instances, the syncopated second bar of the second principal theme in the first movement, not a very elegant phrase at the best, is repeated without definite variation nearly 50 times, not counting reflections! Personally I can take no interest in the presumed nobility and grandiloquence of the classic form or the emotion of structure. In this particular work, the form decidedly and obviously controls and cramps the thinking.

'It is possible however to raise even a weakness of theme to importance by raising questions of colour. Daring experiments in harmony might have atoned for much, but Sir Edward has deliberately abandoned any attempt to achieve the musical culture with which his period has surrounded him.

'In 'Gerontius' he made a splendid and effective start on modern lines. He nearly fell away from grace in the Symphony, but in the concerto makes full and abject apology for his earlier delinquencies. I know no other work of the scope of this concerto in which occur so many melodic progressions built upon the harmonies resulting from successions of thirds and sixes all running monotonously parallel to the melodic line.

'I have not counted the bars but should say they provide the harmonic fare of half the work. Of the seven themes, six are supported by this treatment. This sort of thing is the first acquirement of the student and the simplest and cheapest of all endeavours to fit a harmony to a tune, and suggests that Sir Edward has again been searching the archives of his 'Wand of Youth' cupboard, and found interest in polishing up an old concerto.'

E A Baughan, in the Daily News expressed his disappointment: 'There is a want of climax and this want affects the impression that the work makes as a whole. The composer might well elaborate the conclusion of the concerto and sweep along to a more glowing peroration. The music did not kindle the imagination, although it was evidently intended to do so.

'This is the weakness of the concerto as it seems at a first hearing. Its merits, apart from its workmanship, which is novel and full of interest, is that Elgar has had something to say, something personal, something about his own self. The concerto like the symphony is the history of a soul. I felt that the composer had some definite history of himself to express. Indeed, he almost quoted the music he has already given to the world.

'The introduction of the first movement is a theme which is composed of four sections, each with an organic life of its own but making a continuous melody. The first of these sections is distinctly reminiscent of the 'In the South' overture and was used again in the symphony.'

The Court Gazette added: 'Nor could I find in the music any traces of the feminine influence. Sensuous it is at time – and noble it goes without saying – indeed if it were not for its occasional nobility there would be little in it deserving of the name of character, and it is strenuous, if never passionate. The Termination of the work is not effective and the development of the thematic material does not give the impression of being particularly ingenious or inevitable – at least not for Elgar. Undoubtedly, we heard an extremely interesting and able violin concerto but I cannot say that I think it was as able or interesting as the one by Tchaikovsky or, for that matter, even the Max Bruch in G Minor.'

Ernest Newman in The Nation commented on the popular reaction: 'Enthusiasm of this kind can be kindled by a number of things apart from the value of the music itself and the verdict of first night audiences has not always been upheld by the cooler and remoter court of time. I cannot agree with the bulk of my colleagues that the performance was a fine one, or that Mr Kreisler played particularly well. Elgar's tempo at the beginning of the first movement was decidedly slower than his own marking of it in the score and for some time the movement had an unexpected heaviness in consequence.

'Mr Kreisler, though he polished off all the technical difficulties in masterly style, was, I thought, mostly dull and uncertain in tone and rather dry in emotion. No doubt the responsibility of the occasion had unnerved him a little, and he will make amends later; for one can see that it is emphatically *his* concerto in more senses than it is dedicated to him – he is the only living violinist who combines all the necessary intellectual and emotional qualities with the technical power that the work demands.'

The Musical Standard: 'It is impossible to say we were deeply interested in the work: fully to see the value of the concerto one ought to be a violinist. The vanity of the solo executant is most exhaustively attended to in the latest violin concerto and the result is that we are called upon to listen literally to yards upon yards of palpably manufactured music, as dry, sometimes, as anything Brahms wrote. Much of the first movement is Brahms but the Elgarian scoring somewhat disguises that fact. The slow movement is beautiful but in that beauty there is no element of novelty whatever.'

He liked the cadenza which he hailed as a 'masterpiece' adding the unique accompaniment of the pizzicato tremolando was 'pleasing in the extreme', and he thought that the concerto would be frequently heard but then he added: 'It remains to be seen whether the music is as thematically stale as it seemed to us at the first performance. We know a great deal depends on treatment – a gift of splendid themes would not make a concerto or a symphony. Still, it seems to us that Elgar is becoming very mannered in a thematic sense. We would like to see a little more creativeness on his part.

'Surely he cannot fear we should fail to recognise the Elgar individuality if certain mannerisms did not occur! As the concerto stands it is far too long. It takes nearly an hour to play: it is simply ridiculous that the vanity of the executant should be encouraged in this way. An audience does not solely consist of violinists, gloating over difficulties overcome with supreme ease. We thought the fashion of concerto writing had ended, and that mere display pieces of this kind would in future take up about half the time of the usual concerto. It would be better thus, but Sir Edward Elgar thinks differently. We have nothing but praise for Herr Fritz Kreisler's marvellous performance of the solo music. We dread to imagine what sort of impression the concerto would have made without the advantage of this particular violinist's splendid musical feeling and superb technical dexterity.'

Under the headline: 'A PLEA FOR A MORE CHEERFUL ELGAR', The Truth complained: 'Elgar's greatest works are in no sense popular. I am almost inclined to say they have achieved success in spite of themselves. In these works he concedes nothing to the multitude. Sometimes indeed he tries even his warmest admirers. There are pages in his violin concerto which without being stiff yet have little enough of sensuous beauty to commend them. Not to put too fine a point on it, not a little of Elgar's music is severe to the point of dullness. Brahms himself is not more austere or forbidding in certain moods.

'I doubt myself if much of it will ever attain anything like real popularity – for numerous performances and real popularity are not necessarily convertible terms. The symphony for instance has been given a great many times but is certainly not really popular in the sense that Tchaikovsky's 'Pathetic' is (or was). It is listened to with respect, parts of it please and the public is impressed by it as a whole but it never awakens the enthusiasm of a genuinely popular work; and it will be much the same, I fancy in the case of his new concerto.

'Like the symphony it is a predominantly grave and strenuous work. There are some noble and lovely pages, but also not a few of the less appealing kind. A man cannot get outside his own personality, and doubtless it is one of the secrets of Elgar's success, that he expresses himself always with such uncompromising sincerity: but one cannot help wishing at times that he could bring himself to take a somewhat more cheerful view of existence.

'Why cannot he not give us now a good rousing symphony with rollicking themes, expansively treated, reflecting not the mystery, but the joy of life? No one could do a work of this kind better than the author of the 'Pomp and Circumstance' marches and the 'Cockaigne' overture, but Sir Edward has, apparently, become almost ashamed of the mood which inspired those blithesome creations in his earlier and less prosperous days.

'It is to be regretted not only because one gets rather tired of that almost inhumanly remote and other-worldly atmosphere which pervades so much of Elgar's music in its present phase, but also for the sake of the larger public, who find it still less to their liking. Under this head the situation is rather ironic. After long years we have raised a composer of the first rank. He begins by writing popular works, which catch the public ear, and make him the idol of the masses. Here (it is agreed on all hands) is the real thing at last – a native composer of genius who can write music which the people at large can enjoy. Now he must go one stronger and give us larger works on the same line.

'He does – but lo! the larger works are not on the same lines at all. The public listens eagerly, respectfully, with a pathetic longing to enjoy and understand; but alas, with brave outward protestations has to express itself secretly disappointed and resigns itself reluctantly once more to the depressing conclusion that no good music – or at all events no good music of modern minting – can be genuinely enjoyable.

And Elgar was the very man of all others who might have been expected to demonstrate the contrary! It is not too late however for him to do this yet, and I, for one, sincerely hope that he may see his way now that he has sufficiently attested his seriousness, at least to make the attempt.'

Vanity Fair, under the title 'Velgarity', hoped Elgar had a considerable sense of humour: 'otherwise it is to be feared that he is likely to be overwhelmed by the torrents of snobbery, advertisement and flattery that now accompany the production of his every new work.'

Every editor in London, according to the article, seemed determined that the term 'masterpiece' be applied to Elgar's work, but, 'some of us, when we speak of masterpieces think of the Mass in B Minor, the Zauberflote [i.e Mozart's 'Magic Flute'], the Choral Symphony, the Meistersinger, do not use that word so lightly.'

It then commented that the tendency had arisen in the press to describe a work as a 'masterpiece' a 'work only better than the ordinary which is probably pompous and certainly long. Just as an hysterical invasion scare is the worst possible preparation for a contest with the Germans, so an ignorant, exaggerated, hysterical appreciation of Elgar is the worst possible preparation for a proper recognition and a sympathetic criticism of the music of British composers.'

The concerto was, 'of great length, extreme technical ability, wonderful beauty in places and a passionate addiction on the part of the composer to the indication *nobilmente* which I dislike very much. I always find Elgar somewhat diffuse with a regrettable tendency to hyperseriousness so that the British public who love these qualities would probably endorse my opinion.

'This unbridled enthusiasm is bound to produce a reaction sooner or later and that the cause of Elgar is best served by a total abstention from 'Velgarity' – which denomination, I hasten to add, proceeds not from me, but from Oxford, so that of course it must be quite correct.'

Walter Bernhard in Musical Opinion found the general consensus of criticism 'laudatory in the highest degree. At the same time there are rifts in the lute; and it has to be admitted that in the very few instances where the appreciation can scarcely be described as whole hearted, the notices would appear to be written with marked thought and sincerity. Personally, I found the first movement to be what I should describe as fragmentary; the themes or subjects seemed, to my ears, elusive; and at the end I remained unimpressed.

'The slow movement I admired but not to the extent described in other quarters. Nor could I feel certain as to the influence of repeated hearings. Coming to the last movement, the cadenza struck me as a marvellous inspiration which held one spellbound and I greatly appreciated the rest of the finale.

'Several of the notices leave one with the impression that the writers are journalists first and musicians after – a long way after! To these the music is of less importance than the *'palpitating enthusiasm'*, the composer's *'tall military figure, baton in hand'* – not, you will observe, behind his ear (pen-wise) or between his teeth, and the audience *'as great and expectant, even if not so fashionable as the premier of a musical comedy might have attracted'*.

'This delicious notice (need I say in what paper it appeared?) ends by telling us that *'the huge audience went wild with pride and delight. For a quarter of an hour they called and recalled the man who had achieved a triumph not only for himself but for England, and hailed him with wonder and submission, as master and hero.''*

Bernhard then commented on the various accounts of how many times Elgar and Kreisler were recalled after the end of the performance.

Referring to the Daily Mail's claim that the applause lasted for a quarter of an hour, he said that in order to achieve that they were recalled at least 10 times. The Times, he said didn't give an estimate of how many times they were recalled and the Daily Telegraph said they were recalled 'time without number', while the Chronicle claimed 'many times' – 'whilst the Morning Post critic – evidently a cool, calculating hand (fit he, for stratagems and spoils) – tells us that *'twice after both first and second movements the composer was called upon to make acknowledgements and at the close, he, with Herr Kreisler was summoned back to the platform no less than FIVE TIMES'*(!)

'Not too difficult to count after all for people who kept their heads! Why not temper our enthusiasm with a little sanity? And why not choose our words with due regard to their meaning.'

THE MYSTERY OF THE SPANISH INSCRIPTION

Apart from Kreisler's dedication, Elgar placed a Spanish quotation from Gil Blas above the score: 'Aqui esta encerrada el alma de…..', translated generally as 'Herein is enshrined, the soul of…..' By using five dots, rather than the conventional three to indicate omission, speculation arose about the missing word. Elgar never revealed it however.

The Times first night review commented on this: 'It looks back in more ways than one to the famous 'Enigma' variations and the words 'Aqui esta encerrada el alma de…'suggest that as in them, there is a personal significance in the new work. More than this, there is a theme which reminds us strongly of a theme in the last of the variations [i.e. the thirteenth, or 'Romanza' variation] and it is hard to believe that the same individual has not inspired both.'

The Telegraph, translating the inscription, added: 'But there one must stop. It is not for the outsider to pry into such implied confidences. In the music itself, to which the motto is attached, must the secret be sought, each seeker in search of his own ideal. Who shall say – who has the right to say – what is, to Elgar, the true inwardness of the vigorous, broad, masculine opening theme of the first movement? Or of the seductive, pleading little second subject, the charm of which is never lost during the entire work? Or yet again, who that heard it could refuse to fall under the spell of the exquisite Andante, or the haunting, longing beauty of its melodies, or fail to be at peace in the dreamland they create?

'In the matter of sheer humanness in expression and emotional feeling, of sheer beauty of sound, whether in the orchestra or the solo violin, of fancy or character in the theme, or of mastery of its means, Elgar has here undoubtedly surpassed any previous composition of his own. Of that there can be no question. He has done more: he has, as was said, added a new work to genuine musical literature, and in so doing he – an Englishman – has laid his fellow countrymen under an obligation that all should gladly accept.'

The Westminster Gazette mused: 'It would not be surprising indeed to learn that the whole work had an inner meaning, if not a definite programme, though the composer has wisely kept his own counsel on this point save in so far as he has lifted the curtain by the inscription prefixed to the score.'

The Morning Leader thought 'Here we have an enigma not so dark as that of the Variations for it is easy to guess that the soul is that of Edward Elgar and I should be surprised if the guess does not turn out to be right. The equally obvious remark necessarily follows that, if this is so, the concerto must be akin in emotional range and poetic basis to the symphony – and again the guess will be right.'

THE SECOND SYMPHONY

In 1911 Elgar completed his second symphony, which was first performed at the London Music Festival, held in the Queen's Hall. The crowded three-day Festival programme included four premieres, the English debut of Debussy's 'Ronde de Printempts (Number 3 of the 'Images'), 'Gerontius', Elgar's Violin Concerto with Kreisler as soloist, the Brahms Double Concerto, with Kreisler and Casals, and the Haydn 'Cello Concerto with Casals on his own as well as numerous other works.

Under the headline 'THE TRIUMPH OF SIR EDWARD ELGAR', the Daily Mail preview attacked the 'respectful dullness' which 'hung like a cloud over much of the English music of the last century. 'One only has to recall the names of such representative and eminently worthy English musicians, as MacFarren, Sterndale Bennett, and Barnby to realise their frigid aloofness both from the vital centre of contemporary musical thought and from the national spirit, as compared with, say, Schuman in Germany and Verdi in Italy. Things have so far changed that three of Sir Edward Elgar's works are among the most alluring features of the London Music Festival, a vast feast of remarkable music spread for a musical public whom the question of nationality would probably be the very last to influence.'

The key to the change, the paper believed, was that Elgar had devoted himself to 'the lyrical depiction of emotion', and then it enthused: 'Elgar is our first dionysiac composer. He is a stranger to the too hallowed traditions. He knows more of the living seething organism of the modern orchestra than of the cathedral organ-loft and the associated archaisms. It is a newly opened window of song and through it flows a breeze laden with all manner of delicate spices and odorous deliciousness.'

The symphony appeared in the Festival's final programme on May 24th, along with the premieres of the 'Parthenia Suite' by Walford Davies, and Bantock's 'Dante and Beatrice', an aria by Monteverdi and songs by Schubert. Advanced advertising gave no clue as to the nature of the other new British compositions, merely referring to each as 'New Orchestral Work'.

Recalling the concert in his book 'Elgar as I Knew Him', W H Reed, who led the Orchestra that night, commented: 'For some unknown reason it was not very well attended, although one would have thought that the new work would draw a full house.'

There was, however, a plausible explanation for this – and it had nothing to do with any lack of interest in Elgar's music.

The simple truth was that another major event was also running in London - the Festival of Empire at the Crystal Palace at Sydenham. This had opened 10 days before with a mass choir of 4,500 and a parade of 60,000 schoolchildren and was continuing, six days per week, until October. Newspaper advertising raved: 'All the joys of the open country – all the attractions of the greatest Metropolitan Exhibition ever arranged. Something to do, something to see, something to enjoy every minute of the day, from 10am to 11pm.'

It provided Londoners with every conceivable entertainment. There were exhibitions, pavilions from the colonies, a 'South African diamond mine' 'Canadian logging camp' 'Indian tea plantation' a mock-Tudor village, an Irish village, the 'All Red Route' a mile and a half electric railway – promising a '23,000 mile journey through the Empire for 6d'[£2 today] and many other attractions including free dancing in the grounds, 'Bostock's congress of wild animals', 'River caves of the empire – nearly one mile by water through glorious caves', the 'Eddystone Ride – Mighty Mountain Railway and Water Chute' , 'The Great Fire of London – magnificent electrical spectacle', 'The magic ride', 'The castle of fun', cinema theatres, 'Dancing Motor Cars', 'Circling Waves', 'London in the year 2000' and much more. There was even an international athletics tournament, seen today as the forerunner of the modern-day Commonwealth Games. In rehearsal was the star attraction - a 'Pageant of Empire', due for its first performance in early June and involving 15,000 voluntary performers, a band of 50 players, and a chorus of 500.

This Festival with its myriad of popular attractions and doubtless appealing to many thousands of Londoners was thus running only a short train ride away from the Queen's Hall, on the same evening as the concert featuring Elgar's symphony. Furthermore, the weather was conducive for such an open-air event. May 1911 was unusually hot and during the period when the symphony was first performed, the days were long with considerably more sunshine than average and temperatures reached almost 30 degrees C – the hottest May days for more than 40 years. It is little wonder therefore that attendance at the concert at the end of an expensive three-day musical festival in an enclosed concert hall on a beautiful, sunny, hot, May evening, was below expectation.

Reed failed to mention this.

However, his narrative continued about the reaction to the performance: 'The audience seemed unmoved and not a little puzzled. Was the work so difficult to understand? That the composer noticed the coolness of its reception at this first performance was very clear. He was called to the platform several times, but missed that unmistakable note perceived when the audience, even an English audience, is thoroughly roused and worked up, as it was after the violin concerto or the first symphony. He said pathetically to the author, *'What is the matter with them, Billy? They sit there like a lot of stuffed pigs.'*'

Reed's recollection, written in 1936, has long been the accepted version of what occurred that night. The critics who attended, however, provided differing testimony.

The Pall Mall Gazette said the symphony was performed 'before a large audience'. The Daily Express: 'Sir Edward Elgar, who conducted, and who received a great ovation at the close of his task could not have wished for or imagined a finer introduction to the public for his work than that given by members of the Queen's Hall Orchestra.' The Globe: 'the symphony made the deepest possible impression and was received with unbounded enthusiasm.' The Daily Mail: 'The symphony was received with unhesitating and cordial warmth.'

The Daily Graphic: 'We went to the Queen's Hall last night, we confess, not without a certain sense of misgiving. Was it possible that the new symphony could be all that we hoped and desired? Could Elgar repeat the miracle of two and a half years ago? Would he be able to live up to the standard set by himself? The answer came triumphantly last night from a thousand throats.'

The Referee: 'At the close the applause was loud and long.' The Star: 'At the end the composer who conducted was several times recalled and loudly cheered.' The Evening News: 'The symphony was produced before a brilliant audience.' The Musical Times: 'It was enthusiastically received the composer being frequently recalled.' Glasgow Herald: 'Sir Edward was received with great enthusiasm.' The Western Mail: 'The packed enthusiastic audience readily recognised that the wonderful promise of the great composer is being abundantly fulfilled. This great and glorious production did not weaken the audience's appreciation for the other good things of the concert.' Western Daily Press: 'There was a full house at this evening's concert of the London Musical Festival when Sir Edward Elgar's Second Symphony was given its first hearing…Sir Edward was recalled time after time.'

The Aberdeen Free Press: 'Needless to say the composer came in for an enthusiastic demonstration at the end.' The Scotsman: 'In the interpretation of the composition the Queen's Hall Orchestra played magnificently, conducted by the composer, who had repeatedly to come forward at the close, amid continued cheering and applause.' The Queen: 'The performance under the direction of the composer was admirable, and at the close he received a brilliant ovation.'

For The Times, the symphony: 'may at once be said confidently to be a great deal better than his first and two of its movements undoubtedly reach very near the level of the Variations and the Violin Concerto – that is to say they touch the composer's highest mark. The work was received with much favour, though with rather less enthusiasm than usual, and the composer, who conducted it, was repeatedly called at the close.'

Other critics tended to agree with Reed's assessment of the audience but attempted to provide logical solutions.

The Westminster Gazette noted the numbers of empty seats adding: 'The fact only went to illustrate the difficulty of the concert-giver's business just now, for a new work by Elgar has hitherto been the surest of sure draws.' And The Ladies Field: 'One would have supposed that a crowded hall would have been present but it was one of the thinnest audiences of the week and the symphony was received with no particular enthusiasm. Everybody was careful to say the obvious and to confine themselves to generalities about it. From no one could a definite opinion be extracted.'

The Daily Telegraph sought to explain: 'No doubt yesterday's experience when the third concert in the London Music Festival occurred was, in a high degree, trying to the inexperienced concert goer. For the whole instrumental part of the programme bore the legend 'first performance' and we all are aware that the amateur is supposed to prefer the known to the unknown.'

Referring to the crowded programme, The Musical News commented: 'Three new orchestral works of major importance and all by British composers were given at the concert of the London Music Festival and it was a subject of comment that they failed to attract a very crowded audience. Even in the cheap seats many vacant places were to be seen and it is evident that London is suffering from a plethora of music just now. The composer was more than once recalled but there were no scenes of enthusiasm comparable to those evoked on the occasion of the first performance of the earlier symphony or of the concerto.'

The Bystander, under the subtitle 'The Empty Seat Scandal', reviewed: ''*The Musical World'*, as we know – for have not Mrs [Rosa]Newmarch [who wrote the previews and programme notes for the orchestra] and at least half the Press proclaimed it from the housetops? -has *'awaited with keen interest the appearance of another great work'* from the pen of our leading composer. So keen was the interest indeed, that the more expensive seats of the Queen's Hall at the first production were respectably filled, while not more than one half of the balcony stood empty. So much for the musical world, whose enthusiasm might damp a volcano!'

For St James's Gazette: 'The impression the work made on the audience could not be gauged with certainty from the applause. Till the composer returned to the platform anything like enthusiasm was wanting. After that, however, it ran high and Sir Edward had to respond many times to the calls. But as regards the majority of the audience judgement will be suspended. It was the same with the first Elgar symphony; though with the more recent violin concerto – due doubtless to the popularity of its first exponent, Mr Kreisler – an unmistakable public judgement in its favour was given on the spot. Yet the drawing power of the symphony in the first months of its existence exceeded that of the concerto. The English music-loving public has heard so much of its own ignorance as compared with that of concert-goes abroad that it has not the courage of its own convictions, particularly in the case of a new native work of complex character.'

The People: 'The symphony was warmly received by an audience not half large enough, and the enthusiasm was less marked than might have been expected.' The Manchester Courier: 'The composer was twice recalled, though not so rapturously as his colleagues.'

The Sunday Times, while noting the lack of audience, sought to provide a reason: 'the obvious explanation seems to be that the old aversion of our musical public from musical novelty is beginning to reassert itself. Possibly indeed the inordinate amount of anticipatory description had defeated its own purpose and staled the attraction of the work before it came to a hearing. It is an undoubted advantage that the public should have a general idea of the plan and purpose of a new musical work in the large form but it is a mistake to fill up the cup of expectation to overflowing.'

The Academy cautioned: 'The present writer is conscious of unhappy sensations of inferiority when he finds himself at Queen's Hall in the midst of an eager throng of the rapturous and the hopeful about to hear a new magnum opus by the admirable composer Sir Edward Elgar.

'If he were allowed to hear Sir Edward's clever music without having to accept it as something superhuman, to delight in the beauty of the orchestral colouring, to be charmed by the deft interweaving of themes and the graceful elegance of the lyrical passages: if he might say *'this is very pleasant to listen to, and happy is the nation that can produce so talented a composer'*, he would not feel so wretchedly inferior, so disposed to reproach the Providence which has seen fit to deny him the full enjoyment of the Elgar masterpieces.

'But he knows that he is among those to whom these compositions are very great masterpieces, something sublime and wonderful. For these, a great day has come; they are confident of an hour's exquisite thrill. Breathlessly they listen, their faces excited yet reverent; and there are some who, though they look bored, will, before midnight, have written an ecstatic poem of praise in their journal.

'Is his inability to share in the universal enthusiasm a sign that the age of musical fogeydom has arrived to the solitary who can only enjoy the new symphony with a tempered pleasure? He fears that it must be so, for he knows of a young whipper-snapper, who cannot be more than forty, who thinks Elgar a much greater composer than Schubert, and it is hopeless for him ever to try and reach the platform from which such a judgement can be delivered.

'Yet would he be thankful if his limitations were not so great, if he were permitted to feel the enthralling power of all this music, if he could honestly recognise in Sir Edward Elgar, the profound philosopher, the prince of mystics, the 'sanest of the moderns', as he is told he ought? But on the evening when Elgar's Second Symphony was produced it was difficult to repress an inquiry as to the possibility that the number of the enthusiasts about the composer's music is not increasing, nay, that it may even be diminishing.

'One had naturally supposed that according to the custom, every seat in the hall would be occupied for so great an occasion. This, however, was far from being the case. The gallery, indeed, which is usually besieged by members of what is certainly the backbone of the musical amateur class (for not only do you pay less for your seat there, but you hear better than anywhere else) was almost empty!

'In all seriousness, one suspected that the gallery amateurs had stayed away because they feared to find no room there: otherwise it seems impossible to account for the sparse attendance. While unable to join with the young people who exalt Elgar above Schubert & Co, we certainly look upon the premier of a new symphony by so deservedly popular and eminent an Englishman as an occasion when Queen's Hall should be entirely filled. We believe that the reputation of Elgar as a composer will be all the more fairly established when his adorers have ceased, in speaking and writing about him, to '*toss their splendid epithets about them*' in the way they do.

'It will be time to begin to regard him as a great prophet when we see the depth and extent of the influence he has exercised upon the coming schools of composition, when we see, whether, like Wagner, Brahms, Strauss, Franck, he has founded a school. But we must all admit that he is one of the most interesting figures in the history of British music and we were sorry to see the empty seats at Queen's Hall.'

Elgar supplied the programme notes for the symphony, which Rosa Newmarch digested for the first night programme:

'N.B This is not to be printed literally in extenso: it is only a guide. Phrases may be used if suitable. EE

Symphony No 2

(Motto) 'Rarely, rarely comest thou'

[Spirit of Delight]

Shelley

'To get near the mood of the Symphony the whole of Shelley's poem may be read, but the music does not illustrate the whole of the poem, neither does the poem entirely elucidate the music. The germ of the work is the opening bars – these in a modified form are heard for the last time in the closing bars of the last movement. The early part of the 1st movement consists of an assemblage of themes. The spirit of the whole work is intended to be high & pure joy: there are retrospective passages of sadness but the whole of the sorrow is smoothed out and ennobled in the last movement, which ends in a calm & I hope & intend, elevated mood.

'*N.B. <u>private</u>*

'The second movement formed part of the original scheme – before the death of King Edward; - it is elegiac but has nothing to do with any funeral march & is a 'reflection' suggested by the poem. The Rondo was sketched on the Piazza of S. Mark, Venice. I took down the rhythm of the opening bars from some itinerant musicians who seemed to take a grave satisfaction in the broken accent of the first four bars. The last movement speaks for itself I think: a broad sonorous, rolling movement throughout – in an elevated mood. In the second movement the feminine voice <u>laments</u> over the broad main 1st theme and may not [87] be like a woman dropping a flower on a man's grave?'

In addition to the Shelley 'motto', the symphony carried this: *'Dedicated to the memory of His late Majesty King Edward VII – This symphony designed early in 1910 to be a loyal tribute bears its present dedication with the gracious approval of His Majesty the King.'*

Robin Legge, in the Daily Telegraph had previewed the symphony thus: 'The touch of nature in the [Shelley] poem itself and its slight connection with the Symphony only emphasise what all Elgar's friends know, namely, that he has a love, almost inordinate, of Nature. And I have no doubt whatever in my own mind that when Elgar originally imagined the idea of a symphony around, as it were, the life of late King Edward VII, for him, King Edward was in this case not so much King as an intense lover of Nature, of out-of-door life and all that that implies – a type, not merely a human being.

'Elgar himself has declared the spirit of the Symphony to be a high and pure joy, and those who have felt that in his previous compositions the element of wistfulness, of a kind of mysticism, predominated, will indeed welcome the development, if so it may be called. This of course is not intended to mean that the joy is unalloyed.'

The paper's review – presumably also by Legge –concluded: 'Never before has Elgar given us in terms of music so much of the joy of living as in the opening movement, with all its breezy, blustering sunshine and alternating calms, and its brilliant blaze of colour or such exhilaration as is found in the closing pages which roused the audience to much enthusiasm. Without any hesitation whatever it may be declared that in almost every particular this second symphony is superior to Elgar's first. Nay we are not at all sure that any qualification is necessary at all.

'There seems to be a firmer grip, not only of the symphonic form but of the substance expressed within its confines. And never before has Elgar given us in terms of music so much of the joys of living as in the opening movement, with all its breezy blustering sunshine and alternating calms and its brilliant blaze of colour or such exhilaration as is found in the closing pages, which roused the audience to much enthusiasm.'

He found the Rondo 'remarkable' though confessed to be confused by it, and the finale he found 'surely the most noble piece of pure music that Elgar has yet conceived or at least uttered. It sets its seal at once upon the composer and stamps his symphony as a work of rare and real beauty and significance and a triumph of expression and emotion. Most appealing is the serene and happy ending and most dignified.'

The second movement was already considered then by some, as a funeral march, and possibly some sort of evocation of the state funeral of Edward VII – a notion which still exists today - but the Telegraph critic commented: 'Surely this is a strange misnomer. Far more is it suggested as a poignant, deeply-felt lament in its elegiac pathos and Elgarian introspection. Intimate and immensely solemn, it brings up memories of the earlier Elgar more than any other of the four movements and it made a profound impression.'

The Globe exalted: 'A veritable paean of happiness, a glorious monument of tone, raised in honour of the sheer joy of living: that, perhaps, is the most fitting description. Rarely have we heard music so rich in the very essence of happiness and delight as is that of this new Symphony. In the first movement we have the joy of the springtime of life, overshadowed for a moment by a cloud which soon passes and leaves the air ablaze with rapture and sunshine. The joy of the second movement is less gay and light hearted but it is no less real. It is a joy of peace and contentment rising to the topmost heights of quiet exultation. In the Rondo we have the joy of action and, in a few curious and deeply interesting pages, to which at first it is not easy to find the clue what must surely be intended for the joy of conflict and battle. In the finale we have the very epitome of all joys – a tremendous, overpowering, overwhelming delight, depicted in bold splashes of gorgeous colours.'

The Daily Mail headline hailed the symphony as 'A BACCHANAL RIOT IN MUSIC – ORGY OF COLOUR AND JOY' - and then went on: 'The first movement plunged us with its restless, hurrying twelve-eight rhythm into a mood of wild exhilaration. One formed a mental picture of Bacchus and his train of riotous satyrs in pursuit of Ariadne. Emotionally the movement is a series of climaxes of hysterical, frenzied pleasure with several entrancing interludes of luxurious repose. Most vivid and exciting is the actual end of the movement – there is a blazing crescendo on the brass, the strings flare into arpeggios and in a mad chromatic scamper the wood-wind rushes up to the final chord. It is like a flash of shrieking fauns seen in a forest glade.'

As far as the second movement was concerned, the Mail also dismissed that it was a funeral march: 'Though it is in the tragic key of C Minor it might only have meant the voluptuously descending twilight in a Cytherean isle' while the Rondo – which the critic labelled the Scherzo – 'takes us back to the Aegean bacchanalia.'

However, the critic found the opening of the final movement 'dull' and was puzzled that it seemed to end 'in a tender and serious mood.'

The Referee thought the work 'an invocation to joy' and then went on to label the four movements: '1. The exuberance of joy 2. The sorrow that mars happiness 3. The light side of life, its humour, its contradictions and romance 4. The sober joys of experience.'

The Daily Graphic exclaimed: 'Spring is its fount of inspiration and the Spirit of Delight, whom its motto invokes, hovers over it from first to last. The first movement strikes the prevailing note of the whole work. Spring is its theme - the spring of which artists dream and musicians sing! All that Spring ever meant to a poet is here transmuted into sound – the rising sap, the bursting bud, and wild bird-raptures in the clear March heavens.'

The Evening Times declared: 'Joining hands with Elgar we went away into fairyland. The great English master waved his wand and straightaway we all became happy children, drinking in the streams and streams of melody which chased each other like tiny torrents tumbling down a mountain side'

The Sunday Times however, said this: 'Though the composer repudiates any express programme, he has declared the spirit of the work to be a high and pure joy. But this is hardly the impression of a first hearing. Rather the moods of the work suggest the pleasure that is taken sadly, the high spirits that are forced, the smile that dies away in a sigh.'

And the critic for the Glasgow Herald – who dismissed immediately any connection between the dead King and the symphony, and similarly dismissed a literal connection with the motto continued: 'It must not be thought that this new symphony is just a bustling picture of gaiety and jocundity. The first movement, for instance, full as it is of impetuous energy has a curious cast of introspectiveness.'

As to the quality of the work, the critics were thoroughly divided. Some thought it a greater achievement than anything which Elgar had produced before and derided the sparse attendance. But others differed in their opinions.

The Westminster Gazette critic commented: 'perhaps it is not altogether a matter of surprise that it proved, to some extent disappointing. After the prodigious success achieved by his first symphony and later by his violin concerto, it would indeed have been remarkable if he had been able to go one better again or even to have realised to the full the tremendous expectations which have been built up on those works. This new symphony contains some splendid pages, but it can hardly be said to mark an advance on those earlier works, if, indeed, it is the equal of either. First impressions certainly suggested that in this work Elgar has rather marked time than broken fresh ground.'

The critic did notice, however, one feature of the Rondo which many of the other critics missed : 'A noteworthy feature is the prominence given to a theme from the first movement of a curiously sinister character which is thundered out by the brass with remarkable effect – one of those enigmatic touches with which Elgar loves to pique the curiosity of his hearers.'

The Pall Mall Gazette concluded: 'It tells us nothing fresh. Lacking in an equal lack of distinctiveness to that of the First Symphony it can hardly bear comparison therewith. Emotionally the expression is curiously undecided and there is often a strong air of the manufactured.'

E A Baughan in The Daily News: 'The music is not so genuine an expression of Elgar's temperament as the first symphony and that he has tried hard to achieve a bigness and a strength which are foreign to him. The fault of the new symphony is that it is too apparent. The climaxes are too often the climaxes of mere noise. As a whole Elgar has laid on his colours too thickly in this symphony. He has tried too hard to be forcible.'

Francis Toye in The Bystander, following remarks about the sparse attendance commented that while he generally liked the symphony: 'it is distinctly less pretentious than its much-boomed predecessor. It does not appear to be so earnest or so introspective but it is just as long – which is equivalent to saying it is too long.'

The Wagner scholar John F Runciman, writing in The Saturday Review, while saying that it was impossible for him to give a definitive comment on the symphony until he had heard it again, nevertheless thought: 'The characteristic of the symphony is woodiness. There is no life, no savour or flavour in the themes; and the treatment of them is purely mechanical. There is plenty of the whining tones, but in the case of Elgar this unenjoyable feature comes, I think, not from any fear or funk of life but from a desire to get modernity, up-to-datedness, by a free use of chromatics.

'The best movement is the third – it at any rate has spirit and go. The largo [sic] is a very poor thing: it is pompous and has sorrowful accents, but it means nothing. Throughout the symphony sequences are employed freely, lavishly – sequences, these awful signs of an exhausted invention. Some of my readers will remember how Gounod, in his dreary old age, wrote a dreary oratorio called 'Mors et Vita' which consisted wholly of sequences. The man had nothing to say but the money was forthcoming for an oratorio and the music paper had to be covered with notes. Perhaps Sir Edward will take the hint. He is becoming the legitimate successor of the all-powerful trio of ancient days; and I must say that both Stanford and Mackenzie in their prime did finer work than he has yet given us.'

Runciman, in the same article said this of Debussy's 'Images' receiving its full British premier: '[they are] poor enough stuff. I quite agree with [the journalist] Mr Filson Young who said that no man had ever greater facility of expression and less to express than Debussy. One or two pretty snatches of melody occur, but the bulk of the music is made up entirely of instrumental effects. The miserable whining accents throughout are deplorable. When I listen to such music as this, and to portions of Strauss's 'Salome' and to Elgar's concerto and to the same composer's new symphony, I wonder what on earth the men are afraid of.'

M.A.P. – 'Mainly About People' - a left of centre newspaper founded by the radical M.P. T.P. O'Connor, and whose contributors included George Bernard Shaw, H G Wells, Arnold Bennett and G K Chesterton ran a piece entitled 'THE EXPERTS AND SIR EDWARD ELGAR – AMAZING INABILITY TO RECOGNISE A FUNERAL MARCH'.

This was a satirical review of some of the things which the other papers had written. The anonymous author, who admitted he had not heard the work himself and was merely reviewing the reviews which were on his desk, wished 'to demonstrate the extraordinary unanimity with which these eminent authorities on music agree to differ on the simplest questions of fact.'

After comparing the various differing reviews of the work – some exalting its *'genius'* while others considering it *'unpromising'*, the author then moved to his main point about the second movement: 'Now I should have thought that if there was one thing clearer than another it was the question whether Sir Edward Elgar did or did not introduce a funeral march into his slow movement. If the critics can't tell a funeral march when they hear it, it is really time they emptied their fountain pens and took to pianolas or barrel-organs.

'The Daily Express is perfectly certain that the symphony does contain *'the funeral march of the future'*. It says so in a headline, and it adds: *'But the culminating glory of the new work is the second movement which will probably become established as the Funeral March of the near future. In spirit and expression it is worthy to be ranked among the famous solemn outpourings of the same kind, by Handel, Chopin, Beethoven and Mendelssohn.'*

'There is not getting behind that, and the Star says positively: *'The second movement is a dignified funeral march,'* adding that *'it is built up over strangely persistent figure of four notes with a wide leap.'* The Pall Mall says that the Larghetto (carefully to be distinguished from spaghetto and ghetto) is *'in the character of a funeral march'*. But other critics absolutely deny the funeral aspect of the music. Says The Globe: *'The slow movement has, it is true, been described as a funeral march, but in point of fact it is nothing of the kind...nor can the music itself bear any such interpretation.'*

'The Daily Telegraph admits that King Edward has been succeeded by King George – an important point of chronology – but in a paragraph entitled *'Noble Pathos'* it says that the term 'funeral march' is *'a strange misnomer'*. The slow movement is really *'a deeply poignantly felt lament'* with *'elegiac pathos and Elgarian introspection'* – whatever Elgarian introspection may be.

'I will add one or two remarks on the finale. Thus writes The Globe: *'In the finale we have the very epitome of all joys– a tremendous, overpowering, overwhelming delight, depicted in bold splashes of gorgeous colours. And the music in which these joys are portrayed is extraordinarily vivid and striking. There is hardly a page of the score which is not rich in pliant, supple melodies, of great beauty and strong individuality.'*

'This is surely as final as the finale itself. But what says the Daily Mail: *'The dull opening theme (of the finale) really suggests one of those featureless 'subjects' which the pedagogues invent solely with a view to contrapuntal treatment.'* The Westminster adds: *'This movement is rather tedious.'* If only the critics could be subjected to a little contrapuntal treatment it would greatly simplify the musical columns of the daily newspapers. Over the Elgar symphony these eminent gentlemen have surely surpassed themselves!'

Others looked behind the dedication and the motto for the inner meaning of the symphony, as the critic in the Observer concluded: 'The whole work compels our admiration for being a genuine reflection of personality – the personality (we mean) which consists not in a characteristic use of orchestral colour, but rather in the working of one mind expressed in music. In this symphony we have, what to us seems the genuine expression of a great personality in great music. And for no other reason the work would stand above everything else that Elgar has written by reason of its finale alone.'

Charles Graves in The Spectator reflected at length on the work, noting that there had never been such a diversity of opinions on one work than this, and that some of the critics had been puzzled that the motto from Shelley seemed out of kilter with what they thought had been the general 'joyous' nature of the music.

'To the present writer,' he said, 'the lines of Shelley, so far from being baffling, are admirably chosen, and most accurately indicate the temper and atmosphere of the work. Of joy or gaiety there is little or none; the radiant or serene moments are few and far between, and the attempt to read laughter into the score seems to us an extraordinary piece of misrepresentation.'

The critic in the Musical Standard said this: 'Elgar possesses so consummate a mastery over his means of expression that there is not much room for ambiguity in reading the import of his music. There is nothing whatever in the nature of difficulty or hesitation in his technique, so that we do really get his import direct and unimpeded and some of it in this symphony is so intensely on the darker side of things that we cannot enter into the composer's thoughts without a measure of sympathetic regret and even of recoil.'

He thought the Rondo was a 'masterly piece of work' but added: 'In it occurred passages which seemed to the present writer to approach a state of things only to be described as terrible – terribly in intensity of black import. Possibly this scribe was too sensitive and what the composer may have meant merely as a piece of impersonal scenic work was mistaken by him to be so much of the composer's own personal outlook and as such put down with strength and bitterness. But throughout the symphony one is compelled to admit the seriousness of the composer, he is everywhere in such dead earnest and apparently so deeply personal, that such a construction is not easy to admit. In the light of the whole work the right reading of the quotation from Shelley which is attached to it – 'Rarely, Rarely Comest though Spirit of Delight' – would seem to be that which emphasises the first word with its expressive repetition.'

Two further performances of the new symphony were arranged in early June, with Elgar conducting the London Symphony Orchestra. These were additional concerts, occurring after the end of the normal London concert season.

By this time the unprecedented heatwave with temperatures soaring above 30 degrees C. had settled firmly over the country, further boosting attendance at the open-air British Empire Festival, which by now was featuring full performances of the 'Pageant of Empire' in front of a specially built Greek amphitheatre style auditorium accommodating 40,000.

Neither Elgar performance was well attended, and he forlornly wrote to his publishers after the first: 'No one came to the concert last night so I have told the L.S.O. that I receive no fee of any kind (performing or otherwise) for this concert or for the concert next week – most depressing!'

The Pall Mall Gazette observed: 'It would have been better if the London Symphony Orchestra had been content with the last concert of the regular series instead of embarking on two extra events. The truth is the season is too advanced for orchestral concerts, people are too busy with other things.'

The Times thought the lack of audience was due to the hasty way in which the concerts had been organised 'at a time when more pressing engagements than concert-going occupy the attention of everyone.'

The Daily Telegraph described the audience attendance as 'wretched', but the few that attended, according to the report, witnessed a fine performance, and 'loud and long was the applause at the close that brought the composer back again and again.'

The extra hearings however began to dispel any doubts some critics had for the work. As the Morning Post observed: 'It established once and for all the fact that it is a work of immense resource and power and a worthy successor to the first symphony.'

Elgar conducted both concerts in his new capacity as Chief Conductor of the London Symphony Orchestra with programmes which also featured the 'Corsair' Overture by Berlioz, Brahms' St Anthony Variations, and a concerto grosso by Handel.

Runciman, in the Saturday Review assessed both the music, and Elgar's ability as a conductor: 'As we have lost Richter we must put up with the second best.'

Mentioning that Elgar would recognise 'that experience of a lifetime cannot be acquired in half a lifetime', he then went on to conclude that in his conducting of the Berlioz overture - a work he considered 'absurd' – he came off 'middling well' but added: 'Anyone who plays this piece of purely ridiculous music ought to be half mad.'

Runciman considered Elgar did better with the Handel and Brahms works, but then thought of the symphony: 'I expected an earth-shaking working and heard only what I heard a few weeks ago. It is better music than I thought on first hearing but it is by no means amongst the immortal masterpieces.'

The Sunday Times touched on a theme which had begun to grow at the time of the first performance – that Elgar had disappointed expectation amongst fickle admirers with the new work: 'It was grievous to see such a meagre audience for it indicated that the musical public shares the fickleness of the general crowd. Concert-room patrons expect a composer to 'go one better' every time and when that very unreasonable expectation seems to be disappointed they turn a deaf ear to him at once.'

The Westminster Gazette commented: 'The appearance at the Queen's Hall last night was a clear indication that the public has little taste for serious music just at present. The hall was not a quarter full. It was in truth an amazing exhibition of apathy and indifference of the public. Elgar's second symphony might not be quite the equal of the first (though even this is not quite so certain as was assumed at first) but it is nonetheless a splendid work and the public which made so much of the first symphony should now manifest such little interest in this one is inexplicable.

'Doubtless, however, the circumstances of the season must be held mainly responsible. Certainly, there is nothing in the symphony to warrant such treatment. Like all music of real worth the more it is studied the better is it liked. In sum a very great work indeed and one which is permissible to think has not yet been generally appreciated at anything like its full worth.'

The Musical Standard recorded that the audience was one of the smallest if not *the* smallest that had ever been seen at the Queen's Hall. 'Various reasons have been put forward for the smallness of the audience: it is supposed, for instance, that the Coronation has adversely affected concert audiences and a contemporary states that theatrical managers are bitterly complaining of the poor support forthcoming for their ventures.'

However the critic noted that four days after the second concert, 'a large audience put in an appearance in the same hall, the programme consisting mainly of music by Wagner, Beethoven and Holbrooke. It is true that some critics have spoken unenthusiastically about Elgar's Second Symphony. Was this the principal reason why the audience was so tiny? It may be. Music-lovers must place less reliance on the critical verdicts in the press. We do not request them to turn to us for enlightenment: merely to go and listen to new compositions and judge for themselves.'

The critic reinforced his view of the quality of the music in the symphony having had the opportunity to hear it again and added: 'It is difficult to understand how any serious judge of music can deliberately assert that the second symphony is inferior to the first.

'Surely there is for one thing more *originality* in the later achievement! Its themes are said to be lacking in strikingness. That is not our view at all. We advise our readers to hear the work at the earliest opportunity. They will be rewarded for their pains. For it is a glorious achievement! Why not give some consideration to what *we* say about the symphony?'

Ernest Newman ruminated about the critical reaction in The Nation: 'Some of them said one thing, some another; some of them have said anything; between them they have said everything. It appears that the Second Symphony is an advance on the First. It is also a retrogression. The first movement is much the best; so is the second; so is the third; so is the fourth. What more could a composer wish for?'

Elgar did not attempt to write a symphony again until the very last months of his life.

THE CROWN OF INDIA

In 1912 The World reported: 'Sir Edward Elgar has taken a house in Netherhall Gardens, Hampstead, having been advised by his physician to live as high above the level of the Thames as is compatible with his engagements. The house which is a large and handsome one, has been empty for several years, and the local agents had almost despaired of finding a tenant.

'Naturally, there was the usual rumour that it was haunted. The name has been changed and a Latin inscription removed from the door; and the house is henceforth likely to be haunted by nothing less agreeable than the melodies of the famous composer.'

The Daily Express enthused: 'Lady Elgar, wife of the great composer, dispenses much informal hospitality at their beautiful home in Hampstead where one of the most striking features is the huge music room, where Sir Edward may sometimes be persuaded to sit at the grand piano on a Sunday afternoon and improvise for the pleasure of intimate friends who drop in for tea.

'In the billiard room – billiards is one of Sir Edward's chief recreations – Lady Elgar has arranged a fascinating collection of wonderful trophies presented to her husband at the various musical festivals at which his works have been produced.

'Most attractive of all is the Blue Study – Lady Elgar's special pride – where carpet, chair-covers and hangings are all a lovely shade of deep blue, blue-bound books abound and some fine specimens of old blue Bristol glass give a note of glorious colour. Deep blue flowers are chosen and even the blotting paper in the wide writing pad is a deep shade of blue.'

Robin Legge in the Daily Telegraph drew particular attention to the 'beautiful and very ancient brass front door' and the lamp which had come from a Doge's Palace.

The Westminster Gazette noted: 'Londoners will have learned with interest that Sir Edward has at length finally succumbed, after a valiant resistance maintained during many years to the siren-like enticements of the Metropolis and has taken up his abode in a fine house on the heights of Hampstead. They will be pleased to learn also from an account of his new abode, recently published with its allusions to the wonders of its brass door, beautiful entrance hall adorned with a hanging lamp from a Doge's palace, and the like, that the world goes better with Sir Edward now than in the distant days, when London had so little use for him that he turned away disgustedly to the shires again.'

Under the general title of 'Celebrities at Home', a feature writer in The World, after drooling about Elgar's new home '…we open the door and seem to step from the Trianon to a Georgian mansion…' then gave this impression of Elgar himself: 'To anyone who wishes to cross-examine him, Elgar is the most fascinating and elusive victim. He will, with the utmost adroitness direct the conversation into another channel just when you think he is on the point of answering questions which are of particular interest.

'When asked what he is going to do now, he invariably replies that he has given up composition for good. A few minutes later he will tell you that he is still hunting for a libretto for an opera and that he has studied seventy within the last few months; and when questioned as to the prospects of a national opera in England he will say vaguely that the people will get it when it wants it.'

The first work to appear shortly after the move was the music for the London Coliseum's 'Crown of India' Masque, celebrating the Indian state visit of George V, where, in the Delhi Dubar, he was crowned Emperor. A lavish production was planned - the set, aimed to replicate the Durbar itself, alone costing more than a quarter of a million pounds in today's money.

The Times reported: 'On Monday next Mr Oswald Stoll will produce at the Coliseum, for a run of six weeks at least the 'Imperial Masque' which has been written by Mr Henry Hamilton and composed by Sir Edward Elgar. The idea which grew out of the public interest in the Durbar was suggested by Mr Stoll to Sir Edward Elgar, who, in writing for the first time music deliberately intended to be (in the best sense) popular and for the secular stage, has shown himself, in Mr Stoll's opinion, remarkably alive to the claims of dramatic effect. During the first fortnight of the run the composer will himself conduct the large chorus and the augmented orchestra at each of the two daily performances. In composing the music, Sir Edward Elgar has avoided the usual Occidental treatment of Oriental material, though the score contains ideas drawn from Oriental sources.'

The Standard reviewed the rehearsals: 'Unlike most great composers, Sir Edward Elgar plays his own score at the piano, accompanying chorus and solos with extreme care. He goes over separate bars, repeats special passages and suggests alterations in phrasing, emphasis and light and shade with untiring zeal. Then he will suddenly leave his place at the piano and while a deputy succeeds him at the instrument, beats time with his walking-stick.'

Elgar, the paper commented: 'would commit himself to no special opinion regarding his first definite contribution to the programme of a big music hall. *'It is hard work, but it is absorbing, interesting,'* he said during a pause in the proceedings. *'The subject of the Masque is appropriate to the special period in English history, and I have endeavoured to make the music illustrate and illuminate the subject.'*

The production's Director, Bertie Shelton, enthused to the paper that it had taken a long time before Elgar *'capitulated to the proposals of Mr Oswald Stoll. Many months and numerous visits passed before Sir Edward agreed to do this great work, but now I think he is quite contented in regard to the appeal of his music to future audiences. He attends all rehearsals and works with splendid energy and complete practical understanding. Things are moving very quickly and by Monday week, we shall, all going well, be ready for production.'*

Papers around the country reflected the renewed enthusiasm for an Elgar work. The Eastern Daily Press said there was a 'great deal of public interest' adding: 'That it will be a surpassingly brilliant affair there is not the slightest doubt, and I am given to understand that the score that Sir Edward Elgar has composed will cast a powerful spell over the whole production.'

The Globe mused: 'Noted composers as well as popular actors and playwrights are answering more and more to the demands of the variety theatre. Of late foreign composers, like Leoncavallo and Mascagni, have graced the conductor's chair in the music-hall, but it is a good many years since an English composer of the standing of Sir E Elgar has taken up the baton there.'

The Daily Express wondered whether this was the prelude to an opera: 'Reduced to plain terms, Sir Edward Elgar's position is this: He has written a Masque. If the authorities are to be believed, the Masque was the precursor of opera. Ergo, unless Sir Edward turns tail at the last minute and once again seeks sanctuary in so-called classic forms, England may yet possess an operatic composer worthy of the name.'

The Express then hailed the Masque's first performance: 'Sir Edward Elgar's Great Triumph' and enthused: 'Music has followed the capitulation of the drama and England's leading composer has gone over with England's leading actors to the music-halls. The creator of 'The Dream of Gerontius', 'The Apostles' the great 'Enigma' variations, the two famous symphonies and Herr Kreisler's favourite violin concerto – in short, the man who saved our country's musical reputation – appeared in the waltz king's and the star conductor's special arena and swept all before him.

'While not ignoring the part Mr Henry Hamilton's 'book' plays in the success of the piece, nor the claims of the magnificent Coliseum stage production, the call was for Elgar at the fall of the curtain. It was Elgar's day. It was Elgar's triumph. Time and again he was recalled, and with the performers, with the author, and alone, he came forward and acknowledged the enthusiastic demonstration of approval.'

The Times, after declaring: the 'politics are all right since it has been announced that the 'book' has received Royal sanction,' commented 'the whole, is, of course intended to be symbolical and not realistic, and it is necessary to remember this when a smooth-faced female figure, heralded as *'George by the Grace of God, of that great name the fifth'* enters in triumphal procession. Any other arrangement would be likely to be a still greater shock to loyal sensibilities but it may be suggested that it was not quite necessary to identify the 'King-Emperor' of the Masque so closely with His Majesty as to name him.

'Moreover, the whole might have been made to move more easily by the omission of a good many other lines, though some cuts have been made; probably others will be found to be advisable in later performances. The music to which the Powers of India assemble to receive the 'King-Emperor' in the second scene has something of the energy and culminating power which we have known in the 'Pomp and Circumstance' marches, the Coronation Ode of 1902 and the Imperial March of last year's Coronation. Yet though they reflect these things there is no number in the Masque which excels or even quite evens them. We looked for a second 'Land of Hope and Glory', in St George's Song 'Lift aloft the flag of England' and it seemed laboured by comparison, nor when its refrain came as the climax of the Imperial Procession did it thrill us as it ought to have done.

'Agra's song to India, is one of the best numbers but it is rather hampered by the awkward refrain 'O Immemorial Ind' which does not fall easily into music. Sir Edward Elgar has evidently been anxious that his orchestra should not overpower the speaking voices with the result that the music seemed scarcely important enough, too constantly soft and indistinct.'

The Daily Telegraph felt that Elgar's involvement: 'in what is for him an entirely new role not only gives to this Coliseum production a special significance but may be said to mark an important epoch in the development of the modern variety theatre.'

But the critic then cautioned: 'For obvious reasons a production fashioned on these lines offered the composer of the music far greater opportunities on the pictorial than on the dramatic side. And in this fact undoubtedly lay both advantages and disadvantages. For the whole action of the Masque is symbolical and it was clearly a very difficult task to suggest musically this aspect of the work while recognising in full measure the claims of its pageantry. In relation to the latter all-important feature the production called obviously for broad effects of a kind more direct and 'popular' than those one naturally associates with the Elgar most of us know.'

He sought comparison with 'Pomp and Circumstance' but found it 'less ear-haunting'. He also liked the Agra song, and the 'all too brief interlude occurring between the first and second tableaux. It seemed to us that hardly enough was made of this feature of the music.'

The Standard commented: 'Pomp and Circumstance and Sir Edward Elgar are of course, old friends, but hitherto the composer has been unhampered by stage trappings and dramatic considerations. He seems to be handicapped by the fact that an Eastern subject has to some extent demanded Eastern idioms and this has not contributed to the exercise of that individuality of phrase and terminology which are so peculiarly his. Beyond the opening introduction and possibly the entr'acte – little of which could have been heard except by the first few rows of the stalls owing to the fact that variety hall audiences are not yet accustomed to remain silent between the acts – there are few Elgarisms in the score. Again the melodic line of the only two vocal numbers is not particularly grateful, St George's song being in no way comparable with such a tune as 'Land of Hope and Glory' for instance.

'True the orchestral playing scarcely did the composer, who conducted, justice, but the fact remains that neither in the Processional scenes – which often outvie 'Aida' in sheer brazenness – nor in the dances has he written music which is destined to become popular or to add to his reputation. No doubt the score is to a large measure dwarfed by the spectacle, but the impression left upon the mind by a first hearing was rather perfunctory. It seemed to lack character, and character is, as a rule, the composer's strong point.'

The Daily News thought: 'The plan of the Masque has not given Sir Edward Elgar the opportunity for music he might have been given. The long speeches he has accompanied here and there, but he had to rely, of course, on the marches for the full expression of his talent. He has not tried to give much local colour and has been wise in eschewing it. It is absurd to expect a composer to do his best work for a commission of this kind. Inspiration does not answer to any call-boy yet invented. At the same time if Sir Edward Elgar has not been deeply inspired, he has done his work well, and his music helps to give distinction to the production.'

The Morning Leader thought that the music: 'somehow gave the impression of being better suited to the concert platform than the theatre.

The Times, in a long article discussing the whole rationale concerning British involvement in India condemned: 'This music is not based on experience. It is simply an aftermath of a fortnight of the Delhi Durbar – that is a picture of Englishmen and Indians as they are not and as they hate having, for the moment, to be. Let us have some genuine feeling about things that he has himself lived from the composer of 'Gerontius' and 'Cockaigne'.

This report drew rebuke from Lady Elgar who wrote against the version preserved in the family archives: 'Characteristic of Times – ignorance and stupidity.'

The papers tactfully avoided mention that Elgar - 'the man who saved our country's musical reputation' in the words of the Express – shared the billing at the Coliseum with more familiar music-hall attractions, including Edna Lyle -the 'Australian Nightingale', Gus Elen, the 'Cockney Comedian', the bioscope of the Oxford and Cambridge Boat Race, 'A farce in one Act' called 'After the Honeymoon', and Lipinski's 40 Dog Comedians.

THE MUSIC MAKERS

In 1912 the Birmingham Festival commissioned Elgar to write another major choral work. This time, rather than completing his promised 'Apostles' trilogy he turned to a secular text by Arthur O'Shaughnessy – 'The Music Makers'.
The Festival once again boasted a crowded three-day programme including: 'Elijah', 'The Messiah', The St Mathew Passion, Brahms' 'German Requiem', Verdi's Requiem, 'Sea Drift' by Delius, excerpts from Wagner's Ring Cycle, Elgar's Apostles, the final scene from 'Salome' by Richard Strauss, and a crop of new works. Apart from 'The Music Makers', these included the first British performance of Sibelius' Fourth Symphony, 'Fifine at the Fair' by Bantock and 'The Song of St Francis' by Walford Davies.

'The Globe' complained after 'The Apostles' performance: 'Still pursuing their stereotyped policy the committee saw fit to end the Festival with another oratorio. Perhaps they thought we needed a moral corrective after the secular luxury of 'Salome'. They seem to go on the principal laid down by Byron in 'Don Juan': *'Let us have wine and women, love and laughter: 'Sermons and soda water the day after'* 'Only they give us the doses in the wrong proportion. No amount of wine and other things could justify so many sermons and so much soda water as they inflict on us. This by the way, without disrespect to 'The Apostles'; the protest is simply against the fossilised notion that the last word of a Festival should be given to oratorio.'

As far as 'The Music Makers' was concerned, The Chronicle, quoting the opening lines of the poem – *'We are the music makers and we are the dreamers of dreams. Yet we are the movers and shakers of the world for ever it seems'*, commented: 'If, as it sounds, the verse represents the personality of an extremely violent sufferer from nightmare, we hasten to offer our sympathy to Sir Edward.'

Elgar weaved various quotations from his own previous works into the score including the Enigma Variations, the violin concerto, 'Gerontius', 'Sea Pictures' and the First Symphony, as well as 'Rule Britannia' and 'La Marseillaise'' leading The Birmingham Post to consider the work 'curious in design'

'To illustrate the story of those who have inspired the music, the composer draws from his own works, his quotations from himself being made with considerable subtlety. As in the case of a play founded upon a novel, it is necessary to know the original to appreciate its application, but as Elgar's music is now well known, there is no difficulty on the part of the hearers. There is, of course, much original basis and the manner is more free than any work the composer has yet written. His style with the use of matter, more or less familiar is understandable. Though using recognisable matter, the composer employs it in the best manner. The vocal writing is more graceful than usual, and the chorus showed its recognition of the fact by singing it in a better style than any Elgar work has been sung before.'

The Yorkshire Post referring to the quotations commented: 'These passing quotations and illusions are but one feature of a work which is absolutely new and characteristic of the latest phase in the composer's development. It is, of course, quite free in structure, or, rather the structure of the music depends on that of the poem and its sequence of ideas and indeed it is difficult to imagine a composer of any distinction so reactionary as in a serious work to go back to the old idea of cutting up a coherent and consecutive poem into the series of watertight compartments represented by successive airs, choruses, quartets, and so forth, all complete in themselves.'

The Daily News & Leader found the work: 'A glorification of the poet, the artist, the musician. It is the poet, the author says, which is the real maker of history, the real shaper of the world. It is the poet who foresees and whose word kindles a flame in the heart of his fellow man. He is aloof from mankind and his eyes are fixed on a day that has not yet dawned. There is a note of sadness in his lot for he reads the warning of the new day and he must die.

'The composer writes that he too feels how this is the artist's mission, how these are his tremendous responsibilities and how such is his ultimate fate. This feeling, he says, was uppermost in his mind when he composed the Enigma Variations and hence the theme of the variations in one of the principal subjects and the music makers quoted himself indeed freely.

'The whole is full of characteristic Elgarian beauty and is more easily intelligible at a first hearing than any of his important recent works and its instant popularity would seem to be ensured.'

The Daily Post thought the use of the quotations: 'will probably give rise to a little discussion at first until the novelty of it has worn off. The surprising thing is that composers have not previously seen the new range of expression opened out to them by means of this system of allusive quotation.

'Elgar has greatly expanded the applicability of the principle; the appositeness of the various quotations from his own works in 'The Music Makers' is really remarkable. The 'Marseillaise' too comes in very aptly; but one is not sure of 'Rule Britannia' which comes in a sort of burlesque way at one point. It is said that Elgar's intention here was satirical – not of the tune but of a certain British Government. [The Government at that time was Liberal – Elgar was a staunch Conservative.] Purely musical satire, however, is a dangerous game to play for the chances are that your allusions will be misunderstood by the uninstructed.

'This, however, is a side issue. Some of the quotations not only fit perfectly into the general musical tissue but win a new eloquence from the words with which they are here associated. The work should prove popular.'

The Daily Telegraph also questioned the central philosophy of the Ode: 'Elgar himself has spoken of the suffering of the creative artist; the highest ecstasy of making is mixed with the consciousness of the sombre dignity, of the eternity, of the artist's responsibility, and this, no doubt, makes for the sadness of the mood that pervades so much of the music that counts.

'But I do not find on one hearing of 'The Music Makers' that its note is so much of sadness as of unsatisfied yearning. The composer seems to long himself to be convinced that the music makers are what the poet represents them to be; if they are, then surely here is a case for the most glorious optimism, as of the woman whose children assist in the working-out of the world's destiny. Then again, where the poet speaks in general terms, Elgar appears to look at the personal aspect of the matter.

'The music is often of the most exquisite beauty but though I feel quite sure that the Ode represents Elgar in the highest development of his creative faculty, it is not a work likely to supplant several of its predecessors in the hearts of the generality of admirers of that faculty. Its very mood is against it – this mood of yearning, alternating with a confident mood of massive power, and finally bringing a return to the prevailing lack of confidence as if the subject were greater than the composer could translate into terms of music.'

The Times thought the work: 'touches none of the depths of the composer's really memorable achievements excepting by the way of direct quotation. Yet it deserves and will win popular favour and many performances because of its flued grace and beautifully accomplished workmanship. Sir Edward Elgar, is nowadays in the completest possession of his style of technical accomplishments. He can compose those glowing Elgarian harmonies, that rich orchestral colouring, whether he has or has not a considerable motive behind, just as Bach wrote counterpoint. But the agitated voluptuous feminine nature of Elgar's style makes his really 'occasional' work rather dozing. Where 'The Music Makers' falls short is in the unreality of the theme. The Ode celebrates the feats of the world's poets in forging to ideals and the destinies of their fellow-men.

'This is all very flattering to that charming race of rhymers for whom the most important thing in life is their ballads to their mistresses eyebrows. But did a single member of the chorus who sang those words or one person in tonight's audience really believe them? The fallacy of the poem lies, of course in the fact that poets have nothing to do with 'teaching humanity' or in the building of empires or cities, but solely with the charming of one's finer senses and the enrichment of one's inner life. Music set to this Ode could not therefore be expected to have great strength or sincerity.'

Elgar had written at the end of the manuscript full score 'At Judge's Walk 1912' – a reference to a leafy lane on the edge of Hampstead Heath which even today resembles a country lane in Worcestershire, and doubtless then would have had the atmosphere of the native land Elgar had left behind for his new Metropolitan home.

The day he wrote this, he sent a letter to his intimate friend Lady Alice Stuart Wortley, detailing his mood: 'I wandered alone on to the heath – it was bitterly cold – I wrapped myself in a thick overcoat & sat for two minutes, tears streaming out of my cold eyes and loathed the world – came back to the house – empty & cold – how I hated having written anything : so I wandered out again & shivered & longed to destroy the work of my hands – all wasted - & this was to have been the only real day in my artistic life – sympathy at the end of work.

'*World losers & world-forsakers for ever & ever*'

How true it is.'

This was the last of the Birmingham Festivals. The intended 1915 festival was cancelled due to the War. It was not subsequently revived, and thus ended an Elgarian association which had brought forth his four greatest choral works.

FALSTAFF

The Daily Citizen tracked Elgar down at his Hampstead home to interview him about his projected new orchestral work in July 1913.

"*The subject of it is Falstaff,*' he said, '*and it will be given for the first time at the Leeds Festival early in October under my own conductorship. I have, I think enjoyed writing it more than any other music I have ever composed, and perhaps, for that reason, it may prove to be among my best efforts.*

"*Certainly, the character of Falstaff with its variety, richness and fecundity of feeling and thought, provides ample material for a creative musical work. But it must not be imagined that my orchestral poem is programme music – that it provides a series of incidents with connecting links such as we have for example, in Richard Strauss's 'Ein Heldenlaben' or in the same composers 'Domestic Symphony'. Nothing has been further from my intention. All I have striven to do is to paint a musical portrait – or, rather, a sketch portrait.*

"*The work is scored for ordinary full orchestra and occupies 20 minutes in performance. It is of sufficient scope therefore to enable me to present several aspects of Falstaff's many-sided character. The literary basis of it is taken from 'Henry IV' and 'Henry V' and not at all from 'The Merry Wives of Windsor'. In the latter play we see Falstaff almost solely as a buffoon, but, in all probability much of 'The Merry Wives of Windsor' did not come from Shakespeare's pen at all. As he is pictured in the two historical dramas I have named he appears to me one of the greatest characters ever created – as great as anything in Rabelais.*

"*My composition closes with Falstaff's death when he lies delirious 'babbling of green fields'. It will soon be completed; I have finished all the preliminary sketch work, and of the actual scoring only a little remains to be done. I shall say 'good-bye' to it with regret, for the hours I have spent on it have brought me a great deal of happiness.*"

The piece continued with an impression of Elgar himself: 'When strangers are introduced to Sir Edward Elgar and begin to talk exclusively about music he has a disturbing habit of maintaining an unalterable reserve. It is not that he is unwilling to discuss the art by means of which he has secured a high place among European composers but that he resents being regarded merely as a musician and nothing else.

'He has been a journalist, an orchestra player, a traveller, and a conductor; he is an ardent student of chemistry, a keen critic of literature, a wonderful conversationalist. He will tell you that though music is the one great passion of his life, it occupies only a portion of his time and thought.

'His interests are manifold. Above all he is occupied with life, with the complexity of existence and with the warring forces of the world. His manner is almost the reverse of what one would expect from his appearance. He is tall, well-built but slim: his face is strong with clearly-cut features; his eyes are at once shy, frank, and invincibly honest. But until you have overcome the first shyness with which he meets strangers he is hesitating diffident and nervous. Once you have gained his confidence he talks with eloquence, with fire and with enthusiasm. He has all the sensitiveness of an artist, though few artists have his self-control.

'But there are occasions when even his iron hold on his emotions is insufficient to curb his feelings and orchestra players will tell you that, when conducting 'The Dream of Gerontius' the tears will roll unbidden down his cheeks. No modern composer has been more true to himself, more staunch to his convictions.'

Elgar published a long analysis of the work in the Musical Times, perhaps realising that the subtleties of his writing might create confusion – but was clearly only partially successful. Like the Second Symphony before it, 'Falstaff' left both critics and public bemused.

The Daily Citizen said that 'despite its complexity, the delicacy of its portraiture, and the depth of its psychology, the work made an instant success. 'Falstaff' must be regarded as a departure. In form it does not show any great originality for many recent works have made the symphonic form so fluid, and, indeed, so lacking in recognisable shape that it would be difficult for any composer to fashion it into anything new without making it entirely amorphous.

'So far as the music is concerned it may be said at once that it must rank among the most subtle and most poignant of Elgar's works. Not in the whole range of purely orchestral composition is it possible to find a character painted with such wonderful art, such quick insight and such unfailing power. From the first bar to the last we have exquisite perception of tone values and a most delicate appreciation of colour. The thematic material is as fresh and significant as the harmony. The music glows and lives with human feeling; it is the last word in skilful and sincere character-drawing in music.'

The Yorkshire Post thought: "Falstaff' depends so much on its 'scenario' that it is to be feared those who had not studied the score in the light of the composer's elucidation would find it difficult to follow. The elaboration of detail will of course strike one less as one grows to know the work better but one cannot help regretting that it is so frequently obscured by the copious use of noisy percussion which, even if it were not dispensed with, might conceivably be kept in check. Brilliantly clever the work is without doubt, but its emotional appeal is necessarily small.'

The Times felt the two interludes 'bring a certain artificiality into the design. They are evidently there because the composer wanted contrast and found them the simplest way of gaining it. The first interlude has a touch of irrelevance and in order to get the needed contrast of the second interlude the composer has pictured the scene in the orchard as a sort of summer idyll. He has to bowdlerize the story and forget all about Silence's ribald song.

'Another characteristic of his workmanship makes the progress of the 'study' unsatisfactory. The Falstaff ideas rarely merge into one another and rarely become anything than what they were at the outset. Prince Henry's themes do this much more. The same music under different forms represent him in his first conversation with Falstaff in the brilliantly pictured robbery scene and in the march where he appears as King Henry V. But with Falstaff we are always coming back to the same point; his character is not developed in the music. Moreover, the different personages are not played off against one another with any closeness.

'The score is often very full, but not with a complex texture of ideas. There is rarely more than one melodic idea occupying attention at a time; the rest is supplementary harmony and orchestral effect. This no doubt makes for clearness but polyphonic writing is essential to the life of a symphonic study. Elgar makes up for the lack of it to some extent by constant energy and rapid movement, but in many places there is a great deal of fuss and flurry, while nothing particular happens.'

The Daily Mail reported that 'although the festival audience were chary of applause' 'Falstaff' had a great success. It interests deeply as the work of one of the most accomplished of living musicians in a comparatively untried vein. The result captivates by extreme brilliance and picturesqueness and by a truly fantastic vivacity, the characteristic Elgarian vivacity at its intensest. It is a work of a man arrived at consummate mastery of his means who has contrived a speech that exactly expresses him. Not a page or a line could be mistaken as another's. The new 'Falstaff' has an animation in its succession of scenes of tavern revelry, highway robbery and warfare, broken only by the two little interludes gracefully hinting at old dance movements that cannot surely for long fail to exhilarate all hearers.'

The Daily Telegraph was confused. 'When I have listened to 'Falstaff' I have noted its occasional loveliness and ugliness, for some of his music here is undeniably, though intentionally and appropriately, ugly: but I have not yet fathomed the (to me) mystery as to why what I believe is called in theatrical language the 'fat' of the music, is applied to other folk and their doings, or to description, and not to the protagonist himself.

'I do not think even Elgar has written more complicated music and it is for this very reason that I wish a greater conductor than he had explained his complications last night, for much of the wonderous maze of detail in his score did not become audible to me at all. Yet in spite of this I heard more than enough to cause me to realise that here again Elgar has given us a masterpiece of music, and I firmly believe that if he will take his courage in both hands and perpetrate a good deal of judicious pruning – say, cut some five or more minutes, so to speak from his score – his work will be vastly improved and be infinitely quicker in its appeal.'

The Festival day began with a morning concert with Verdi's Requiem in the first half, and a second half featuring a cantata by Bach, Beethoven's 7th Symphony and the premier of Butterworth's 'A Shropshire Lad'.

The evening featured 'Dante and Beatrice' by Bantock, the prologue to 'Mephistofele' by Boito, a Verdi aria and the 'Falstaff' premier in the first half, with the premier of Hamilton Harty's 'The Mystic Trumpeter', a group of songs by Wolff, some unaccompanied choral pieces by Cornelius and finally Mozart's G Minor Symphony in the second.

Ernest Newman in The Birmingham Post criticised this 'overcrowded' programme, complaining: 'they have added to our difficulties by placing three novelties in the same day.'

'Falstaff' he thought: 'will take some time, I imagine, to play itself into popular favour and that for two reasons. In the first place it is based on a rather copious programme, and unless the audience knows every detail of this, even to the extent of following the suggestions of two simultaneous themes, it will necessarily fail to make a coherent whole of the work. In the second place, the style of the score shows us in many places quite a new Elgar and one that the public, used to the old Elgar, will not assimilate very easily.'

The Standard considered: 'It is programme music naked and unashamed that he has sought to woo. Although he advises us not to treat the connection between the literary basis of his study and the music too literally, the comments and quotations with which his published analysis of the themes is studded are so circumstantial that his warning become futile. One has little hesitation in saying that this immensely clever work is handicapped by being judged in relation with the programme.

'It is bewilderingly complex, uncannily resourceful orchestrally speaking and not infrequently overpowering resounding. Brass, more brass, and still more brass would appear at times to be the composer's cry. The work as a whole would greatly gain by compression, especially in its earlier stages. There are a few moments when Elgar almost achieves beauty and many minutes of sheer downright ugliness. Heard under the direction of the composer, the score seems overweighted with detail, much of which fails to come through, though it is possible, Elgar failed to make the most of it.'

The Nation also complained: 'It is surely not necessary to place three new works in one day's programme; and it is certainly neither necessary nor desirable that the most important of them should be timed to finish at so late an hour as to make it practically impossible for a critic to do justice either to himself or to the composer.

'Elgar devotes, perhaps, the best part of a year to thinking out a work like his 'Falstaff'. The critic is then expected to tell the world all about it, and to pass some sort of judgement upon it, at about 10.30 one night, with the knowledge that he has several other things in the programme to discuss – sometimes including another new work, as happened at Leeds – and that if he is much more than half an hour over it all he runs the risk either of his message not getting over the wires in time or of it being mutilated beyond recognition by a tired and hurried telegraphist at one end and tired and hurried compositors at the other.

'If the composers have a grievance against the critics, the latter have still more cause to be aggrieved at the festival executives. To my mind the attendance of the critics at every concert of these festivals is a mere newspaper tradition that has no ground in reason. The opinion of the critics themselves – and they may be supposed to know something of the inside of the case – is that if the country as a whole really wants to know what happens at Leeds or Sheffield in a particular week of the musical year, the local reporter could easily supply all that was wanted; while the critics, instead of wearing themselves out in listening to some seven hours of music each day, most of it too stale to call for discussion, should attend on the performances of new works or performances of old works that were likely to have some feature out of the common, and should write carefully, and if need be, copiously about something that was really worth writing about and reading about.

'The present foolish system simply wears the better men out to no purpose except that of advertising the festival; and in the crowd of ordinary things, the extraordinary thing has to suffer. On the 'Falstaff' night for example, we first of all had to listen to Mr Bantock's 'Dante and Beatrice' and then to two long and tiresome vocal solos before Elgar's work came on; and after it we had to wait another forty minutes or so, during part of which time, half of our impressions of 'Falstaff' were driven out of our heads by a new work of Mr Hamilton Harty's.

'The only thing that really concerned the newspapers, their readers and their critics on that evening was 'Falstaff'; and it should surely have been a very simple matter so to arrange the programme that the critics could have got away from the hall an hour or more earlier and with their impressions of the work still undimmed. As it is, I can remember no new work of importance that has been treated more hurriedly and with less credit to the critics than 'Falstaff' was by every one of us last week.'

The Manchester Guardian's critic, A J Sheldon, echoed the sentiment: 'For some reason the two most important novelties of the festival were crowded into the middle of the concert. As a result, I can only give the most imperfect account of Mr Harty's and Sir Edward Elgar's new compositions. If one were to search for a subject that, at first sight, would seem to be the most unlikely for Sir Edward Elgar's muse, one need not travel farther than Shakespeare's Falstaff. Yet he has done it and has given us a work teeming with interest – one, too, that will require many hearings for its full unravellings.

'The insight, the matchless capacity for thinking in music shown in the work are beyond all praise. In the most vivid manner, Sir Edward Elgar sets before us an unsurpassed skill in orchestral device a tone picture of Falstaff as he appeals to him. I do not venture too much in declaring it the greatest composition in this form as yet written by an Englishman.'

THE WAR YEARS

As early as January 1906, Elgar had been a signatory to an open letter to the Daily Telegraph headlined: 'ENGLAND AND GERMANY'

The letter deplored anti-German feeling expressed in various newspapers, and drew attention to the dual affinity between the two countries in the fields of science and the arts and added : 'A war between the two Powers would be a world-calamity for which no victory could compensate either nation; and we emphatically declare our belief that the levity with which certain journalists occasionally discuss such a possibility is the measure of their profound ignorance of the real sentiments of the nation.'

Apart from Elgar, the letter was also signed by Thomas Hardy, Walter Crane, Israel Zangwill, William Strang, Alfred Russell Wallace, William Rothenstein, Michael Rosetti and many others.

It appeared above a similar letter from German scientists and scholars, including Richard Strauss, Engelbert Humperdinck, Joseph Joachim, and Siegfried Wagner.

Political events proved differently.

When war eventually broke out, Elgar was initally reluctant to get involved in any propaganda effort against Germany – the country he loved and to which he had owed so much – eventually only persuaded by the German army's invasion of neutral Belgium, an act which caused national horror in Britain.

He remained ambivalent however. As far as the war was concerned, his attitude was contained in a letter from which a passage is often referred concerning Elgar's desperation at the fate of the horses in the war. But his reaction to the fate of the people was also contained in the letter: '"Concerning the war I say nothing – the only thing that wrings my heart and soul is the thought of the horses – oh! my beloved animals – the men – and women can go to hell.'

Elgar' first wartime production was 'Carillon' - an orchestral accompaniment to the poetry of Emile Cammearts which premiered at the Queen's Hall in December 1914. The piece struck accord with the public.

The Daily Chronicle said: 'The music has caught the exact spirit of the poem, its pathos and its proud, defiant feeling.' The Daily News commented that: 'the heart-broken cry of the patriot poet weeping for his ruined country and declaiming vengeance has inspired Sir Edward Elgar to one of his loftiest utterances. There is a bigness of outline in it, a subordination of detail to the whole and a strength of melodic outline which he has not always achieved.'

The Star: 'A peculiarity of the work as it now stands is the absence of music during the delivery of the greater part of the poem. In this Sir Edward has realised my unuttered wish when I have been straining to hear words through too-loudly played illustrative music. What Sir Edward has written for use during the recitation greatly deepens the effect. Between the stanzas are most sympathetic and subtle interludes which prepare the listener for the sentiment of the next stanza.

'The work is such a masterpiece of its class that to emphasise any particular portion seems to give a false impression of its completeness as a whole. It was magnificently played by the London Symphony Orchestra under the composer's direction and at its conclusion Sir Edward and Mr Cammearts made so many entrances and exits to the platform as to suggest they were doing 'sentry go'.'

The Observer: 'The composer, by the simplest of means and a sure technical guiding hand has produced one of the most effective and stimulating things of its kind in existence. Not that there is anything very original about any portion of the material employed – the carillon theme is the conventional four notes of the descending scale, with alternating accents by reason of the triple time employed, and the simple swinging melody a statement of some curt phrases that have been almost too frequently utilised for both sacred and secular purposes – but the sheer spirit and glowing excitement of the fabric with also its moments of poignant undemonstrativeness had all the effect of a clearly inspired utterance. Both composer and poet had wonderful receptions and it was quite evident that most of those present would have gladly had the work repeated.'

The Daily Telegraph: 'Nothing more mordant than this fine poem has yet resulted from the war. It could not have found a more sympathetic English composer to emphasise its meaning. Elgar has grasped the 'sense' of the poem and expressed it as only he of native composers of today could have done.'

'Polonia', a 'symphonic prelude for orchestra' followed in July 1915 in response to the German invasion of Poland and was first performed at the Polish Victims Relief Fund Concert organised by Paderewski, who wrote to Elgar expressing his thanks: 'I heard your noble composition on two different occasions. Deeply touched by the graciousness your friendly thought and profoundly moved by the requisite beauty of your work.'

The Daily Mail observed: 'The themes are not all Polish. There is one at the beginning which is Elgar's own, and its mingled dignity and tenderness bear the hallmark of his personality and yet it is in complete harmony with the national atmosphere of the work as a whole. The Polish themes themselves which are used have been chosen with a view to contrast and the first of them is nobly wistful while the second breathes the spirit of martial ferocity. Their emotional meaning is intensified by the rare skill with which they are scored. As the work progresses with growing excitement one notices familiar traits of Elgar's style and the mixing of the British and the Polish is interesting though sometimes it must be confessed the two elements seem hardly congruous. A very happy touch is an interlude in which one of Chopin's best-known melodies creeps into the score united with a theme from Paderewski's Polish Fantasia. It is not only a fine tribute to the two great musical patriots of Poland, but musically very striking.'

He changed direction in Christmas 1915 producing songs and incidental music for the children's play 'The Starlight Express' starring Charles Mott. This was based on a book by the occult and mystery writer Algernon Blackwood, who also produced the script for the play.

Lena Ashwell, who produced the play at the Kingsway Theatre, was enthusiastic about Elgar's involvement. In an interview she gave to the Referee she said: 'I think I would rather produce a play like this than do anything else on the stage. Although producing a play in war time has its minor difficulties in the way of procuring materials and getting them delivered, the serious difficulties have solved themselves. The first serious difficulty might have been the music – the play needed music – but when I took the script to Sir Edward Elgar and he promised to write it I knew that that difficulty was overcome before it had arisen. And now it is so wonderfully part of the play that it has grown to be much more than incidental music.'

The Pall Mall Gazette thought 'the thing as a whole was unsatisfactory. It was a success of esteem, one of those productions about which a certain amount of courage is needed, to be candid. Quite pretty in its fancy, it simply does not prove a good play. It does not show dramatic imagination. Where it should be just humbly telling the audience a story, leaving them to make their own conclusions, it is preachy and pretentious. It pretends to be meant for children but is canvassing all the while for grown-up sentiment. For each ten minutes of genuine action there are half-hours wasted over explaining and repeating a symbolism that is for the most part familiar and obvious.'

The Morning Post noted much of the music derived from the 'Wand of Youth' suites: 'The whole is an accompaniment of perfect appropriateness. He enters completely into the particular mood of the piece. It has stimulated his imaginative vein to the full'. The paper particularly liked the songs: 'Here great variety of treatment is shown even to the point of downright frivolity and all of it is admirably reproduced by Mr Charles Mott.'

The Yorkshire Post found the charm of Elgar's music 'unquestionable. Little of this is heard during the delivery of the text, for Elgar shows rare discretion in accompanying the spoken parts: but what there is fits the situation like the proverbial glove, deepening the meaning by subtle suggestion, by musical phrase and tone colour.' The Daily Chronicle, found Elgar's music 'a little mournful at times.'

The Observer thought: 'There are times when the theatre is detestable. Not on account of petty annoyances, like curtains that go up twenty minutes late, and plays that are insufficiently rehearsed, and programmes that loudly proclaim themselves to be free, yet cannot be had without payment – in order that this or that theatre can make a good show in the Red Cross donation lists.

'It is detestable because it stretches out its great paws to grasp exquisite little things and crushes them; because instead of roaring you as gently as any sucking dove, it whispers you like a bull; because the more it tries suggestion, the more hopelessly it proves limited to the statement of action, action, action.

'Here is 'The Starlight Express' a charming fantasy – a dainty dream between sleeping and waking. The theatre grabs at it and the 'Starlight Express' itself – that 'train of thought' – becomes a set of wobbly black curtains with spangles on them. The delicate fancy becomes a heavy sermon and the denoument about as probable as the conversion of Scrooge. A producer of genius might perhaps give us a little of 'The Starlight Express'. A merely clever and experienced producer might still make something of the present representation. There is Sir Edward Elgar's music to go upon and Mr Charles Mott's superb singing. Even so, the theatre would have hard work to prove that it is not, in cases like this, detestable.'

The following January Elgar produced 'Un Voix Dans le Desert', another Cammearts' accompaniment, performed with stage backdrop at the Shaftesbury Theatre. The poem created the idea that there was a thatched cottage which had somehow survived in the middle of no-mans-land and from it, at the height of the fighting, emanated a young girl's voice, singing a plaintive song looking forward to a time when peace might return. A somewhat absurd vision of what was actually happening in the killing fields of France and Flanders.

The Westminster Gazette commented: 'In spite of the fact that a scenic setting was provided it hardly proved the equal in point of effectiveness of the famous 'Carillon'. It is a somewhat novel idea to combine music, speech and song in this fashion, in conjunction with a stage setting; and if the whole thing is less effective than might have been anticipated this is due chiefly perhaps to the excessive restraint which has been exercised by the composer.

'Unlike that of the 'Carillon' Elgar's music is in this case so exceedingly unobtrusive that it might almost be non-existent; and this is, of course, a pity since it is only the music which affords any justification for the production at all. Such as there is of it is quite pleasing, but it is so slight and unimportant that the whole thing hardly seems worthwhile.'

The Pall Mall Gazette added: 'One wonders, after all, whether a composer of Sir Edward's calibre might not be better employed than in supplying music for a situation that could almost be met by a little vague improvisation.'

The following May saw the first two of three settings of Laurence Binyon's poetry. The finished production, 'The Spirit of England' was to be Elgar's last large-scale choral work.

'To Women' and 'For the Fallen' appeared at Leeds, preceding 'The Dream of Gerontius'. Elgar conducted the Leeds Choral Union.

The Sheffield Daily declared: 'Never since 'Gerontius' has Elgar given us music that carries so unmistakable a ring of sincerity throughout the whole course. In that work he told us he offered the best that was in him. In 'The Spirit of England', for that is the full name of the complete work he has given his supremist art, music that cuts to the very essence of living, vivid poetry and which with magical veracity expresses the unuttered thoughts of the people.'

The Yorkshire Observer commented: 'Here is no banal outburst of Jingoism but the utterance of a scholar and a gentleman. And that, moreover without a trace of pedantry. There are, indeed, plenty of subtle touches in the scores – unusual progressions and modulations, overlappings of the melodic line which may supply the curious with matter enough for study and admiration; but the main structure of the pieces is fairly simple and readily understandable, being in effect that of an accompanied part-song – a very elaborate part-song thanks to the variety of subjects and rich orchestration especially in the second instance but still belonging to that genus usually grateful to English concert-goers. What in the new pieces presents some obstacle to immediate acceptance is the close incorporations of the poetry with the music. The two fit like the hand in a well-chosen glove and can scarcely be separated for a single instant without loss of the true effect.'

A few days later, the programme was given in the Queen's Hall, London, and then repeated every day during the week in the afternoons and evenings, with proceeds - £160,000 in today's money - going to the Red Cross.

Ernest Newman in The Birmingham Post thought 'For the Fallen' showed Elgar in 'his finest vein'.

'One admires the works not simply because they crystallise some of most poignant emotions about the war but that they crystallise those emotions into very beautiful and expressive shapes. Their value, I imagine, will still endure long after the war is over. The 'For the Fallen' is as moving a piece of music as Elgar has ever given us – a work of passionate sincerity and a beauty that is by turns touching, thrilling and consoling.

'Into a short poem of eight stanzas he has packed not only great intensity but an astonishing variety of expression. The emotional basis of the music is proudly elegiac with moments of soaring rapture. The climax is a magnificent outburst. It takes a lifetime of incessant practice to attain a touch at once so light and so sure as this.'

The Evening Standard added: 'It is rumoured that Elgar thinks his latest work his greatest. It may be so, though it is dangerous to take a poet's or a composer's opinion on such a point, the critical faculty working very erratically when one's own work is in question. If Elgar really said this, he probably means that the three war poems of Laurence Binyon he has strung together and has set as a choral-orchestral trilogy moved him mightily as they turned themselves into tone under his hand and that he is conscious of the result being a piece of sincere personal expression. This one can well believe for the two sections heard yesterday at the Queen's Hall do not sound like a well fashioned occasional piece as did 'Polonia' a few months back, but, like 'Carillon' have the ring of instinctive utterance.'

The critic however found that 'For the Fallen' 'had lines in it that are mere clichés – the commonplaces of the war poet. Elgar's setting redeems even such lines as these however.'

The Observer thought 'For the Fallen' 'will probably prove to be the greatest expression in music, attributable to the call of the hour, given by any composer of any nation.'

The final part 'The Fourth of August' appeared in October 1916 receiving scant critical attention. Ernest Newman in The Musical Times however thought that Elgar 'has voiced the best that is in us. For the first time in the lives of many of us, we find ourselves indulging in a national hatred and not seeing any reason to be ashamed of it: for the hatred is not so much of that of a mere enemy as that of an immoral something that has become for the first time in history incarnated in a whole nation. For that foulness, Elgar has hit upon a peculiarly telling symbol in 'The Fourth of August'. It sounds the same fine note of hope and pride as its two predecessors – a spiritual pride that has nothing in common with the strut and swagger of the commoner 'patriotic' verse and music and a hope that always shows itself unconsciously in the mounting curves of the melodies and the sequences.'

After 'The Spirit of England', containing Binyon's time-honoured Remembrance Sunday words:

'They shall not grow old as we that are left grow old

'At the going down of the sun and in the morning we will remember them'

Elgar changed direction again – writing songs for the music-halls.

THE FRINGES OF THE FLEET

In 1917 Elgar composed 'The Fringes of the Fleet' for a summer variety show at London's Coliseum Music-hall. The four settings of Kipling poems, celebrating the war-time contribution of British coastal vessels, were sung by four baritones dressed as sailors against a theatrical backdrop of a tavern on a dockside.

The show, originally booked for one week only in June, proved popular and ran throughout the summer, before embarking on a provincial tour. Elgar conducted every performance – twice nightly with matinees on Wednesdays and Saturday – and shared the stage with such acts as: Cyril Clensy (impersonator), Baisdon (the talking comedy cyclist), Molly Butler (dialect comedienne) Mademoiselle Dalmere's Table Circus of performing cats, rats, monkeys and canaries, and Vera Caine (female boxer). There were also some theatrical interludes such as Haslam and Lady in their matrimonial burlesque 'Smiletones' and Dr Nichols and Company in their 'screaming farce' 'It's up to You'.

Elgar's appearance was, however, the star-turn on the bill, with newspaper advertisements announcing triumphantly: 'Sir Edward Elgar will conduct in person'.

The printed programme for the performances also regaled the fact that Elgar was appearing with a poem and cartoons showing the four 'jolly jack tars' in performance. The opening of the poem read like this:

'Four Rough and Ready Sailor men
You see upon the stage
Though no-one in particular
Today they're all the rage
They're called the 'Fringes of the Fleet'
And tell you all in song
About their life upon the Sea
In language rather strong
They started out upon their trip
Upon a day in June
('Twas Rudyard Kipling wrote the words
And Elgar set the tune)
Sir Edward Elgar, I should say
That gallant chevalier
Of whom the ladies all exclaim
'Oh, isn't he a dear !''

Such a production, with the composer of 'The Dream of Gerontius' taking to the stage twice nightly in the company of female boxers, impersonators, comedians and the like, naturally bemused some critics but the majority expressed staunch support for Elgar's decision to perform.

The Manchester Guardian commented: 'Our tendency as a people to identify an artist too rigidly with his material has until quite recently prevented a full recognition of the personality of Sir Edward Elgar who is at the Manchester Hippodrome this week, conducting ('in person' as the theatre-posters state in careful detail) some of his own compositions.

'We came to know Elgar first of all through his 'Gerontius' preferring it to other of his works, probably because of the inordinate national predilection for oratorio and it was generally taken for granted that the man who could write such super-earthy music as 'The Dream of Gerontius' must of necessity be himself unsubstantial and febrile. Consequently, the surprise expressed in many quarters at his appearance and reception in the music-hall can be understood. But true Elgarians have always known our greatest composer – and he really stands with the *very* greatest – to be intensely human.

'Since 1914 it would seem Elgar has deliberately simplified his art and broadened it to a communal pattern in order to gain a point of contact with the people. The result has been some of the most inspiring patriotic music ever written. Elgar is the only English composer who has attempted fairly and squarely to tune his melody to the time and to serve his country by the expression of its convictions and emotions concerning the war. He could not wholly fulfil this task without venturing into the music-hall which is beloved of our soldiers and has become the place of all others for the expression of popular feeling.

'It was with no loss of dignity therefore but rather with a new accession of it that the composer of 'The Dream of Gerontius' came forward to conduct the meagre and too little competent orchestra at the Manchester Hippodrome yesterday in his setting of Kipling's war ballads. One felt he had become a follower of Dibdin and the older ballad writers who made the story of our country the pride of their music'.

The Leicester Daily Post reported: 'Visitors to the Palace this week have an opportunity which is not often vouchsafed them of seeing the foremost English composer conducting his own music.'

The Illustrated Leicester Chronicle commented: 'The appearance of the greatest of living English composers, Sir Edward Elgar, at the Leicester Palace this week, is an event of more than ordinary interest. Some folk of old-fashioned notions probably think that artistic dignity has received a rude shock through celebrated musicians having consented to perform at music-halls.

'Why such ideas should find expression I do not understand and for my part I am glad that there are men like Sir Edward Elgar who apparently recognise that the fulfilment of their art need not be confined to the circumscribed limits of the concert hall. It is the opinion of those who follow the signs of the times that the old ballad concerts are passing away and that the leading singers and instrumentalists will be more and more attracted to the best halls.'

'Sir Edward is of a quiet, retiring disposition, and shrinks from publicity but I imagine he is a man of broad democratic views and sympathies, and intensely human.'

The Manchester City News felt that 'it is fitting that works so typically national in character should receive their first welcome in that great national meeting place of all classes, the music-hall. Posterity, in accord with present-day opinion will undoubtedly acclaim Elgar as the most typically English of all our great national composers.

After the provincial run, the show returned to the Coliseum in November 1917 with The Era commenting that it was 'one of the finest productions ever seen in the music-halls.'

But by the end of December, Kipling, unhappy at the production, put a stop to the performances and the physical pressure which Elgar had endured by conducting night after night began to take its toll on his health. Rumours began to circulate that he was unwell and some of these reached the press with one correspondent noting: 'There have been rumours of late, some of them rather alarming concerning the health of Sir Edward Elgar. I am more than pleased to hear there is no foundation for them whatever. Sir Edward *has* been ill, though not seriously and is now on his way to complete recovery.'

Elgar spent time in a nursing home. When he left, he recuperated at the remote woodland cottage in West Sussex which Alice had found for him. This was 'Brinkwells' and it was here that he was to compose his three chamber works, and the 'Cello concerto – his last great works.

THE CHAMBER WORKS

The first work produced at 'Brinkwells' was the Violin Sonata, first performed by W H Reed and Landon Ronald in London's Aeolian Hall on March 21st 1919.

The Times noted it: 'breaks the silence the composer has maintained since the beginning of the war and breaks it in a manner which everyone will welcome. The absence of a work in this form from one who leads modern British musical thought was much to be deplored. Its style in its general effect may be described as new to this composer. It is less marked by individual characteristics common to his works and indicates an extraordinary expansion of means. The work is a worthy addition to our literature, while, as far as its author is concerned, it reveals a development and a softening of style that cannot fail to win its acceptance on the best of grounds, grounds that can ignore all the adventitious aids of preliminary description and discussion, namely its own merits.'

The Morning Post considered it: 'one of the composer's most vital and poetic works.' The Referee concluded: 'The impression left after the finely worked up conclusion is a keen desire to hear the work again.'

According to the Musical Times: 'The large audience (which included a good sprinkling of well-known fiddlers) recalled the composer and player again and again.' But The Referee, noted: 'The audience was not as large as might have been expected.'

And L Dutton Green commented in the Arts Gazette: 'I could hardly restrain a cry of indignation on entering the Aeolian Hall. Imagine the announcement of a new sonata by Ravel in Paris, by Richard Strauss in Berlin or, in times gone by, by Brahms in Vienna. Why, weeks beforehand it would have been impossible to find a single seat; and here was a new violin sonata by Sir Edward Elgar, one of the greats of all times and perhaps the greatest living composer, at the piano one of our best conductors, the leader of one of our orchestras as the solo violinist, and, for shame ! a half-empty hall. It seems incredible, yet it is a melancholy fact.'

Ernest Newman in The Observer noted the poor attendance might be due to many other performances on the same night which attracted large audiences but added : 'when a new work by one of the greatest of living composers – and he an Englishman and a Londoner – is given, out of London's seven millions there cannot be found enough music lovers to more than half fill a small hall, holding, I suppose, at the most a few hundred people. A phenomenon of this sort is very distressing.'

'I, living in the provinces, naturally wanted to see what my London colleagues had said of the sonata. I went through all the provincial editions of the London papers on the day after the performance. I found one small notice of the work. In The Times I found an announcement to the effect that the work had been produced the preceding day and that a full account of it would be given in Monday's issue. I twice searched the columns of the Monday's Times, in vain however, for that account.

'Either it was not in the provincial edition that I had or it was so small and buried in so out-of-the-way a corner of the paper that one would require an hour's work with a microscope to find it. All that my researches brought me then, was one short notice of the sonata in the whole of the London press. It does not seem to have occurred to those responsible for the 'make-up' of these papers that the production of a new work by Elgar was a matter of interest to musicians all over the country.'

Shortly after the Violin Sonata, Elgar completed his String Quartet and Piano Quintet which were first performed at London's Wigmore Hall, on May 21st 1919 together with another performance of the Sonata. W H Reed was joined by Albert Sammons, Raymond Jeremy and Felix Salmond for the Quartet, and William Murdoch played piano in the Quintet. Again, the press coverage was scant.

The Times commented: 'The interest aroused by the news that Sir Edward Elgar was addressing himself seriously to the composition of chamber music was perhaps a little damped down when the sonata for violin and piano made its appearance a few weeks ago and proved to be neither startlingly new nor of the kind which goes straight to the heart of the ordinary listeners. Still there was something elusive about it which might be taken to herald bigger things and these bigger things have now arrived.

'The dominant impression left by the succession of the three works was one of ascending power. In the Sonata and the String Quartet one recognises the Elgar we have always known: in the Sonata one discovers Elgar a little disconcerted by finding himself with only one violin and a piano instead of an orchestra; in the Quartet, Elgar happy in the recovery of the full emotional sonorousness of strings. But in the Quintet and more especially in its ample first movement, there is something more; it seems impelled by a stronger force and an energy more muscular and less nervous than that of the Elgar we have known.'

The Daily Mail considered: 'Undoubtedly these three works are a precious enrichment of English chamber music which up to recent years was so poor and even today has not much of European importance.'

It found the Quintet 'better than Dvorak or Brahms, but though somewhat more modern than they who can imagine it to have existed without them? It adds refinements to the one and richness to the other and yet it ends by cloying. The composer in fact still indulges in those reiterations and repetitions which today seem the bane of classical music.

'And withal there is in so much textual richness hardly anything pungent. In the Finale one positively craved some stridency from the strings, which never came, or some novel sonority from the piano (Sir Edward's piano-writing is above all conventional – he has no doubt scorned to learn from Liszt). Yet the work will assuredly give just pleasure to many audiences and would, too, to great numbers of players if it were not so difficult.'

The Morning Post commented: 'It was striking to notice the evidence the pieces afforded of the composer's gradual adaptation of his methods to the form. In the Sonata and the Quartet he is inclined to cling to orchestral writing; in the Quintet he shows that he has grasped the proportions, with the result that although there is much that is notable, much that is inspired in Sonata and Quartet, it is in the Quintet that this great musical mind speaks with the assurance that makes his work a significant contribution to modern British chamber music.'

Robin Legge in the Daily Telegraph found the Quintet 'the least attractive of the three works, in spite of the supreme beauty of its slow movement. It is long since even Elgar has given to us a work of such sublime beauty as the Quartet which is purest most characteristic Elgar from its first to its last note'.

The Pall Mall Gazette questioned the wisdom of playing all three works in the same exclusive programme: 'we do not think Elgar is a composer to whom one can easily listen attentively for two hours. The test was a severe one more likely to show the composer's weaknesses than his good qualities. Each one of the nine movements in turn seemed too long in proportion to its content, especially as in most of them the thematic material was of less interest than the incidental passages, in spite of the fact that the latter were often constructed upon sequences. It is difficult for Elgar to leave a sequence as it is for a bicycle to leave the tramlines.

'The Quartet is written thickly and therefore lacks clarity, though not robustness. The writing for piano is not good in the Sonata and scarcely better in the Quintet, but the latter being less polyphonic in design, is, on the whole the clearest of the three works. It has moments which would suggest that the composer was dwelling upon reminiscences of one of his visits to the South.

'The slow movement of the Quartet has a true Elgar melody. It is a pity that the three slow movements finish 'en queue de poisson' [come to an abrupt end], muted, except in the Quintet, where the mute is kept for the finale. It was this repetition of similar devices that gave an impression of monotony. Each work and especially the Quintet would stand a much better chance.

'There was a moderate audience and if the critical or professional section were deducted it would furnish a sad comment on the interest we take in the doings of our premier musician. On the other-hand the reception could not have been more enthusiastic.'

The Evening Standard found 'the moods of these works are very varied. Like all Elgar's works they have a good deal of quiet mystic feeling, but they are like Dr Johnson's friend who tried to be a philosopher, in that 'cheerfulness will keep breaking through'.'

The Sunday Times sought to explain the lack of audience: 'It is very much regretted that the programme at the Wigmore Hall on Wednesday should have been given in the busiest week we have known for five years. A concert of such significance demanded more consideration than it could possibly receive, if only because Elgar has but just come forward as a writer of chamber music.' But he added: 'Each work left one gasping with admiration particularly at the beauty of its slow movement and each needed hearing again and again.'

The Times thought: 'Elgar's music is always autobiographical; but the life is not completed; it is the present which one looks for most eagerly in his latest work and not the past. What has he to say now and have the years stamped their meaning on him in any profound way? It was the failure to find this through the greater part of the new works which made one impatient before the end of Wednesday's performance, yet mercifully it is not altogether absent.

'The first movement of the Piano Quintet has a breadth of view, one might almost say a manliness of expression, which has never appeared so clearly in anything he has written before. It was perhaps prefigured in the finale of the Second Symphony, but not maintained. So much of Elgar's symphonic writing has hinted at great possibilities and almost wilfully obliterated their impression. He has clung to a wayward elusiveness in the Violin Sonata. But in the Quintet, after a few questioning phrases he puts all this behind him and launches boldly on a high enterprise from which he never seems to turn aside until the movement is completed.

'It was this movement rather than the two which followed it which seemed to raise the Quintet to a higher plane than either of the preceding works; and more than all else convinced us that Elgar is still a force amongst the many currents of the music tide.'

THE 'CELLO CONCERTO

Elgar's 'Cello Concerto was first performed with Felix Salmond as soloist at the inaugural concert of the London Symphony Orchestra's first proper post-War season in the Queen's Hall on October 27th 1919.

Elgar conducted the concerto but the rest of the programme, *including* Borodin's 'Heroic' Symphony, Wagner's 'Forest Murmurs' from *Siegfried and* Scriabin's 'Poem of Ecstacy', was directed by Albert Coates, making his debut as the orchestra's new Principal conductor.

Ernest Newman reviewed the concert in the Observer. After praising Coates' performance of the Scriabin 'that we are not likely to have bettered anywhere or at any time' he added: 'It went a long way towards compensating us for our disappointment over the new Elgar 'Cello Concerto – a disappointment, not with the work but with the presentation of it. One never expects a first performance to be an ideal one, and Mr Felix Salmond, admirable artist as he is, may well be forgiven for feeling and showing the responsibility laid upon him.

'But we should like to have an explanation of the failure of the orchestra. There have been rumours about during the week of inadequate rehearsal. Whatever be the explanation, the sad fact remains that never, in all probability, has so great an orchestra made so lamentable a public exhibition of itself. On Monday the orchestra was often virtually inaudible and when just audible was merely a muddle. No one seemed to have any idea of what it was the composer wanted.'

The blame for this, according to Lady Elgar's diary lay firmly with the Russian-born Coates.

'October 26th: 'to rehearsal at Mortimer Hall – horrid place- the new work, *'Cello Concerto, never seen by Orchestra* – Rehearsal supposed to be at 11.30. After 12.30 - A. absolutely furious – E. extraordinarily calm – Poor Felix Salmond in a state of suspense & nerves – Wretched hurried rehearsal – An insult to E. from that brutish, selfish, ill mannered bounder A. Coates.

'October 27th: to Queen's Hall for rehearsal at 12.30 or rather before -absolutely inadequate at that – That brute Coates went on rehearsing 'Waldwben'[i.e the Wagner piece]. Sec[retar]y remonstrated, no use. At last just before one, he stopped & the men like Angels stayed til 1.30 – A wanted E to withdraw, but he did not for Felix's sake – Indifferent performance of course in consequence E. had a tremendous reception & ovation.

'October 28th: still furious about rehearsals – Shameful. Hope never to speak to that brutal Coates again.'

Taken alongside Lady Elgar's unequivocal ire, Newman's review has long been the accepted version of the event: that the orchestra were under-rehearsed, the concerto was given a substandard performance, and that, apparently, Coates was to blame. But Newman's words do not seem to tally with those of other reviewers present at the performance.

The Daily Mail said this: 'Certainly it is the most beautiful 'cello concerto in existence. It is a new sort of concerto, a new and surpassing metamorphosis of an old form. The successful concertos of modern music, like those of Liszt and Tchaikovsky oppose the solo instrument in a kind of duel with the orchestra. Schuman and Brahms tried to interweave the two. This is Elgar's way, but he soars above those writers.

'One of the supreme beauties of this work is the placing of the solo in the orchestral picture. Quite early in the first movement this relation is established with ravishing beauty. The Scherzo which has a most original opening, is playful, but yet playful in the particularly intimate, introspective way, which is the emotional range of the whole. The short Adagio brings intenser loveliness. It is music of honeyed sweetness like the scent-saturated evening air of a garden.

'The Finale starts with quiet good humour. But this movement has the great surprise of all. For as it seems naturally reaching its close, the mood of soft autumnal happiness changes with a pang. A sharp and bitter note of regret, almost of pain, the pain of retrospect and disillusion is uttered. Music has never expressed anything more intimate, and on this the strains fall and die.'

And of the performance, much maligned by Newman and posterity, the Mail said this: 'Mr Felix Salmond, the soloist, was nervous, but played with the right beautiful velvety tone which was not so scratchy even in the semiquavers of the Scherzo. The composer conducted and was warmly acclaimed, but such music is not the sort that 'brings the house down'. One sacrificed the pleasure of hearing Sciabin's 'Poem of Ecstacy' to allow the strains of the concerto to vibrate a little in the memory.'

The Daily Chronicle commented: 'an excellent performance of the concerto was given.'

The Globe: 'Mr Salmond played beautifully throughout.'

The Westminster Gazette: 'The concerto, which was conducted by the composer, had in Mr Felix Salmond an admirable exponent of the solo part and was most cordially received.'

The Sunday Times: 'Mr Felix Salmond played very finely as also did the London Symphony Orchestra.'

The Daily News: 'The solo part was played by Mr Felix Salmond with fine understanding and fluent technique. Sir Edward Elgar, who conducted, received the most cordial welcome and was loudly cheered and many times recalled at the close.'

The Referee: 'The solo part was played with apparent complete understanding of the composer's intentions and rare executive skill by Mr Felix Salmond, and the composer, who conducted, had the entire sympathy of the orchestra. The reception of the work was enthusiastic.'

Criticism was reserved for the music itself.

The Westminster Gazette commented: 'For some reason or other, which has never been made quite plain the majority of existing 'cello concertos are hopelessly dull affairs. How therefore does Elgar's new concerto stand in this respect? Has he succeeded in overcoming the difficulties which have floored so many of his predecessors in this troublesome form? I should be disposed to answer at once 'Yes' and 'No'.

'Certainly, he has managed to give his soloist much better chances than he usually obtains and to write a 'cello concerto in which for once in a way there is never the least difficulty in hearing the 'cello, so that to this extent the answer must be 'Yes'.

'On the other-hand this result has not been obtained without considerable sacrifices in the matter of the general orchestral facture and a corresponding diminution in the general brilliance and effectiveness of the work, so that to this extent in turn the answer must be 'no'.

'There is a wealth of fine ideas and beautiful music in this new work of Elgar and yet taken as a whole it left, on a first hearing at all events, a not completely satisfactory impression. Again and again the feeling suggested itself that in his praiseworthy desire to avoid at all costs the fault of 'covering' the solo voice he has failed to do full justice to his material – the result being an impression of flatness and tameness and triteness, where forcefulness, energy and brilliance seemed rather to be demanded.'

The Times: 'It is not a work to create a great sensation; it is perhaps the least rhetorical work Elgar has ever written. Indeed, a moment or two of virtuosity in the solo part is remarkable because it stands out from its context.'

The Daily Telegraph: 'What the whole work seemed to lack was exaltation.'

The Sunday Times: 'It must be admitted that there are dull moments.'

But perhaps one of the most perceptive comments, in the light of the knowledge that this was to be Elgar's final exercise in large scale music, and the nature of the times which were changing rapidly around him, came from the Pall Mall Gazette: 'The British public had not yet adjusted to the Elgarian musical idiom. There was a time which most of us can remember when audiences only too well accustomed to the sound of organ pipes in the orchestra, hailed Elgar as a deliverer, and insisted, perhaps disproportionately upon hearing him as often as they might. Then they heard the modern pipes of Pan, and discovered that, whatever else he might be Elgar was no Pagan.

'Meanwhile the times had become Pagan and the fervour of an Elgar symphony ceased to attract, even in its right proportion. Thus, we have the balance disturbed alternately in both directions, and the question arises whether the new outburst of Elgarian activity will restore it.'

Shortly after the first performance of his new Concerto, Elgar wrote to his friend Nicholas Kilburn: 'My pen has been idle for months – so much the better for prosperity and posterity.'

THE DEATH OF ALICE ELGAR AND BEYOND

Alice Elgar died on April 7th 1920. The Times obituary, 'COMPOSER'S DEVOTED HELPER' presumably based on information provided by Elgar himself, recited her biography and paid tribute to the work she carried out on his behalf, laying out scores to help him with his writing – 'he would come down next morning to find as much of the form ready as he could fill in during the day with the orchestral parts. There is not a full score of his which she has not laid out in this way.'

It also mentioned her own literary talents – as a novelist and poet, providing texts for some of his songs, and learning languages fluently: 'she electrified the orchestra in Turin by making a speech of thanks for him in Italian. But whatever she might have done in the way of literature she gave up in order to help him.'

She had been ill for some time, but from the evidence of correspondence Elgar failed to realise how serious her condition had been. In one letter, written less than a month before she died he commented: 'She is only now beginning to be her active self – she gets out much as usual but easily tires, however, she is progressing well while I retrograde in evil – perhaps.'

The effect her death had on him can be seen from another letter written on May 6th 1920: 'I am still a stunned and broken man. I am no fit company for decent human beings at present.'

The conventional wisdom has thus maintained a notion of a devoted loving couple, destroyed by her death – and Elgar, so devastated by the event that he never again composed a major work.

Rosa Burley, in her book 'Record of A Friendship' however provided an alternative view: 'There is no doubt that her death after thirty-one years of their married life came as an overwhelming blow to him but it was not in reality precisely the kind of blow which has been described by most of his biographers.

'That Alice had devoted her whole life to Edward is beyond question. She really did worship him with a blindness to his faults, and indeed to his occasional cruelty to her, that seemed almost incredible. But it is equally true that, while relying on this devotion, he was in the first place rather impatient of its blindness and in the second uncomfortably guilty over his debt to her. Her death accentuated the conflict in his soul and left him completely stunned.

'Their marriage had been in many ways irksome and irritating. Many of the friends whose wealth had dazzled Edward in later years had barely concealed their contempt for Alice, but Alice's extremely conventional standards of correct conduct had already made an indelible impression on him and throughout his life he had been at immense pains to maintain a façade of married bliss.

'So stunned was he by the blow, so withdrawn into himself that no one at Severn House dared to approach him even when the undertaker had to be interviewed. I was in the house at the time and, realizing that something had to be done, I went into the study and told him as gently as I could that he really must pull himself together.'

Whatever the explanation, it is a fact that after Alice's death, Elgar produced no more major works. In the vacuum which was thereby created, performances of his existing music also seemed to be falling out of favour. This has long been attributed to the emergence of new music from both British and overseas composers, coupled with the belief that Elgar's works were seen as old-fashioned, coming from a pre-war colonial past.

Another cause was however suggested in this article in the January 1921 edition of The Musical Times. It quoted a 'leading journalist' who commented: 'Elgar's Violin Concerto does not appear in our concerts as often as it should do, mainly, I think because of the performing fee that is charged. So, at any rate I was recently told by one of the half-dozen greatest of living violinists, who assured me that he admired the Concerto and would be glad to play it everywhere but that it was simply impossible for him to pay the fee for the privilege of doing so.'

The Musical Times article defended the charge but as the magazine was published by Novello's who had applied the fees in the first place, it was hardly objective. It admitted however that the concerto had 'rarely been heard' since 1914 adding: 'we are glad to see that the neglect of Elgar's works is being discussed.'

While naturally ruling out that their own performing fees were to blame, they offered two explanations:

'1. Audiences don't want them

2. Conductors won't play them.'

The performing fees issue had festered for years. In 1912, The Globe reported: 'According to an interview in 'Musical America', [Belgian Violinist] Mr [Eugene] Ysaye said: 'I should have liked to play the Elgar here but I finally abandoned it because of the endless difficulties I had with the publishers and the enormous royalties they were asking. The composer himself is so effectively bound hand and foot that he can do nothing to aid the artist. It seems a very foolish thing to me that it should thus become the fashion to hinder the propaganda for a new work. And the Elgar concerto is a great work – the finest thing in its way, I claim, since the concerto of Brahms.''

The paper published a rebuttal by Novello's, claiming that the most they had asked for was 'seven and a half guineas' [about £625 in today's money] for each performance– and that in each occasion two thirds of the fee had gone to Elgar.

It concluded: 'When we consider how small is the possible money compensation for such an effort of the creative musician as the Violin Concerto of Sir E Elgar, limited as it is by the comparatively few executants of capacity sufficient to give it effective performance, there is something churlish in the attitude of the world-famous executant as revealed in yesterday's correspondence. To contrast the fees of the man who composes with those of the man who plays is to realise one of the world's inequalities.'

Robert Lorenz, in the Daily Telegraph, stirred the debate: 'The position of Elgar continues to reflect great discredit on those responsible for moulding, or, rather, making mouldy our concert programmes.'

Lorenz then listed a number of people and organisations which he said were to blame, including the publishers Chappell, and Sir Henry Wood. Chappell were to blame because they promoted orchestral concerts, while 'Wood's record in regard to Elgar's symphonies since the war, is, in my opinion, a thoroughly bad one. He gave the First Symphony three years ago at a Promenade concert, at which, owing to particularly foul weather, the hall was quite empty. To my knowledge, he has never since ventured to play either of the symphonies, in London at any rate. This is a great pity, because Wood is really at his best in Elgar; in-fact much better than in some other composers in whose works he fancies himself more, such as Beethoven and Wagner.'

Jointly, he accused Chappell and Wood for producing programmes that possessed 'too little imagination,' then accused Albert Coates and the London Symphony Orchestra: 'The post-war record of this orchestra in regard to Elgar's larger works, is absolutely pitiful, and Coates, who has been the regular conductor, must be blamed for favouring second-hand Russian works at the expense of our own masterpieces.'

Finally, he blamed the public: 'not the public that fails to appreciate Elgar, but the fully appreciative section which refuses to give vent to its enthusiasm. In no country are music lovers so tepid or so cowardly as in this. Under the banner of 'good form' they tolerate in music every conceivable form of insult that they would not dream of tolerating in other spheres of life. If only a few thousand music-lovers would understand that, by merely wanting Elgar's music and saying so, they can have it, we should be miles further on the way to salvation.'

Lorenz concluded by making a plea for readers of his article to write to the Telegraph to express their views in Elgar's favour: 'Sheer weight of numbers is bound to tell in the end, and no power on earth can hinder the consummation of a reasonable and practical ideal.'

The plea sparked correspondence to the paper. The composer, Charles W Orr, wrote: 'I am sure he is only voicing the opinions of thousands of music-lovers who feel that the neglect of such masterpieces as the two symphonies, and 'Falstaff' is nothing short of scandalous. When one considers the amount of decadent rubbish forced on us in the course of a season – outpourings of congenital idiots from Paris and Moscow, and contrasts the neglect of our own great genius, it gives one very furiously to think.'

Orr's letter produced rebuke from Algernon Ashton of Maida Vale: 'Every now and then a correspondent crops up protesting against the supposed neglect of Elgar and the latest is Mr Charles W Orr who laments the omission of the 'greatest of our composer's' two symphonies. Surely these complaints are hardly justified considering that Elgar's symphonies have had frequent performances ever since they were written. Moreover, every musician knows only too well how extremely difficult it is to obtain even a single hearing of a symphony. Many fine and magnificent works, far finer and more magnificent than any of Elgar's compositions are utterly neglected and ignored nowadays.'

Ashton was a composer and Professor of Piano at the Royal College of Music. One wonders whether the 'many fine and magnificent works' he was referring to might have included his own – a question also considered by correspondent J Kenneth Davis: 'It would be of interest to know what works Mr Ashton has in mind. At all events, and whether or not one agrees with this statement it cannot in itself be held as justification for a neglect of Elgar's symphonies.'

R W S Mendl added: 'There is no excuse for neglecting the symphonies. Why should Saint-Saens' Third Symphony be given a hearing to the exclusion of Elgar's two symphonies?' D C Parker of Glasgow sadly reflected: 'If Elgar were a movie star or a boxer more public attention would probably be conferred upon him. One would be sorry to have to admit that if Elgar had seen the light of day in some far-off town, that had he borne an exotic name his music would have been found of higher value.'

M V Salaman contributed: 'The musical world is yearning for Elgar, but what it gets from the LSO are contortions like the 'Rite of Spring' and horrors like the lunatic 'Woodwind Symphony'. It is incomprehensible.'

Kenneth Wallace of Bristol however raised once again the question of the alleged high performing fees. Bristol it seems had not yet heard a performance of the 'Enigma' Variations more than 20 years after its composition: 'I do know that a Bristol audience would have had an opportunity of a first hearing of the Enigma Variations last season, had not an extraordinarily large performing fee been asked.

'So far at least as the Provinces are concerned it is possible to give very attractive programmes without paying any fees at all and even then to lose money. When Elgar's music obtains such a hold on the public that supports symphony concerts that all expenses can be covered in addition to the fees, then we shall no doubt hear more of it. In the meantime we must put up with our old friends until the Elgar copyrights become extinct.'

Harold Rawlinson added: 'In my opinion I do not think we shall ever be able to look forward to many public performances of Elgar's greater orchestral works while his publishers demand such heavy performing fees.' He then suggested putting on two exclusively Elgar concerts featuring both Symphonies, both concertos, 'Falstaff' and other works but added that they would cost 'about £1,000' [about £40,000 in today's money].

The composer and arranger Rupert Erlebach agreed 'with those who protest that the performing fees for many Elgar works are exorbitant.' But he added: 'I think the reason for comparatively infrequent performances of these works lies in the extraordinary difficulty and complexity of the scores themselves. Even in large modern works like 'The Rite of Spring', those of Prokofiev, Strauss or Ravel there are many pages of comparative simplicity, where the conductor may 'cut' at rehearsals, thus saving much valuable time. But this can hardly be done with Elgar.'

Novello's – via their publication The Musical Times hit back: 'There is no mistaking the general feeling that the neglect of Elgar's orchestral music is a scandal, though there is considerable difference of opinion as to the cause. One correspondent in The Daily Telegraph drags out the old bogey of the performing fee. As we showed in an article on this subject in the Music Times of January 1921 the performing fee is not to blame.

'For only four of the orchestral works published by Messrs Novello is there a fee – the two symphonies, 'Falstaff' and the 'cello concerto. Are the violin concerto, 'In the South' and the 'Introduction and Allegro for Strings' played nearly as often as they should be? Even the 'Enigma' Variations are far less heard than much inferior and less popular music. Clearly the fact of there being no fee does not help these works. On the other-hand the violin concerto was very frequently performed before the war, despite the performing fee. The fee was taken off in 1914 since when the work has been rarely played.

'Finally there is the fact that Elgar's No 1 received during the two years following its publication more performances than any other symphony. The fee was no obstacle then and is not an insuperable one now, despite the economic difficulties of concert-giving.'

The issue appeared again in the Strand Magazine. In an article entitled 'Herr Kreisler Talks' he said of 'The Dream of Gerontius': 'I have been told that Elgar sold this sublime work for a trifling sum – twenty pounds, I think it was.'

Novello's replied, via The Musical Times: 'In ordinary circumstances the details of a transaction between a composer and publisher concern nobody but themselves. As however, a definite and inaccurate statement about such a transaction has thus been made in a widely-circulated magazine, and the usual privacy broken we feel we have no option but to make known facts usually treated as confidential: The sums received by Elgar in respect of 'The Dream of Gerontius' turned the four-figure point some years ago, and the royalty payable to him (which was part of the consideration) is still running. As Herr Kreisler's statement was admittedly based on hearsay, it is a matter for astonishment that he should have given it wide publicity without first making enquiry as to its truth.'

Whatever the explanation, performances were becoming scarce and poorly attended. In June 1922, Elgar conducted a performance of 'The Apostles' at the Queen's Hall in aid of the Westminster Abbey Restoration Fund.

The audience was so sparse that George Bernard Shaw protested to the Daily News: 'It would be an exaggeration to say I was the only one present. My wife was there. Other couples were visible at intervals. One of the couples consisted of the Princess Mary and Viscount Lascelles, who just saved the situation as far as the credit of the Crown is concerned as it very deeply is.

'I distinctly saw six people in the stalls, probably with complimentary tickets. In the cheaper seats a faithful band stood for England's culture. My object in writing this letter is simply to gratify an uncontrollable impulse to let Sir Edward Elgar and the Leeds Choral Union know that I am unspeakably ashamed of their treatment.

'I apologise to them for London society and for all the other recreants to England's culture, who will, I fear not have the grace to apologise for themselves. And finally I apologise to posterity for living in a country where the capacity and tastes of schoolboys and sporting costermongers are the measure of metropolitan culture. Disgustedly yours. G Bernard Shaw.'

The Daily News' lamented: 'the hall was more than half empty. The afternoon, it is true, is not a good time for choral concerts but the attendance was disappointing nevertheless.'

The Sunday Times commented: 'Mr Shaw in his justifiably angry outburst has said all that needs to be said on the smallness of the audience at Thursday's performance of 'The Apostles'. The sight of Queen's Hall was indeed a disgrace to London.'

However, 'The Man in the Street' writing in the Daily Sketch demonstrated how much times had changed in post-war Britain: 'One way or another we have certainly been getting it in the neck during the last forty-eight hours or so. Several persons who should, I suppose, be treated with profound respect, have constituted themselves judge, jury and Crown prosecutor rolled into one, tried us for various offences and have found us guilty of each charge brought against us.

'There is f'rinstance Mr C R W Nevinson, the artist, whose puzzle pictures are supposed to possess amazing significance for those capable of discovering a world of meaning in things apparently meaningless. Mr Nevinson has been telling us just what he thinks of post-war civilisation and presumably expects us to crawl into a corner and hide our diminished heads. Mr Nevinson has only made £2,000 in the last four years, so he thinks there is something seriously amiss with people who prefer 'hot baths and a limousine' or 'an enlarged photograph of one of their hideous babies' to his pictures.

'Then there is Mr Bernard Shaw who having attended a performance in the Queen's Hall of Sir Edward Elgar's 'The Apostles' and been disgusted at the smallness of the audience, has written to the Press announcing: 'I apologise to posterity for living in a country where the capacity and tastes of schoolboys and sporting costermongers are the measure of metropolitan culture.'

'Various other people have given us to understand that they are more or less ashamed of us and that we are a decadent race. At the conference of the Church of England Men's Society at Leicester, Dr G S Hughes stated that 'Public opinion has changed for the worse in sex matters,' and in support of this statement mentioned 'the demand for easier divorce' and 'the inclination to be sloppy and sentimental over the unmarried mother.'

'And if all this were not enough, we are informed by one newspaper that 'leading biologists assure us that there is no evidence that the physical type of existing races has improved during the historical period of about a hundred centuries.'

'I suppose we should all be feeling thoroughly miserable when we contemplate this record or our manifest imperfections and iniquities – but are we?

'I'm not for one. I refuse to institute odious comparisons between my own physique and that of a gentleman who may have lived a hundred centuries ago. I am equally determined not to feel ashamed of myself for failing to buy Mr Nevinson's pictures. Nor can I bring myself to feel that I am a person of loose morality because I refuse to adopt the Victorian attitude towards the unmarried mother by treating her as an outcast and a moral leper.

'If this indicates a change for the worse in public opinion, I can only say that I would rather be numbered among the sloppy sentimentalists than among the stern unbending churchmen who mistake frightfulness for righteousness. So much am I the victim of 'crushing materialism' that I even refuse to become indignant over the failure of the multitude to rush to the choral performance at Queen's Hall which gave Mr Bernard Shaw so much pleasure and has caused him to become so excited.

'If the occasion was so very important why did not Mr Shaw let us know in advance by writing an article about it? If our intellectual leaders neglect to keep us informed of these matters, we can scarcely be blamed if we know less about them than we do about the Derby and the Cup-finals.'

While such debate continued Elgar wrote little. He orchestrated a Fantasia and Fugue by Bach and a Handel Overture, then composed incidental music to Laurence Binyon's play 'King Arthur'– some of which was earmarked in 1933 for use in his unfinished Third Symphony.

And his attitude towards all he had ever done could be seen from a letter to the Daily Telegraph. Published under the headline 'The Dream of Gerontius – a Real Appreciation' he wrote: 'It will be readily understood that during the more than twenty years that 'The Dream of Gerontius' has been before the public I have received much praise and blame; as far as I can gather the latter predominates, but I may be wrong.

'Such appreciation as comes under my notice usually takes the form of a letter mentioning with much unction, the 'great spiritual uplift' &c, and suggesting the prompt sending of anything from 5s to £5 to pay for seats to hear and a copy or two of the work to follow a performance. But now at last comes the only testimonial I have ever cared to receive; this is from a remote part of New Zealand.

'A lady has been touring and singing, with pianoforte accompaniment, much English music; her selections include the 'Angel's Song': on hearing this a little boy was so delighted that he sent me a message: 'I wish he would could come to stay with us – I would give him my pup.'

'The breed is not specified but that is not material; I long for that pup and if legislation had not interfered with its landing, I would go and fetch it.'

THE FINAL YEARS

During the 1920s Elgar semi-retired making only infrequent public appearances. One of these was to conduct a massed choir at the opening ceremony of the British Empire Exhibition in the specially constructed Wembley Stadium on St George's Day 1924. The year also saw him appointed Master of the King's Musick.

The Daily Telegraph covered the rehearsals in bitter weather during March: 'Grey haired, tall and distinguished of appearance Sir Edward Elgar took his stand on Saturday on the platform of the loud-speaker to rehearse some of the music for the Royal opening less than a month from now. It was our greatest English composer's first experience of conducting a great band, or orchestra by means of the microphone in an open-air arena, and probably the experience was a strange one.

'There will be no greater occasion of the year than the solemn and imposing opening of the exhibition by the King and Queen. Hence the presence of Sir Edward Elgar in one of the bitterest winds of the year to test the acoustics properties of Maxwell Ayrton's great open-air theatre; the greatest coliseum ever built in ancient or modern times.

'Great effects and great music are called for in such a magnificent setting. So, Sir Edward Elgar realised when he mounted the band platform placed on the western side of the Stadium and called upon the Band of the Royal Military School of Music from Kneller Hall to sound the note 'G'. With the musicians were the massed choir of the London Church Choirs Association of some 200 voices.

'The choir cheered the veteran conductor as he mounted the steps. The National Anthem was the first thing Sir Edward desired to test. He wanted the singers to shorten and sharpen their words so that each word could be carried distinct and ennobling to the microphone, and thence by cable to the amplifiers, whence it is conveyed by another cable to the great sound projectors massed on a high platform and transmitted into the Stadium like an invisible sea of sound.

'To the musicians, Elgar called out *'Hit it! Hit it!'* Lieutenant Atkins, Director of Kneller Hall, added with a younger, louder voice *'Attack with the beat'* and again the massed choir and band filled the Stadium with the opening bars of 'God Save Our King'.

"Hit it! Hit it right from the first note!' demanded Elgar and then to the boys he added a note of advice which boys and men alike might follow: *'Stand up like men! That is the only way to sing the National Anthem.'*

The effect was very fine. How much more imposing it will be on St George's Day may be imagined, for on that occasion, in addition to the performers here referred to there will be the massed bands of the Brigade of Guards and a combined United Kingdom choir of 2,000 voices.

'Before he left, Sir Edward took the band and choir through Parry's 'Jerusalem' and Mr Sidney Nicholson rehearsed 'The Old Hundredth'.'

Apart from music he wrote especially for the Wembley event - 'The Pageant of Empire' comprising eight songs and an 'Empire March'- there was little else forthcoming. But in 1928, he produced incidental music for Bertram Matthews's play 'Beau Brummel', which ran at Birmingham's Theatre Royal in November of that year.

The Birmingham Post commented: 'One began to fear that no more music would come from his pen. He has broken silence however and in the way least expected. Not that Sir Edward is new to the theatre; the music to the 'Starlight Express' and 'Grania and Diarmid' found him at home there.

'Some of the incidental music to 'Beau Brummel' will find its way into the concert-room. Sir Edward can still draw on a store of melodies of the characteristic Elgarian type – so characteristic indeed that a mere phrase can be said to declare its origin. Their character of course is not entirely derived from the melodic outline, for their sequential treatment and harmonic progressions contribute towards their individuality.'

Most of Elgar's music disappeared at the end of the run with only a Minuet surviving. The Birmingham Post's report thus provides a rare description of what Elgar produced.

'A Prelude of some length leads into the first act and there are shorter introductions to the later acts. Much music, however, is heard in association with action, to sustain an atmosphere or heighten the tension of a dramatic moment.

'The music to the second act, indeed, plays a more than incidental part, for the act is unified through the music as well as through the action. But the play as a whole is musically unified through a minuet through whose courtly eighteenth-century strains one seems to catch a suggestion that in Beau Brummel a period found the last of its representative types. The period of the play is 1818; therefore when in one of the entr'actes the music breaks into a gay waltz, there is no sense of anachronism.

'The minuet is certain to find its way into the concert-room, and a fine suite could be made from music scored with masterly economy of means and the art of a great mind taking its ease in small things. Melodrame is a feature of the play, and the music accompanying Brummel's fine death scene enhances its poignancy; its wistfulness carried a reminder of the marvellous music of Falstaff's dying moment's in Sir Edward's tone-poem.'

The Daily Telegraph added a further clue: 'In the vivacious music of the introduction, in the charming Minuet or when the orchestra accompanies the action with some sweet melody 'en sourdine' [quietly] the deftness and the individual touch are clearly evident. It is a score which someday perhaps, Sir Edward may turn into a little suite. If he should ever do so, 'The Wand of Youth' will have a worthy companion.'

The Birmingham Gazette commented that though the music 'had not anything startlingly original to say it is endowed throughout with the composer's own particular charm of expression. A little minuet tune haunted the play and this, together with some phrases for clarinet stay pleasantly in the memory. The music between the second and third scenes of the third act had something of the character of programme music. Its irresistible rhythm carried us along the High Road near Bath with Beau Brummel and his servant. The music with its delicate suggestiveness played a large part in heightening the effect of the dying scene in the last act.'

Elgar conducted the first night, and received, according to the Birmingham Mail 'almost reverential rapture.'

It was another two years before anything more of substance came from him – this time in the form of a test piece for the Crystal Palace brass band competition – a work which we know today as 'The Severn Suite' – or 'Severn Sweet' as the Sunday Pictorial called it - originally written for brass band and later adapted for full orchestra.

The press paid the event little attention but were much more animated by the arrival of the fifth Pomp and Circumstance March which appeared in September of 1930 at a Promenade Concert in Queen's Hall, which also included music by Weber, Richard Strauss, Grieg and Cesar Franck. The emergence of a new, and brilliant, orchestral piece from Elgar prompted the papers to hope that this was a new beginning.

One, unidentified paper made the unsubstantiated statement that: 'It was announced at the death of Lady Elgar – the marriage was an ideally happy one – nine years ago, that Sir Edward would never compose again. It is a fact that he has composed practically nothing since then, and certainly no major work, for some incidental music to a play cannot be counted as such. Perhaps we may now hope for a third symphony or another concerto.'

The Daily Telegraph noted that the hall was crowded with all seats sold for the concert, and that 'no recent musical announcement could have given greater pleasure to a vast number of people than the promise of a new military march by Elgar.

'One dares to say that war has little to do with the inspiration of the new work. For this is happy music: militant if you like, but with not memories of the horrors of bloodshed. You may visualise as it pleases you, cheeky, care-free young soldiers on the march, glad enough to be disciplined, glad to be in the sunlight, rejoicing in the possession of health and high spirits, laughter in their hearts. The effect of the whole was exhilarating.'

The Observer added: 'The appearance of a new work by Sir Edward Elgar is something to await with eagerness. Time and opportunity have acquainted us with the profundity, and equally with the scope and varied character of his achievement. His fancy has ranged widely and his liberal sympathies found expression in ways that often may have seemed extremes of contrast. But it is this quality that has given his creative work its unique breadth of appeal; for in his music there is significance for all kinds of listeners, those who feel for the symphonies or those who are stirred by the Pomp and Circumstance marches.

'Elgar's intention had been to write six of these marches. The fifth was heard for the first time at Queen's Hall last night. Like its fellows it is music for special occasions. Or it may be called a laureate piece, the sort of thing that comes with particular aptness from The Master of the King's Musick. The work is richly and heavily scored, is finely rhythmic, and has, as well, a typically Elgarian tunefulness. The audience received it with great enthusiasm.'

Press speculation that Elgar was composing again gained momentum. In December 1930 the Evening Standard announced: 'Sir Edward Elgar is engaged on a new choral work. It is to be full sized and will, I imagine, rank with his masterpieces.'

What did emerge was the 'Nursery Suite', the last work of any substance he completed. Dedicated to the Duke and Duchess of York and the two Royal Princesses, Elizabeth and Margaret Rose, it received its first de-facto performance in the HMV recording studio at Kingsway Hall.

Elgar conducted the London Symphony Orchestra and the rehearsal was attended by the Duke and Duchess, as well as a large group of luminaries including George Bernard Shaw, Landon Ronald, Sir Barry Jackson, the actor Cedric Hardwick, various people from HMV and a group of music critics.

Herbert Hughes, in The Daily Telegraph describing the event: 'On Saturday morning it was my privilege to hear this new and lovely work in rehearsal for the first time, the rehearsal being preliminary to a recording. The occasion was privilege indeed. Here were experts on duty versed in the science of the microphone, making their preparations for a great event. Here were instrumentalists of the London Symphony Orchestra grouped about in the stalls, the auditorium oddly transformed by long strips of heavy material hung from the circle balustrade.

'Here was [Conductor] Lawrence Collingwood, busy with band parts; here was little 'Freddy' Guisberg [sic] [the legendary producer], moving about noiselessly as usual, his manner always that of one who is in some secret hush-hush expedition with a smile like that on the face of the Mona Lisa.

'In the artists' room – the rehearsal has not yet begun - I meet Sir Edward, looking a good ten years younger than the 74 years he reaches next week. He is standing by a table on which some music is lying. On his left is 'Willie' Reed, who has led many a Three Choirs meeting, trying over, very gingerly a cadenza that occurs towards the end of the new suite. On his right is Gordon Walker, one of the finest flute players in the world, trying over an important solo part in 'The Serious Doll' – the second movement. Sir Edward marks time with one hand, indicating the rhythm as the player reads the exquisite page for the first time.

'In a few minutes the composer and his colleagues are back in the hall. A photograph must be taken by flashlight before the first run-through. The Master of the King's Musick seats himself at the desk. 'Bring Collingwood into the picture,' says Sir Edward. Collingwood, modestly protesting is brought forward and the cameras click. The serious business begins. With miraculous ease these players read the new score.

'As I come away it seems to me that the composer was no more delighted than those fine players who realised that they had a new masterpiece under their fingers. The composer may call this nursery music; but those of us who have ears know well, that this score, written for the Royal Duchess and her children is the sublimation of eternal youth. There is a philosophy, a metaphysic in this music that comes from one of the subtlest intellects of our time. These moving contrasts of sadness and gaiety have only been expressed in this music because they have been deeply felt. Like Verdi in his day, our Elgar appears to grow younger and more masterful as the years pass.'

That October, Elgar made one of his, by now, scarce appearances in London, to conduct the second symphony, in an all-Elgar programme which also featured Henry Wood conducting 'Cockaigne', the 'Cello Concerto, with Thelma Reiss Smith as soloist, and Parry Jones singing part of 'King Olaf'.

Considering the criticism in the 1920s at the alleged lack of interest and the scant number of concerts featuring Elgar's music, the audience reaction this time was interesting.

'Crowded House at the Proms', declared the Daily Telegraph - 'splendid tributes offered to him by the audience which filled every part of the Queen's Hall. Significant, too, was the close attention with which each movement of the work was followed throughout, as though the audience was determined to miss none of its subtle and often glowing beauties. The enthusiasm at the close was overwhelming and Sir Edward had to return several times to the platform in response to the demonstrations.'

The Daily Mail agreed, but made an interesting observation, considering that so much has been made of audience applause at Elgar premiers in the early years of the century: 'The symphony was listened in silence. The new fashion, by the way of 'no applause between movements' does not suit Elgar's symphony, the first movement of which, with its concluding full orchestral glissando, demands applause. At the end of the splendid performance there was an ovation – an abused word, but it really was an ovation this time. No man on earth but must have felt touched by such tribute by assembled thousands.'

No further large-scale works were to come from Elgar, but in March 1932, Anton Dolin produced a ballet to the music of the 'Nursey Suite', choreographed by Ninette de Valois. Elgar attended the first night, and, according to reports, received a 'rapturous reception'. Also present, unannounced, was the Duchess of York.

One anonymous report bore reference to Elgar's love of the theatre, and, along with many others hoped that this ballet might bring forward more theatrical productions from his pen. However, it did remark that although he was a 'frequent playgoer, his preference, strangely enough, is for revues and musical comedies. Not long ago he was seen in a local theatre in his beloved West Country, intently watching a touring company perform a review entitled 'Curls and Camisoles.'

The ballet featured a succession of well-known nursery characters, such as Little Bo-Peep and Georgie Porgie.

Herbert Hughes, in the Daily Telegraph commented: 'This making of ballets of music already composed is an arbitrary business. More often than not it is worlds away from the composer's vision. I have not asked Sir Edward Elgar what he thought of Little Bo-Peep and Georgie Porgie, and Jack and Jill gambolling to the magic wiles of the choreographist [sic], Ninette de Valois; or of the Prince and Princess so handsomely impersonated by Anton Dolin and Alicia Markova. One may be sure he was not thinking of the Three Bears when he was writing the Waggon music or of the other strange things that could happen.

'What matters is that it was a most animated show and that the audience whistled and cheered with delight. When it was over Miss [Lilian] Baylis brought Sir Edward onto the stage and the curtains rose and descended many times before the audience realised there is a limit to the number of times even the Master of the King's Musick can bow to his acknowledgements.'

That same year the BBC paid £1,000 – about £45,000 in today's money – to commission his much anticipated Third Symphony. The move was applauded by George Bernard Shaw in a letter to the Times, written rather exotically from The Blue Train, paying tribute to Sir John Reeth, the BBC's Director General, but he added: 'Is it not a pity that Sir Edward has had to wait so long for the advent of a public administrator capable of rising to the situation ?'

An unattributed press cutting in the Elgar Birthplace Archives, cites a visit by a correspondent to Elgar's Worcester home where he was given an idea of what the symphony would be like. : 'It is easy to understand how rumours have become attached to the new symphony for no work since the pre-war years has been so eagerly expected by English musicians. The symphony is growing fast. After the first week of the Malvern Festival I paid a visit to Sir Edward at Worcester and was privileged to hear a few episodes from the work.

'Sir Edward brought out several sheets of manuscript and, going over to the piano, warned me that I should get no idea of the orchestral sonority. 'This for instance is for strings,' and he played an extended theme built on sequences and sang the melody as violins would sing and phrase it. 'These chords are all for the brass, and here violas have the theme.'

'And so, in spite of the warning I began to arrive somewhere near to the actual sound of the music. 'Here's another tune; the fiddles will love this,' and again he played and sang the melody, straining as if to transmute pianoforte into violin tone there and then. All the time he seemed to be regarding the music as the creation of another mind, something that he had discovered by chance and had taken lovingly to himself. It has always been so with him.

'The Third Symphony has possessed the composer ever since he began it some months ago. It is designed like the first two symphonies and the Violoncello Concerto, in four movements. Each movement is based upon splendid thematic material, which, without being reminiscent of earlier works, carries the unmistakable imprint of the composer's mind. I cannot speak of the development sections, but in the themes themselves there is abundant and appropriate material for that subtle mind to work upon.

'The symphony has an impressive opening, strong and direct, and each movement appears to be tempered with an austerity which is not found in the other symphonies and although something of that influence is felt in the Violoncello Concerto, here it moves with greater force, not beneath the burden of a sorrow. In the harmony there are new sounds. They are borne neither of theory nor of the environment of contemporary experiments, but of necessity.

'When first the Angel of the Agony episode was heard, Elgar was known to be a pioneer in harmonic invention. The creative process has never since stopped, and now, out of his own independent imagination, comes this renewal of harmonic thought. There is in it nothing outrageous or far-fetched, but somehow one thinks it has never been said before quite like this.'

Another visitor was the correspondent from the Daily Express who claimed that he'd 'surprised him at lunch in his manor house deep in the country where he has retired to compose the work.'

Elgar's home, Marl Bank, large but hardly a manor house, was not too far from the Worcester City Centre.

He apparently commenced the interview by declaring: *'Don't talk to me about music, talk to me about something I know – horse-racing – I've studied it all my life.'*

The correspondent painted a picture of how he found Elgar: 'Spick, span and debonair, in perfectly pressed brown tweeds, his white hair and dragoon moustache curling onto an alabaster skin, he sat between two spaniels at the table in a low beamed room giving on to that garden county of England. The telephone rang. He leaped to answer it. I had heard that he never answered telephones – that his life was completely inaccessible.

"*King Oscar won'* – he ejaculated. *'Good. I was on it and on the second. How much? Splendid: then I'm in clover. That was my bookmaker friend,'* he confided, returning to the table and increasing my astonishment at this supposedly austere personage.

"*I know them all. But this one was specially introduced to me on the racecourse, and what do you think I found him doing? Studying the score of the Second Symphony between taking bets. He had it off by heart and asked me to sign it. I would have signed anything for the boy, except a cheque of course, which would have been careless.'* Sir Edward could not help winking.

'The limit of fastidiousness is Sir Edward Elgar, from the selection of his shirt, which harmonises with his suit, to his long pale hands, as dimpled and as slender as any young woman's, to the ultimate phrasing of his music, where an acute sensitiveness defines the broad sweep of his work. He strode about the room brimful of vitality.

"*I am a literary man; I only resigned the Presidency of the London Library when I came into the country. And I am a chemist. My music is mostly written in flashes when I'm out fishing. I then dig it from the basket weeks later.'*

'He fell into a silence and his dogs talked to him. They are his inseparable companions. Suddenly he hummed a snatch of melody and rose. A sharpness had come into his voice: *'I have work to do, a great deal of it.'*

"'Yes, the Symphony – I pressed eagerly. 'How many movements has it?'

"*Movements? Symphony?* he echoed, leaving for his study across the passage. *'I know of no symphony. I'm writing an opera.'*

This year saw the collaboration with the 16-year-old Yehudi Menhuin with the Violin Concerto resulting in the celebrated recording they made together, and the live performances in London and, in the following year, Paris. The overseas trip saw Elgar's visit to see the invalid Delius at his home at Grez-sur-Loing, near Fontainebleau.

The Berrow's Worcester Journal covered the event, mentioning that Elgar had taken some records of music by Sibelius and Hugo Wolf as a gift for his fellow composer, but none of his own.

"*Delius would not want to hear my music*,' he said in his modest way.'

The paper quoted from an interview that Fred Gaisberg, of HMV gave to the Press Association following the meeting: "There was something of pathos in that meeting. Yet I have never seen two men with so much joy at being together again. Both of them are old and one is blind and stricken with paralysis. Yet in the two hours that they were together they seemed completely to recapture their lost youth.

"They talked of happy days together at Leipzig, of concerts where they had listened together, and of music they had created and played to each other. They were really like a pair of boys."

Another unattributed report stated that the two composers were 'old friends. Distance has prevented close intercourse; but they have much in common beside the bond of nationality.'

The Daily Telegraph printed Elgar's own account of the meeting which discussed Delius's love of Dickens, Elgar's own literary suggestions and his new-found interest in flying.

He concluded: '*The time passed all too quickly and the moment of parting arrived. We took an affectionate farewell of each other, Delius holding both my hands. I left him in the house surrounded by roses and I left him with a feeling of cheerfulness. To me he seemed like the poet who, seeing the sun again after his pilgrimage had found complete harmony between will and desire.*

'*In passing through the pine-scented forest of Fontainebleau on the way to see Delius, I had come to a turn of the road leading to Barbizon. The scent recalled a scent of romance of 1880, and I nearly – very nearly – turned to Barbizon. After my visit to Grez I decided to go to Barbizon, but when I passed the crossroads the longing had passed away. That belonged to the romance of 1880, now dead. My mind was now full of another romance – the romance of Frederic Delius.*'

References to Elgar's meetings with Delius over the years remain scant – they certainly encountered each other in 1909 when they both conducted their works at the Hereford Festival. Yet Gaisberg's comments suggested that they were much closer friends than any hard evidence has supported – particularly his statement that they had spent what would seem to be some time together in Leipzig.

Available evidence places Elgar in Leipzig between December 31st 1882 and January 18th 1883. Delius is known to have attended the Leipzig Conservatoire between 1886 and 1888. There appears to be no evidence that Elgar travelled to Germany during that period, which would mean that they could only have met in Leipzig during the earlier time, when it is known that Delius, forced to work on behalf of his family's business, neglected his duties to visit the major musical centres in Germany. Whether this is the case is open to speculation.

However, there appears no doubt that Elgar and Delius enjoyed a friendship long before their meeting in 1933. A letter Elgar wrote to Sir Adrian Boult in advance of that meeting made reference to his excitement at the prospect of meeting 'my old friend Delius' and from the nature of the records which Elgar took as a gift, he appears to have knowledge of the other composer's musical preferences.

After the French trip, Elgar's health deteriorated. He had an exploratory operation which found he was terminally ill, and he entered the South Bank Nursing Home, south of Worcester. While there, in early 1934, Elgar directed an orchestra in London in a recording of some of his works via a telephone link from his sick bed.

The event excited the press. The Daily Mirror reported on January 23rd: 'Tired of idleness after many weeks of illness, Sir Edward who is nearly seventy-seven suggested to His Master's Voice Company that he should make a record of the triumphal march from 'Caractacus', one of his earlier works which has never been recorded.

'Two telephone lines specially tested for the wide frequency of an orchestra were rented from the G.P.O. and in the St John's Wood studio, the London Symphony Orchestra, seventy strong, conducted by Mr Lawrence Collingwood, played the march. With a special loudspeaker at his bedside, Sir Edward heard the orchestra and through the microphone commented on the playing and made suggestions and criticisms.

'When the piece had been played once, Sir Edward said: '*I want all the tune you can get out of the clarinets and oboes in that figure. La,La,La,*' hummed Sir Edward, ' *that is how I want the tune brought out.'* Then he added: *'that's a nice noise to make, my voice is like a crow's.'*

'When the record had been made, Sir Edward asked the orchestra to play his 'Woodland Interlude', and after listening to it he remarked *'I want it very much lighter and a slower tempo.'* The orchestra played it through again and Sir Edward expressed his satisfaction.'

He died a month to the day after this.

It is fitting, however, considering this journey through his lifelong relationship with the press, to note that one of his last letters was sent to a journalist - written via dictation to Edward F Corbett, who wrote a local heritage column in the Berrow's Worcester Journal under the pen-name 'Stroller'.

In his letter, Elgar urged him to consider an article based on his favourite area of Worcestershire – the places he remembered as a boy growing up all those years ago:

'…The Teme to me is the very heart of Worcestershire, that is to say from Worcester through haunted Shelsley – the valley of the Shelsleys is the most romantic bit of the Shire – as far as (say) Orleston where my interest ceases or wanes.

'The majority of Worcestershire people know nothing, except what is seen from the bridges of the most distinctive & picturesque feature in their county: the 'gorge' between Knightsford Bridge and Martley Bridge…'

THE AFTERMATH

Elgar's dying wish to be cremated and his ashes scatted at the confluence of the Rivers Teme and Severn, just south of Worcester, was ignored, presumably because it was not in accordance with Catholic tradition. Suggestions of burial in Westminster Abbey were similarly rejected, also on account of his Catholic faith, so a compromise was reached by burying him with Alice at Little Malvern.

The funeral was to be 'secret'. The Daily Dispatch quoted Elgar's daughter Carice: 'The late Sir Edward Elgar expressed a definite wish that the funeral should be absolutely private and that neither the day nor the place should be known. He was anxious there should be no mourning or flowers.'

Nevertheless, the news got out and a photographer managed to sneek in to record the event and the photographs he took that day made several papers. The ceremony involved very few mourners, mainly drawn from members of Elgar's family together with long standing friends such as W H Reed, Ivor Atkins and Hubert Leicester. There was no music and no mourning clothing. Only a small bunch of daffodils, sent in by two lady well-wishers, bearing the legend 'From two lovers of the symphonies and Falstaff' were placed on the purple-draped coffin.

The Bristol based Western Daily poetically described the scene, though one wonders where the information came from considering that the event was supposed to be secret and private: 'In the secluded Roman Catholic church of St Wulstan's no organ sounded a Te Deum in honour of the great composer. There was no choir. Not a bell tolled to summon the mourners, nor to mark his passing.

'There were no visible signs of mourning. The score of intimate friends who followed the purple-draped coffin wore the garb of the every day world. Sir Edward's only daughter stood at the graveside in country tweeds, light coloured stockings, a brown hat and a grey fur coat. And there were no fears. Dry-eyed, the mourners watched as Sir Edward was laid to his rest.

'The congregation numbered less than a score. The brief service, read in Latin, was conducted by the Rev G C Alston. With him were youths who held the incense burner and the Holy water. Another youth held a gleaming cross at the foot of the purple and gold covered coffin. Candles cast a gentle radiance over the church.

'In a few minutes those present passed out into the sunshine to the churchyard. In a sheltered corner, a moss-lined grave, lying immediately beside that of Lady Elgar, who passed on 14 years ago, had been prepared.

'With the smoke of the incense rising on the still air and only the murmuring voice of the Priest breaking the silence, the funeral service was brought to an end.

'Even as the mourners walked away slowly, the sky became overcast and snowflakes fell gently onto the coffin with its bold embossed cross. For a moment, the spreading valley of the Severn and the steep slopes of the Malvern Hills were hidden.

'*'I am a Worcester man and proud of it,'* Sir Edward once said and now he lies side by side in Worcester soil with his partner in life.'

When Alice had died, Elgar buried the regalia of his honours with her. Romantic notions of grief, loss and tribute have surrounded this gesture ever since but the innate sense of rejecting ostentation which hallmarked his own funeral, may have been the real reason. Alice's Times obituary, doubtless based on his testimony, had noted: 'he broke his resolve to remain 'Mr Elgar' all his days, and took whatever honours came his way for her sake.'

Elgar's death received the usual obituaries and tributes. Fond myths which have surrounded Elgar's story ever since were also now invented.

The Evening Standard announced 'The romantic story of Elgar's life' which discussed Elgar's upbringing, his self-taught musical education and his alleged shunning by musical society as he tried to establish himself: 'He was wholly apart from the school of which his somewhat older contemporaries, Stanford and Parry, were the prominent representatives. If the advantages which such composers enjoyed had at the same time drawbacks, they were at least saved from being cold-shouldered. Undoubtedly Elgar was cold-shouldered. '*When I entered the musical world of London in the 'eighties,*' he said in a speech last year, '*I wrote letters to eminent musicians in an attempt to get recognition for my compositions. Fred Cowen (now Sir Frederic) was the only one who replied."*

Such a 'romantic' notion of the struggling genius attempting to gain support from the hierarchy of his art, and receiving nothing but rebuff, is certainly very endearing – particularly with the knowledge of hindsight.

But in any creative field, then and now, the famous are routinely bombarded with requests from wannabes seeking assistance in their careers – not least Elgar, when he himself became famous. Even in the early days, long before his Knighthood and when he only had the honorary Doctorate of Music from Cambridge to adorn his name, autograph hunters were tersely dispatched with printed cards worded: 'Dr Edward Elgar gives his autograph at the request of personal friends only.' During his time at Brinkwells, the handyman, Mark Holden, was tasked, according to W H Reed, with emptying the waste-paper basket – 'when the daily torrent of circulars, requests for autographs and begging letters overflowed'. One wonders whether the waste-paper basket contained similar requests from unknown musicians 'in an attempt to get recognition' for their fledgling careers?

And was it not the same Fred Cowen – the only one who had replied to his own 'begging letter' when he was an unknown - who Elgar had cruelly slighted with his ham-fisted attack on conductors when Professor at Birmingham?

The Daily Express summed up Elgar's life thus - glossing over some of the minor details of the actual facts: 'Born in 1857 in Worcester, he was the son of a Roman Catholic organist who kept a music shop. His parents were poor, he was self- educated and at one time conducted bands in county asylums. He was first brought into prominence by Richard Strauss, who declared he was the greatest living composer when he heard the 'Dream of Gerontius' in Germany in 1901.'

Everybody's Weekly ran a headline: 'His First Audience were Lunatics' and then commenced: 'Fifty-five years ago a poor man of twenty-two made his first bow as a conductor before the inmates of Worcester County Asylum. His orchestra was composed of the Asylum attendants and the music played was a composition of the young conductor. Ten years later this young man with many compositions to his credit came to London. Like Wagner in Paris with the score of 'Tannhauser' in his pocket, Elgar went from pillar to post to meet everywhere with discouragement. And as Wagner left Paris for Dresden, so Elgar left London for Malvern. While he was living there as a conductor and teacher this brilliant son of a Worcester organist was composing mighty music and in the end, as always happens, the world stopped to listen.'

An incisive assessment of Elgar and his place in the history of music came from Van Norman Lucas.

Writing in a publication called 'G R's Weekly' he wrote: 'To his own generation of musicians he was an enigma. To the present generation he remains as a noble and living monument of the past. His was a lonely figure: as Gibraltar stands, towering and massive and lonely in the surrounding sea.

'Indeed it is easy for us, in the welter of post-war music to forget how much of the freedom now enjoyed from the deadening restraint of the dons we owe to the bitter warfare through which Elgar fought to his final eminence – and to the acknowledgment won from a startled Europe that good could come out from England.

'Historically he stands between the end of an epoch, and the beginning of something new, the end of which is hidden from us. He belongs to the old, yet the old, with a few exceptions, knew him not. That much at least, of the new, we can recognise. Ours is an age of experiment, much of it of great interest but of its nature insecure and unstable. Elgar was content with established forms.

'The two symphonies, 'Falstaff', the 'Enigma Variations', 'Gerontius' and the violin and 'cello concertos are works which will rank among the great music of the world; and there are, in the conscious and deliberate national music, great sweeping melodies – sentimental, vulgar if you wish, as many of them are - that will thrill while lives a man who can thrill and be inspired by the glory that once was England's.

'A last word on this national question. Elgar was a great creator of music who would have won for himself respect, admiration and recognition had he been born in Czechoslovakia or Timbuctoo.

'He was English of the English and brought to the music of Western civilisation something which only he, the individual and the Englishman could bring. It is therefore common to talk of his music as essentially English. It is somewhat ironical that the essential English were almost the last of the nations of Europe to recognise his greatness.

'In truth, Elgar's music is essentially Elgarian. He wrote as an Englishman in the language of the far wider culture of Europe. He is a great musician for all time. He was a great patriot of an age before patriotism had narrowed to nationalism, before men had to wear coloured shirts to be conscious of their heritage.'

An article in the Guardian recalled other aspects of Elgar's character: 'A writer recalls the master's pleasure in new clothes, in which, he said, he found fresh inspiration when composing. He had pride too in his appearance we are told and would often tease his friends by demanding of them (half in earnest) if they did not think he looked like a guardsman.

'He enjoyed the pleasures of ordinary people and on one occasion meeting the writer referred to confessed that he was on the way to see a review *Clowns in Clover* for the twelfth or fourteenth time – he couldn't remember which.'

Clowns in Clover, ran at the Adelphi Theatre in the West End for 588 performances between 1926 and 1927. It featured a long list of songs including: 'Goodbye Mr Gloom', 'I Can't Get the Rhythm', 'Sarsparilla Bodkin' and 'There's a Trick in Pickin' a Chick Chick Chicken'.

Personal reminiscences also filled the papers.

Robert Buckley in the Birmingham Gazette recalled his first meeting with Elgar during the 1880s when W C Stockley, in whose Birmingham orchestra Elgar played, sent out a request for Buckley to meet him.

'When I arrived, he brought forward a friend named Elgar, whom he formally introduced, and, the ceremony over, said: *'I think him a clever fellow and I want you to give him a lift in the Gazette'*.

'My first impression of my new friend was his shyness and his superior intelligence. We became intimate: I lent him books, he lent me books. We corresponded and I wrote him up in the Gazette, until jealous musicians persuaded Alexander Still, the Gazette editor, to interview me concerning my alleged raptures.

'I remember the central idea of his remarks thus: *'I do not question your judgement, but you will remember that over-praise is apt to damage rather than assist.'*

'Having a free rein, I continued my weekly comments until the production of 'Gerontius' after which the grumblers held their breath. Elgar was an omnivorous reader of good literature. *'If musicians would read and assimilate the great poets they would write better music,'* was a favourite aphorism of his creation.

'As a man he was grave, courteous, sincere and at time humorous. He could also be crushing when meeting with vulgarity, impudence or indecency; which he would chastise with such scorn that the criminal at the moment of concussion regretted the indestructability of matter and wished himself well out of the universe.

'He had a quaint dislike for the connection of art with the commercial things of life. In a long letter he wrote: *'I was invited to the Wagner memorial celebration, but I respectfully declined. Too commercial! The progress of art and not the piling up of money, in a case like this should be the great object in the foreground.'*

'Arriving unexpectedly one day, I was met by Elgar's wife. She said Edward was at work, but that she would tell him I was there. *'Send him in!'* he cried, and entering the sacred enclosure, I found Elgar in his shirt-sleeves and with a penknife vigorously scratching out on a manuscript score.

''Hard work composing,' said I, 'when you have to doff your waistcoat.'

''*I'm not composing; I'm decomposing,*' he replied. Then, with a roguish twinkle, he, looking up, added: *'Perhaps you don't think I scratch out enough?'* And as I merely smiled in reply, he continued: *'Perhaps you think it would be better to scratch it all out?'*

'This was after the arrival of 'Gerontius' in 1900, a work not at first appreciated by reason of its novelty. *'We must advance,'* he declared. *'To follow slavishly our predecessors is not the best art. We should strive to better as our ancestors strove to do better, and more or less succeeded. For though we may not accomplish the glory of actual and complete novelty, we should have done our endeavours to show and lead the way.'*

'Concerning 'Gerontius' in its early days, Elgar wrote to me: *'You have seen the big wreath given to me after the performance at the Lower Rhine Festival of 'Gerontius' when all Dusseldorf was said to have risen to the work. The most reverent performance so far, and therefore the best. Next comes the Sheffield performance. And you will note this fact – that there is no record of any work by a British composer ever before having been given at these festivals. Hail me, Buckley boy, on the conquest of Germany !'*

Horse-racing legend Somerville Tattersall in the Horse and Hound, highlighted Elgar's love of the races. Tattersall recalled Elgar staying with him for the spring meeting at Newmarket in 1933 and continued: 'from the age of thirteen he had taken an interest in racing and longed to see Newmarket, but that visit was his first and writing to me at the end of the year he said, *'I never expected Newmarket, even for a moment, a reality but you made it so and most pleasantly so. This alone makes 1933 one of the really bright years.'* I feel sure that he often went racing quietly – not in the Club enclosures – though I never saw him on a racecourse until last year. He certainly followed form carefully.'

Referring to that spring Newmarket meeting, Tattersall added: 'He asked me whether I thought Gold Bridge would give Golden Legend the weight. I did and backed the top weight; he backed Golden Legend – a 5 to 1 winner – and then motored off 130 miles to Worcester. I never met Sir Edward till December 12th 1932, at his own house, Marl Bank, Worcester, which he described as his 'last little haven before the end'. He sent his car over to Birmingham to fetch Yehudi Menuhin and his father and me to lunch. His first question to me was, *'What do you think of the Free Handicap?'* A dog sat on either side of him at lunch. He had several others, mostly spaniels.

'At the end of December I sent him two records of Chopin's nocturnes played by Pachmann. He then wrote an entire letter in pencil, thanking me and saying how overjoyed he was to hear that the Worcester race committee talked of naming a race after him. He said: *'Here is fame at last!'* At Newmarket he had been talking of giving a clock-tower to the stand at Worcester. He thought that would be better than *'some silly monument to him'*.'

Tattersall quoted only one phrase from the letter he received from Elgar. This was written on December 28th 1933, and is probably the last letter Elgar ever wrote – its content is telling:

The full text reads:

'My dear Tattersall

'All good wishes for 1934. I should be ungrateful if I did not at once thank you for the records: Pachmann was among the great artists.

'I wish our race meeting was something worthy of your stable!

'I am overjoyed - Colonel Payne [of the Worcester Race Club] *wrote yesterday that the Club will name a race after me! Naturally it will only be a £100 selling plate (!) but it is fame at last and will (D.V.) remove the stigma of the symphonies, concerti etc etc.'*

The composer Havergal Brian, in the P[erforming].R[ights]. Gazette recalled the first performance of 'King Olaf': 'The few who assembled in the Victoria Hall, Hanley on that chilly October morning for the launching of 'King Olaf' took part in the most historical ceremony in English musical history. Owing to a misunderstanding, Edward Lloyd missed his train and did not sing in the final rehearsal. In the first big tenor solo, Willy Hess - who was leading the orchestra – seeing Elgar's temerity and scenting danger, jumped to his feet and saved the situation. Elgar was grateful ever afterwards to Willy Hess. In spite of an indifferent performance 'King Olaf' won by its intensely musical inspiration, rich and sumptuous orchestration and a dramatic impulse hitherto unsuspected from an English composer.'

Fritz Kreisler in the Daily Telegraph remembered the first performance of the Violin Concerto: 'I went to see him in Worcestershire and found him at white heat. The sheets of his manuscript had been flung one after the other on the floor, which was strewn with them.' This echoed a similar anecdote he had given to the Strand Magazine some years before: 'I was in the composer's study. Scattered all around the floor were the sheets of manuscript where the composer had dropped them to dry as they came from his pen. We picked them up between us, numbered them hurriedly, and I set them, still barely dry, upon the music stand, picked up my violin and played.'

As far as other aspects of Elgar's character were concerned, Kreisler, as reported in the Worcester Journal, found him 'not easy to play with'.

'In his enthusiasm during performance of rehearsal he would forget everything around him in face of the beauty of his own work. On one occasion during a rehearsal he went on conducting his concerto for several minutes before he noticed that the soloist, who was Kreisler himself on this occasion, had stopped playing.'

Fred Cowen recalled in a letter to The Times: 'Like most musicians his nature was a simple one. He was not in the least conceited, though his constant and marked depreciation of his own music might lead one to imagine that this was the case. Elgar was sociable when one got to know him, easily amused and fond of outdoor and indoor games, of which, indeed, he was often the instigator.'

Gerald Lawrence, who had directed the 1928 play 'Beau Brummel' for which Elgar wrote the incidental music, wrote to the Daily Telegraph: 'We had our dress rehearsal on the Sunday night, and everything that could possibly go wrong went wrong. Misfortune culminated with the entire collapse of the scenery at the end of Act II. This caused me to go completely 'off the deep end' for about a minute and I do not think I repeated myself. Elgar, at the end of the outburst, rapped on his desk with his baton, and said: *'Gerald, you have not kept one word for me to say to the orchestra!'*"

Walter Willson Cobbett, the great sponsor of chamber music and instigator of the Cobbett Cyclopaedia, recalled an incident with Elgar's String Quartet involving the Worshipful Company of Musicians: 'It was the outcome of a commission originally offered to Elgar with an honorarium of 50 guineas [about £4,000 in today's money], but at the moment of publication [in 1919] so many years had elapsed that he refused to accept it. I suggested to him that he should write a piano trio, that being a form that British composers of the first rank had unaccountably neglected, and so square matters.

'He accepted, mentioning casually that he had already a trio in portfolio. However, years wore on; it did not make its appearance, and I ended by inducing him to accept the honorarium which I considered to be really his due. Thus, this famous quartet came to be entitled to be considered as a commission of the Musician's Company.'

A short report in the Edinburgh Evening News succinctly summed up Elgar's character: 'He was one of those rare men who was a genius without the eccentricities of genius. He liked going to the theatre, put money on horses, did cross-word puzzles on the train, and was a diligent reader of newspapers. He was always well dressed. Elgar decked himself out fastidiously before he started to compose.'

An amusing anecdote was supplied to the Worcester Daily Times from the actor Sir Cedric Hardwicke from his book 'Let's Pretend': 'When at a south coast resort where he was conducting a music festival, Elgar chanced to meet an old school friend who had come down to play in a croquet tournament. For a while they talked of boyhood days. Then the friend remarked: *'By the way, weren't you awfully keen on music at school?'*

'Sir Edward admitted he was. But when the first question was followed up with the enquiry *'Did you keep it up?'* the composer was so surprised that he could scarcely stammer a reply.'

Another similar anecdote was run by the Weekly Dispatch: 'Sir Edward Elgar called one day at a music shop to buy some lined music paper. The assistant took a friendly interest in his quiet customer and kindly told him how the paper should be used.'

The American born Shakespearean actress Mary de Navarro, who lived at Broadway, Worcestershire with her musician husband Antonio, and had been friends with Elgar for more than 25 years recalled, in a letter to the Times, how he rarely used to pass her door without calling in. 'He would frequently arrive with an unpublished record or two as a present. Once he came with the proof-records of his magnificent 'Falstaff' and marched about the room acting the part with much spirit, now and then breaking off to explain the different scenes portrayed in his music.

'Another time he brought us a record of Moszkowski's Malaguena and danced me wildly about the room while it was being played.

'He saw good in all sorts of music, even in good jazz. Two years ago Sir John McCormack [the great Irish tenor] was staying with us and Sir Edward came over for a long day. He was in brilliant form. He played a great deal, with the orchestral effects that characterize a composer's piano-playing, and he accompanied McCormack in parts of 'Gerontius'. It was an unforgettable day.

'He was full of life and fun and loved chaff. Some years ago, Sir James Barrie [author of 'Peter Pan'] was coming to lunch. We knew he liked being alone with us as we did with him. Sir Edward happened to ring us up and propose himself for lunch on the same day. My husband laughingly told him that two O.M.s at one meal would be more than an ordinary household could grapple with, but he replied *'I don't care a hoot who the other O.M. is. I am coming.'*

'He arrived early, very smartly dressed. He had beautiful feet and was wearing patent leather shoes and white spats. While we were chaffing him about them Barrie stood at the door showing visible signs of dismay. *'Who is he?'* he whispered. 'Elgar'. *'Oh'* with a look of relief, *'I don't mind him. I've known him for years.'*

'We had a very lively lunch. Sir James does not care for music. So, Elgar, turning to me, said *'After lunch, Mamie, we'll bind Barrie to an arm-chair and put him to death to slow music.'*

Sir James looked at him and answered quietly *'I'd rather be trodden to death by your buskins,'* [i.e. Elgar's patent leather shoes]. This retort delighted Elgar.

'Yet for all his merriment and exuberance there was a certain largesse, a distinction about him that marked Elgar as a great man. Last December, before leaving Broadway for two months, I visited him in the Nursing Home in Worcester. As he lay on his bed he looked more beautiful than I had ever seen him look before.

'He was much thinner his noble forehead and his hands were pallid, but otherwise his colour was fresh and clear. He held my hands and said: *'I am a very sick man. Do you realize? I am a very sick man.'* Then he smiled and asked me if I motored over in the 'Straight Eight' (he used to chaff me about it and say that it was the only straight thing in our old place). I told him I had and that I would come in it when I returned and drive him over to stay with us at Broadway. *'I should love nothing better,'* he said.

'He spoke of how, when he stayed with us, he would ask me to blow for him while he extemporized on the organ in our music room each evening about sunset. I told him that I had put the baton with which he had conducted the first performance of his violin concerto into the hand of the bronze Antinous, which stood between the two pianos; and how a little while before, when [pianists] Harold Samuel and Myra Hess were about the play on them, I had told them to play at their best as Elgar was conducting.'

'He smiled. *'I am glad I am not forgotten,'* he said. He kissed me good-bye. *'I believe it IS good-bye'.*

'And, as I looked back at him from the door I knew that it was for the last time. Leaving him, I felt that the direction 'nobilmente', so often met with in his works, might serve as a fitting motto for the life that informed them and above all for that life's close.'

But perhaps the final comment from those who personally knew Elgar came from Ernest Oldmeadow, Editor of the Catholic magazine The Tablet. He had been friends with Elgar from the very early days and had published a version of what was to become 'In Haven', the second of the 'Sea Pictures' song cycle, and the Minuet for Piano, in a quarterly arts magazine he edited called The Dome.

Oldmeadow recalled an encounter at Hereford shortly after 'Gerontius' had received its triumphal performance at Dusseldorf: 'So far as I remember, there was some Kappelmeistermusik grimly awaiting us and Elgar was fortifying himself with a pipe. A London music-critic came up and joined us. He was one of the type familiar enough thirty years ago, when men with only a dabbling knowledge of music or painting could get positions as music-critics or 'art critics' so long as they wrote stylish English and made no howlers.

'This particular critic began talking about 'the technique of composition' and asking for opinions on it. At last Elgar had had enough. I forget his exact words; but he said in effect that he never bothered to think whether his technique was 'developing' or not. A composer, he added, moves on from one composition to another, always striving to master more and more of the means of expression with the result that what an outsider might call his technique undergoes changes and makes headway; but it is his works in themselves that preoccupy an artist, and not some art-critic's abstraction, dubbed 'technique'.

Oldmeadow considered this 'robust, creative spirit' in Elgar which 'estranged him from the type of critic who will not accept as a true artist any man who is not highly self-conscious. The ugly music-makers of today give many of us the impression that they are writing for one another and for an intelligentsia terrified of being a day behind the fair, rather than for simple mankind. Whether Elgar was serious when he declared that he did not read newspaper critiques of his works I cannot say. But it seems to me that much of his music will live because he made it beautifully; and things of beauty will be joys for ever.'

Despite these appreciations, Elgar's reputation had been under attack for decades, mainly in academic books and papers. The effects of this still persist and expose the ephemeral weakness of any newspaper article seeking to defend him. A book remains available for study for many years forming opinion lasting for generations. A newspaper article exists for just a few brief hours before the next edition appears.

In 1907, Ernest Walker of the 'Oxford School' of criticism, denounced Elgar's 'hot-house type of emotionalism', his 'forced pseudo-impressiveness', and a tendency to 'allow colour to hide content'.

In the 1917 'A History of Music', the Irish Protestant composer Charles Villiers Stanford issued this scant dismissal: 'Cut off from his contemporaries by his religion and his want of regular academic training, he was lucky enough to enter the field and find the preliminary ploughing done.'

At the time The Queen magazine replied: 'Singularly unhappy and unjust is the brief discussion of Sir Edward Elgar. Why a composer's religion should cut him off from his contemporaries, none but the most intolerant of bigots can imagine. Lack of academic training is not a total loss to a man of genius, and it is quite certain that those who ploughed Elgar's field (whoever they may have been) did not provide him with the seeds of his inspiration.'

Fine words, perhaps. But they were gone when the next edition arrived. The book, on the other hand, inventing its long-regurgitated notions of deficiency through lack of academic training and a Catholic religion was reprinted in 2018.

In 1921 J F Porte's biography received this in the Musical Times: 'From literary and critical points of view it is easily the worst book of the kind I have so far come across. It is ill-written, banal, and in several respects shows deplorable want of taste.

'One almost wonders whether the pages were read in proof, so slovenly is the composition and punctuation. Almost at random my eyes light on such gems as these: *'On his art he could cover a wild (sic) field of discussive matter'*. *'No composer had a more faithful propagandarist (sic) than Elgar did in Richter'*

'Of 'Salut d'amour' and 'Mot d'amour': *'We do not know whether Elgar was under any amorous influence at this time, but both pieces betray a curious earnestness to outline their subject'*

'As an example of muddled expression and bad taste look at this: *'There are many parts of the libretto of 'Gerontius' which seem fanatical to us: for instance we believe in the existence of 'Purgatory' as much as we do Jack's Beanstalk, or Alice's Wonderland, but the whole is vivid and imaginative, Elgar's music fitting in exactly with the words'*

'And there are at least two other passages in Mr Porte's discussion of Newman's poem that will make a good many readers feel disposed to hurl his book into the dustbin. I could go on and fill columns with puerilities drawn from this amazing volume. For amazing it is. We may equally conceive an equally bad book written on a great contemporary painter or writer, but we should be astounded if it found a publisher. Evidently the intelligence of the musical section of the reading public is rated very low.

'Our sympathy goes out to Mr Porte's subject. Elgar has been none too well treated by his generation and should have been spared this wounding in the house of his friends. Well may he say, *'Save me from my propoganderists"*

But these words would also not last beyond the next edition, and Porte's book was reprinted in 2015.

In the 1924 German 'Handbuch der Musikgeschichte' – still widely available - eminent scholar Edward Dent, successor to Stanford as Professor of Music at Cambridge explained that Elgar: 'was a Catholic, and more or less a self-taught man, who possessed little of the literary culture of Parry and Stanford. To English ears, Elgar's music is too emotional and not quite free from vulgarity. His orchestral works – two symphonies, concertos for violin and 'cello, and several overtures – are vivid in colour, but pompous in style and of a too deliberate chivalrousness of expression.'

Dent repeated himself again in 1931, in an Italian musical journal in which he began by discussing Liszt: 'In England the best musicians have a real horror of him. The only composer who shows traces of his influence is Elgar, and Elgar, despite his brilliant style is repugnant to many English musicians by reason precisely of that chevaleresque rhetoric which badly covers up his intrinsic vulgarity.'

Robert Lorenz defended Elgar in the June 1931 Musical Mirror, noting that Dent, at this time, was Chairman of the International Society of Contemporary Music: 'This is, I imagine what happens,' he added. 'When German, French, or Italian musical lexicographers require articles on modern British music, what better man can they turn to than the excellent Professor Dent, about whose qualifications for such a purpose they have no idea, but whom they have met at social gatherings and have been able to talk to without an interpreter. He may be just the man for the job; besides he is readily accessible and to ask him will save all the bother of finding out whether anyone else might possibly do it better.

'It is difficult to speak with restraint of Professor Dent's habit of wilfully misrepresenting British musical opinion abroad. Had the late Peter Warlock [i.e. the composer Philip Heseltine] and myself been aware of this Italian article, we should have considered it on account of its downright offensiveness even more deserving of exposure than the German article.

'I rather fancy that an Italian who reads Professor Dent's remarks will conclude that an Elgar work meets with rather a mixed reception in this country. How far this is from the truth, every concert-goer knows.'

The letter concluded with a limerick, along the lines which his friend Warlock, prone to writing such things in the most offensive language, might have been proud:

>'Our public to misrepresent
>
>Is the aim of a critic named Dent
>
>What he daren't say at home
>
>Is foisted in Rome
>
>As accepted by common consent'

Dent's opinions have resonated with generations of music students. His many books are still freely available today and continue to form musical opinion. Lorenz's letter appeared in a long defunct musical journal.

Lorenz had also signed a 'Manifesto' protesting against what Dent had been writing about Elgar which had also been signed by the composers John Ireland, E J Moeran, Peter Warlock, and William Walton as well as other luminaries including George Bernard Shaw. This appeared in an edition of Musical Times more than 80 years ago and lies untouched and generally forgotten in the archives.

In 1955, the reference book 'The Record Guide' said this: 'Boastful self-confidence, emotional vulgarity, material extravagance, a ruthless philistinism expressed in tasteless architecture and every kind of expensive yet hideous accessory: such features of a late phase of Imperial England are faithfully reflected in Elgar's larger works and are apt to prove indigestible today'.

In 2007, Michael Kennedy, in a Daily Telegraph article celebrating the 150th anniversary of Elgar's birth noted: 'For the Elgar centenary in 1957, the number of celebratory concerts was not remotely on the scale of this year's. The superficial public image was still that of a musical Colonel Blimp - he even looked like a colonel or a country squire.'

He added that 'the majority of academics and critics,' still subscribed to the estimate of his music contributed by Dent. If there had been change, he said, it was still patchy. 'Perhaps as a reaction to the well-orchestrated avant-garde campaign in the 1960s and 1970s to persuade us all that salvation lay with serialism and the new wave of Boulez, Stockhausen and others, a number of Romantic and post-Romantic composers whose names had not been mentioned (except in derision) in many university music departments for decades came storming back into public favour, supported by long-playing recordings and, later, compact discs - Mahler (he had a foot in both camps), Bruckner, Strauss, Rachmaninov, Puccini, Sibelius and Elgar.

But, added Kennedy: 'remember - the celebrations on the weekend of his anniversary are an English phenomenon. There will not be wall-to-wall Elgar on Austrian Radio or in Italy, France and Germany. America has its Elgarians but they are not a major force.'

Elgar's will was published in May 1934, and the press were surprised that despite his position in the world of music, his estate grossed only £13,934 [about £750,000 in today's money] and nett at £9,104 [about £450,000].

The Birmingham Mail along with many other papers quoted Elgar's text, written in 1932 which contained an element of bitterness: 'I regret that owing to the sudden collapse of everything artistic and commercial, I have found it necessary to revoke the will which I had previously made and to make this present will. I leave nothing to any charity as I have given everything possible during my life and I much regret that it is now necessary for me to cancel the legacies which it had been my purpose to leave to servants and friends and institutions.'

The Glasgow Bulletin noted: 'Sir Edward Elgar has not died a rich man. In these days not even the Master of the King's Musick is a 'best seller', musically, and the earnings of composers are lower than any other artists. Conductors too win glory rather than wealth and the late Mr Percy Pitt, conductor at Covent Garden and the Queen's Hall for many years left only £31 when he died last year.'

However, the Glasgow Daily Express reported: 'It will be found, I think that Sir Edward Elgar has died a rich man, although at the height of his creative period, he was a comparatively poor one. Gramophone records were almost the sole cause of the transformation. Elgar's gramophone royalties amounted to thousands of pounds a year for many years. In addition he was paid large sums for conducting while the records were being made.'

Elgar's death led to speculation as to the fate of the unfinished Third Symphony. The Daily Sketch reported: *'Although the manuscript of the unfinished symphony is almost complete it is like a 'jig-saw puzzle,'* said a close friend, *'and only his master mind could have assembled it. Now it is a mystery – a masterpiece lost to the world.''*

Despite this, by the autumn, papers were reviewing the unfinished symphony and asking whether it might in the event be completed. At that time everyone agreed that this was an impossible task, given the fragmentary nature of the sketches Elgar had left behind and his comments in the last days of his life as reported by W H Reed that 'no one should tinker with it.'

The Daily Telegraph featured a photograph of Elgar's daughter, Carice with Sir Adrian Boult looking over the sketches at Broadcasting House and stated that they were to be placed in the BBC archives. 'Only a few bars have been orchestrated and there is an incomplete sketch of the first movement. There are a few fragments of other movements. No attempt is to be made to put the symphony into a form suitable for performance.'

Some of the sketches were subsequently published – first in W H Reed's personal reminiscence 'Elgar as I knew Him', and then in a special edition of the BBC magazine 'The Listener'.

In a Daily Telegraph feature following these publications Ernest Newman applauded this move but added: 'I respectfully suggest, however, that this is not enough to satisfy our legitimate curiosity about the work. What all students of Elgar would like to have would be a volume containing the whole of the material relating to the symphony that can be discovered.

'For the serious purposes of musicology we need every fragment of music that relates to the symphony, however enigmatic or chaotic it may appear at first sight.

'There need be no fear that someone will 'tinker' with the music, as Elgar dreaded, and try to complete the symphony from the material thus made available. The laws of copyright will make that impossible for the next half century or so. I venture to suggest therefore to the BBC that they bring out, if only in a limited edition, a volume containing the whole of the sketches, not in facsimile but in a form that the student can follow without qualifying for a visit to the oculist.

'What Elgar's Third Symphony would finally have been is a subject upon which it is, and will always be, utterly futile to speculate: the many secrets of the organic joining up with these fragments died with Elgar.'

The argument over whether the sketches could or should be worked into a performing version of the Symphony raged for decades, with the custodians of Elgar's copyright adhering to his reported wishes. However, as Newman had speculated, copyright of published work eventually runs out, and as both Reed and the BBC had published the sketches in 1934, the limitation under EU law was 2004 – 70 years after Elgar's death.

The realisation that the sketches would then be in the public domain and therefore anyone might be able to attempt to complete them into a performing version led to permission being granted to the English composer Anthony Payne, who had taken a keen interest in the matter for many years, to see if he could complete a performing version of the music.

He did, and to great acclaim the 'Elaboration of the Sketches of Elgar's Third Symphony as Realised by Anthony Payne', otherwise now known as the 'Elgar/Payne Third Symphony' received its first performance in the Royal Festival Hall, London in February 1998. The work has now received performances around the world and taken its place in the regular concert repertoire.

Another of Elgar's wishes was that the nation should acquire the humble country cottage where he was born at Broadheath, near Worcester, as a memorial to him. In the wake of the grief which had apparently struck the nation following his death – which led, of all things, to a London telephone exchange being named after him - this idea gained momentum. – The plan was that the cottage should be bought by the Worcester Council, and a fund developed so that it could be run as a museum. One local councillor, however, declared that the £400 asking price – about £20,000 in today's money - was far too much for the ratepayers of Worcester to be expected to pay – and anyway, 'hardly anyone would know who Elgar was, unless they were told'.

The Daily Telegraph became the central depository for donations. In its initial announcement, it said Elgar was 'still unrecognised in this country in 1901. 'This was in spite of the fact that both the 'Enigma Variations' and 'The Dream of Gerontius' had then been written. Elgar's reputation only began to be properly appreciated here when in 1902 'Gerontius' was received with acclamation in Dusseldorf.'

For some weeks later, the paper printed lists of subscribers and amounts given. The Telegraph itself donated £105 (about £5,000 today). Robert Meyer contributed £25 (£1,200), Landon Ronald £15 (£800), while Adrian Boult and Vaughan Williams gave £2 each (£100). Kreisler gave £25 (£1,200) and Barbirolli £5 (£250). HMV gave £105 (£5,000) while other contributors included Herbert Howells, Arnold Bax, Bernard Shaw, Johnson Forbes-Robinson, Henry Wood, W H Reed, Somerville Tattersall, Barry Jackson, Haydn Wood, Hamilton Harty, Malcolm Sargent and many hundreds more – the majority from the general public - with the smallest donation being six pence (£1).

The Birthplace opened as a memorial museum in 1938. Since September 2017 it has been in the stewardship of the National Trust who hold it, initially, on a five-year lease.

As far as other tangible monuments to Elgar are concerned, Great Malvern features an Elgar statue in the centre of the Town, and still retains (as privately-owned homes, not open to the public), Elgar's two houses – 'Forli' and 'Craeg Lea' – as well as his studio where he taught violin and where he first met his wife Alice. 'Birchwood Lodge' at Storridge, just outside Malvern, where he wrote 'The Dream of Gerontius' and several other works, remains, as a privately-owned house, not open to the public, nestling in the woods which inspired him. Various schools and colleges also retain memories of his teaching activities in the 1890s. The majority of the buildings belonging to the County Lunatic Asylum, at Powick just outside Malvern, where he was bandsman in the 1880s have been largely removed to make way for a modern housing estate, though some of the original buildings can still be seen.

In Hereford, his home 'Plas Gwyn' has been converted into private apartments and from the outside looks much as it did when he lived there between 1904 and 1912. There is also a statue showing him with his bicycle 'Mr Phoebus' near to the Cathedral.

'Brinkwells', the thatched cottage in the remote woodlands near Fittleworth, West Sussex, where he composed his three chamber works and his 'cello concerto, still stands in countryside retaining the magical atmosphere which inspired him at the end of the First World War. It can be viewed from a public footpath which curves around it but it is not open to the public. The studio which was across the garden from 'Brinkwells' and in which he wrote his music, was removed to the nearby village of Bedham and two wings were built on to it, converting it into a bungalow.

In London, the house in Avonmore Road, Kensington – again a private residence - where Elgar and Alice lived in rented rooms between 1889 and 1891 bears a blue plaque recording the fact that Elgar lived there. 'Severn House', his mansion in Hampstead was demolished in 1942, but a small memorial has been placed on the house which replaced it.

Elgar's daughter, Carice, donated some autograph full scores of his major works to those Universities who bestowed honorary degrees on her father. Falstaff is thus at Cambridge, Introduction and Allegro for Strings is in Yale University, USA, the 'cello concerto is at the Royal College of Music but the majority of his manuscripts and letters are now housed in the British Library in London. Another major archive, including Alice Elgar's original diaries are housed at Birmingham University and a large corpus of material is still held at the Birthplace museum, though many manuscripts and other material were transferred from there to the British Library in 2018.

The City of Worcester's Elgarian legacy has also included a statue in the High Street. Worcester Cathedral features a memorial plaque and stained-glass window. Considering the controversy stirred up by the Cathedral authorities in 1902, this is ironically based on the theme of the Catholic inspired 'Dream of Gerontius'.

Places where Elgar lodged as a young man in the City are still extant, some identified by plaques placed by the Elgar Society, but the Elgar Brothers Music Shop at Number 10 High Street, Worcester, where his much vaunted self-taught musical education largely took place, was demolished to make way for a department store in the 1960s. Marl Bank, on Rainbow Hill, Worcester, his 'last little haven before the end' where he died, was demolished in 1969 to make way for three blocks of flats called 'Elgar Court'.

Printed in Great Britain
by Amazon